LEGENDARY BIJU

The Man and Mission

LEGENDARY BIJU
The Man and Mission

Major K P Mohanty
Editor-in Chief

Assisted by
Board of Editors

Kaveri Books
New Delhi - 110 002

First Published in 2002
Second Impression 2022

ISBN-10: 978-81-7479-054-3
ISBN-13: 978-81-7479-054-5

Published by
Kaveri Books
4832/24, Ansari Road
New Delhi-110002 (India)
Tel: 011-23288140, 4707 2321
E-mail : info@kaveribooks.com
kaveribooks@gmail.com
Website: www.kaveribooks.com

PRINTED IN INDIA

M.M. RAJENDRAN
GOVERNOR OF ORISSA

सत्यमेव जयते

RAJ BHAWAN
BHUBANESWAR-751 008

Nov. 26, 2001

MESSAGE

I am happy to know that Editorial Board is compiling and editing a biography of Late Biju Patnaik in English for the readers of national and international level.

Late Shri Biju Patnaik was one of the brilliant sons of the Motherland and his contribution towards National Development, particularly in the field of education and industry, is everlasting. His sacrifice for the nation, his patriotism and philanthropic activities and noble mission will enrich the pages of history. I trust, the enduring achievements of Biju Patnaik will be a source of inspiration for the generation to come.

I wish the publication all sucess.

(M.M. Rajendran)

Acknowledgement

We acknowledge with gratitude the help and assistance rendered to us by the Editorial Board. Rakesh Goel of Kaveri Books, New Delhi is to be thanked profusely. He is a very uncommon publisher, who is available at all times to render assistance at every stage and in every way. Shri Suresh Bhusan Patnaik and Shri Hadibandhu Das have provided excellent secretarial assistance to the editorial board. The editors Prof. Swadesh Ghosh, Prof. Jagdish Kumar Patnaik, Capt. Debasis Das, Dr. Srinibas Pathi and Dr. Nishamani Kar, were modulators, mind setters and workers of tremendous zeal and enthusiasm. Late Banka Bihari Das contributed a paper in Oriya just two months before his demise. When we (Dr. J. K. Parida and I) met him at his place, he accepted us with such hospitality which cannot be described. He spoke on Biju Babu for an hour. We could not record it. We were not prepared for it. He mistook our request and wrote in Oriya. However, his writing was translated into English by Capt. Debasis Das. We regret that we would not be able to hand over our publication to him now. But his encouragement has always been a guiding force.

Our regrets are many. It should not be spoken out. That will not pay in any way. All desires and expectations cannot be fulfilled. The whole world is like a Pandora's box. However, our esteemed contributors have indebted us in contributing papers and write-ups without which Biju's Biography would have remained a 'dream' not come true.

Major K. P. Mohanty
Editor-in-Chief

Khurda, Orissa
March 05, 2002

Biju Patnaik : So Many Things To Say and Do
(March 05,1916 - April 17,1997)

Biju Patnaik and his Wife Gyan Patnaik

Biju Patnaik with his Father Laxminarayan

Prem, Geeta & Navin

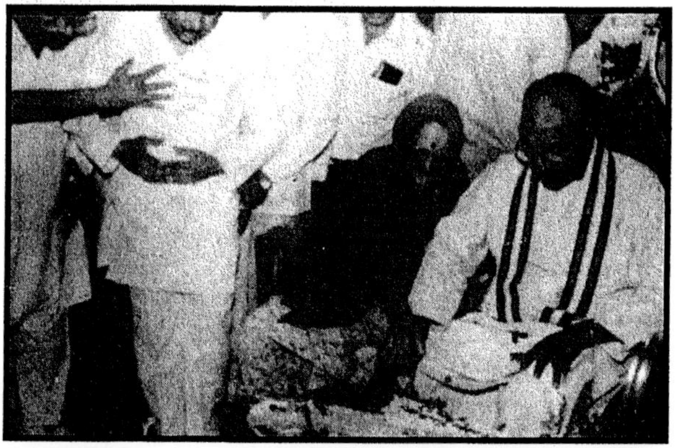

On the Occasion of 79th Birthday Celebration

Biju Patnaik with Mr. John L. Painter,
The High Commissioner of Canada

Inaugurating a Children's Festival in Bhubaneswar

Remembering the Past Biju Patnaik enjoying the Moments with Oriya Paikas

Biju Riding a Cycle after 58 Years Passed Memory

Contents

Preface

Why Biju's Biography ?

Orissa remembers Utkalmani Pandit Gopabandhu Dash, Utkal Gourav Madhusudan Das, Krushna Chandra Gajapati, the Maharaja of Parlakhemundi, Biswanatha Das, Harekrushna Mahatab and Biju Patnaik with reverence as each of them has moulded the destiny of this tiny little State in some way or other in both pre-and post-independence period. Orissa once moved the heart of the Father of our nation when he was greatly shocked, experiencing for himself the poverty of millions of people living in it. It is said he was a half-naked Fakir, as he was once called by Winston Churchill, for he made a promise that unless every individual in India has adequate clothes to wear, he would wrap himself with pieces of Khadi as necessary to cover his nakedness.

Orissa had a rich and glorious past; its culture was superb; its temples were world famous; its beaches were romantic and attractive; its mineral and forest resources were abundant. Still it remained a State predominantly poor throughout 19th and 20th centuries. All the personalities cited above have created history for the State in their own way, but Biju Patnaik associated himself intensely with Orissa for about forty five years till he passed away at New Delhi on 17th April, 1997, without a crown on his head. The people of Orissa showered love on him more at his demise than during his life time and the affection, regards, condolences, hysteria expressed during those days after his death were unprecedented.

Biju was physically tall, had a towering personality, seldom bowed down and was always in an adventurous mood. He had a peculiar bent of mind, was over-zealous and had a desire to industrialise Orissa, to spread science education, to improve the economic viability of Orissa and to bring the all-round development of Orissa at the time without being conscious of his limitation and the limitation of potential energy of the State. His whole life, childhood, youth, growth as an industrialist, becoming a business magnet, a cabinet minister at the Centre, Chief Minister, Leader of Opposition of Orissa, a King-maker of the country for a considerable period and above all an undisputed leader of Orissa was legendary and if one reads it, it would sound like a fiction.

Many of us in the Editorial Board were not personally known to him, but were enamoured of his adventurous one-in-many personality and therefore decided to compile and edit a biography to make him immortal to the readers at the national and international level.

Current affairs, for that matter the history remembers many heroes, personalities and persons of eminence and this memory inspires generations after generations. Cleopatra, Napoleon and Mahatma Gandhi — all these are remembered. Gandhiji's ideal, way of life, inspirations and preaching, will probably remain a source of living light for centuries to come. Biju may not be remembered as much as Napoleon or Gandhiji, but will remain a source of inspiration for generations to come as he exhibited his unending zeal and enthusiasm to think and to work for the Oriya people, who formed no insignificant part of the Indian Union. We thought of editing a biography not of a traditional pattern. Therefore, we wrote to many persons of eminence who were closely associated with Biju Babu, to project a picture of him dispassionately. We were disappointed as quite a few of them failed to respond. What a shocking apathy of people ? We only regretted but we could not do anything otherwise. But we were grateful to those who came forward to contribute their 'write up' at their earliest convenience. A generation is growing now which stands on as it is and does not bother for the past nor is worried for the future. A person dies in a family, his associates forget him or her even prior to the period of mourning. In our days of fast life, probably these developments are a natural phenomenon and it will continue for sometime till we are greatly involved in fast or faster life. Where is the time for us to remember a person who has already passed away and who would not benefit us physically in our day to day life.

II

I knew Biju Patnaik through some occasions. It is an invaluable memory. He was the Chief Minister of Orissa. A Conference of Association of College Teachers of Non-Govt. Colleges of the State was scheduled for one evening. A few other distinguished guests were there along with him. The venue was the hall of Christ College, Cuttack. We were delegates to the Conference and were eager to listen to him. The meeting began. The sound system failed. Biju Patnaik came down from the rostrum, fondled the sound system and made it functional and again took his chair and waited for his turn to address the gathering.

It was really something unthinkable in those days in this country with a strong colonial background. A Chief Minister, may be after independence, ought to be a King of Kings, not merely the Presiding Officer of a Council of Ministers.

The second occasion when I met him was when he was the Chief Minister of Orissa in the first five years of the nineties. By then he had already grown with age. He was lacking his usual spirit to meet people, to talk to them and to interact with them for the future of the country. I had been to his office to invite him to grace the silver jubilee function of a ladies' hostel of the College in which I was the Principal. His Private Secretary was R. N. Patra, an IAS, who was a classmate of mine. I got the consent of Biju Babu to come to the College with the good offices of my friend. Before I met him, I witnessed an incident, which is still fresh in my memory. A parliamentary delegation was scheduled to call on him and to exchange ideas on some very very important problems of the country. The entire office was ready for the purpose. Biju Babu was himself present. The delegation was well received and introduced to the Chief Minister. The members of the delegation were delighted to meet a grand old personality of the time of our freedom struggle. There was a lot of hope of exchange of views and interaction. But suddenly the meeting ended as soon as the tea was served. He got up and said 'good bye'. The parting words were 'visit Orissa, see Lord Jagannath, enjoy the beauty of the sculpture of Konark, experience the beauty of Puri Beach, go back with the good memory of Orissa". I was quietly standing in the crowd at this time and could observe the disappointment of the members of the delegation. It was very much unbecoming of Biju Babu. I have thought over it several times and found no answer. May be, he was disillusioned with the present day generation of M.Ps and did not want to waste time discussing with them.

He kept his word and came to Banki College on the appointed date. He was five minutes earlier than the scheduled time of arrival. Everybody knew his punctuality throughout his life and many have been embarrassed on several instances when he has reached in time and his hosts were not ready to receive him. I remember an interesting incident with regard to his sense of punctuality. He misbehaved with a host when nobody was ready to receive him when he was to address a meeting at the appointed time.

In the Silver Jubilee function of Rani Suka Dei Chhatri Nibas, he addressed a crowd of ten thousand people inclusive of students, local people, and others who came there from a distance of 25 to 30 miles to listen to him. It was his first visit to the area as Chief Minister. It was always his habit to be impatient when the crowd did not listen to him with rapt attention. He preferred to interact with people through a question-and-answer session. I was sitting next to him, interrupted him and requested him to complete the speech; otherwise it would be a long session which would tell upon his ill health. He stared at me, I got frightened and I thought that he would give me a push and tell me to stop interpolating. But that did not happen and he quietly accepted my advice and spoke for some minutes, thanked the people and ended his address.

With his long and vast experience of life as a statesman, sometime he was unable to bear the irrelevance of talks, proposals and suggestions. He was more anxious to know the remedy of a malady and was expecting proper and appropriate briefing. He was very angry and rude, when bureaucracy was dilly-dallying with a problem in the usual manner which it inherited from the days of Britishers. It is told that the top officials of the state were afraid of proposing a thing if it would not be appreciated by him. He was very fast in thinking and doing a thing, and others were not able to keep pace with him. There was a wide gap between his functioning and the functioning of the bureaucracy which he was leading.

III

Apart from personal acquaintance with Biju Patnaik, many of us were aware of his multi-faceted personality which we want to record in this publication for the benefit of our readers.

In the sixties when he was the Chief Minister of the State there was a proposal to hold the annual session of the Indian Science Congress, under the auspices of Utkal University. The Chief Minister's office called a meeting of the Vice-Chancellor and other top officials of the State to discuss linking up coordination of holding the Congress. At that time Vice-Chancellor Dr. P. K. Parija was his revered teacher. He called back Biju and enquired what made him to call the conference when the University was the host. Biju Patnaik agreed and asked all concerned to assemble in the University within thirty minutes to attend the meeting for coordination under the Chairmanship of the Vice-Chancellor. Biju Babu was himself available for the purpose. What magnanimity of a statesman and what respect shown by him to an old teacher! Such attitudes are rare these days.

The State was undergoing a resource crunch in the nineties. As the Head of the Government he issued directives regarding restrictive uses of government vehicles, particularly on Sundays and public holidays. The people in the capital city of Bhubaneswar were surprised and amazed when they witnessed that the Chief Minister himself was riding a bicycle (on some occasion in the cycle rickshaw) to reach the Orissa Secretariat to attend to his duty on holidays. 'Example is better than precept' was his motto. Such activities of his had a tremendous impact upon the people and his followers.

For the cause of the community or for that matter for the sake of communal harmony, he risked his life on one such occasion, which readers ought to know. At Rourkela, the Steel City of Orissa, communal violence broke out and took an ugly shape. On knowing it he immediately reached there and proceeded on foot to meet the mob in fury. The law-and-order authorities were preventing him to move about in such a manner, but he proceeded, met the mob and put it under control. Biju Patnaik was always courageous, whether it was the cause of his own personal life or a cause of the nation. These are some of the small incidents but had a tremendous impact on the people living in the present-day society.

You may call it a drawback or weakness of his personality: Biju Patnaik was never secretive. He preferred to remain open to the people at large. He was more frank to his opponents than to his followers. He appeared before a Judicial Commission, known as "Famous Khanna Commission". There were some allegations of financial improprieties against him. He boldly appeared before it and said "Excuse me, your Lordship, such improprieties shall be committed a number of times for the sake of the development of my State". The Commission was surprised and horrified to listen to such a statement from one against whom it would pass a verdict.

In the days of 1962, i.e. during the Chinese aggression, he was nominated to assist the then Prime Minister Pandit Jawaharlal Nehru in matters of defence. The Defence portfolio was handled by another person of repute late Y B Chauhan. Biju Babu was sent to the USA to explain our need. Our relationship with the USA was not that cordial. He met their leaders, people and the press. On queries he spoke out our strategy without hiding anything. The national press was very hostile to him on this issue and criticised him. He did not care it and said "secret dealings have been out-dated now."

One must admire his patience. In defeat, in crisis, and in disadvantage he always remained cool and calm. He has fought elections, sometime contested from several seats at a time, and faced debacles everywhere. People have thrown him out and rejected him out-right. But he has accepted it humbly and resolved calmly to come out of it. Had it been any personality other than Biju Patnaik, he would not have risen at all. For a long time, he became a king-maker both in his own

State and at the Centre in New Delhi. After the one party hegemony of the National Congress at the Centre in India was over, Biju Babu became a crisis-manager to establish many governments at New Delhi consisting of various heterogeneous groups. The leaders of such groups were sometimes not on talking terms. Biju Babu would meet them, hold midnight parleys and get them to sit at one table and to draw up a strategy to work together to run a government. When he was also in the National Congress, the 'High Command' was deploying him for many arduous tasks either for the sake of the party or for the sake of the country. Therefore, on his demise, tributes flowed from all quarters and sentiments were expressed in a very uncommon manner. During his life-time he nourished a special love for the youth, particularly for the student community. He was simply not able to tolerate the difficulties faced by the students. He gave priority to their education, particularly to Science and Technology. He encouraged them in Sports, adventure and all sorts of courageous endeavour. He said "Oriya students should not be cowards". But there was a *fait accompli* too. He faced severe opposition from students during their agitation in 1964. It turned violent and became a mass movement. He had to leave his Chief Ministership due to their agitation. Wherever he went, he faced hostile students and he accepted their anger, their brick-batting and throwing of shoes and *chappals* at him.

The same Biju Babu, when he again took over the reins of the State in 1990, V P Singh, the then Prime Minister, introduced the reservation of seats in service and in educational institutions for other backward classes on the basis of the Mandal Commission findings. The students joined the people for a state-wide agitation, Biju Babu had to maintain law and order. But he very tactfully dealt with the matter and won the hearts of the students. He was not willing for the reservation of seats for the students belonging to other backward classes in educational institutions. He insisted that reservation should be made on economic backwardness. Perhaps, he was the first politician of independent India, who declared in unequivocal terms that 'The Poor have no caste'. He started a debate over it both at the national and state level. He often met the students and had a direct dialogue with them. He called for a two days conference of heads of institutions, student representatives, political leaders, professors, youth leaders and educationists to discuss the problem. He presided over it with patience and listened to every argument. Like a judge, he was making queries. Such measures adopted by him pacified the students. Inevitably, the student community reposed faith in him. Unlike many political personalities of his time he was very cordial to his opponents. He was friendly to them. While taking a decision, he would consult them without exception. He was very alert for their welfare and well-being. He was praised for such an attitude towards them. But during the second spell of his Chief Ministership with his failing health, he was not available to many. He was devoid of interaction with those who do not agree with him. There was not much opportunity. Therefore some of the decisions he took about them were unlike those to be taken by Biju Patnaik.

In this biography writers have written about him and about the various aspects of his personality abundantly. We do not want to repeat them. Biju charismatically dominated the State of Charismatic Orissa as a whole for a long period with his charming and persuasive, although unbending, personality. He was loved earlier, is remembered now, and shall be remembered for years to come. Our failing to draw up an accurate biography will be our regrets, but he remains as he was and as he is.

Major K.P. Mohanty
Capt. Debasis Das

My Reminiscencess

1

Rabi Ray

I met Biju Babu for the first time at Wellington Hospital, New Delhi (now Ram Manohar Lohia Hospital) in 1967, when he came to inquire about Dr. Lohia's health who was seriously ill, almost in a stage of coma. He subsequently died. It was almost his daily routine to come and see Dr. Lohia in the hospital. He would be there for the entire day talking to hundreds of workers who came from different parts of the country to see him. I was really touched by his humane and affectionate feelings towards Dr. Lohia. Those who were familiar with the history of the "Quit India Movement" of 1942 launched by Mahatma Gandhi were well aware of the fact that Biju Babu along with Dr. Lohia, Jayaprakash Narayan, Aruna Asaf Ali and Achut Patwardhan kept the flag of 1942 movement flying after Gandhiji's arrest. Biju Babu was a young pilot then. He was courageous enough to make the supreme sacrifice by actively responding to the clarion call of "Do or Die" of Mahatma Gandhi. He was arrested and put behind the bars along with other leaders.

Biju Babu joined Congress after he returned from the jail. Jayprakash Narayan and Dr. Lohia who were heroes of the 1942 movement founded the Socialist party. The Socialist party and the Congress were ideologically poles apart. I had been in the Socialist party from my student days. Hence it was but natural that I had no political relationship with Biju Babu till he severed his relationship with the Congress party in 1971 and formed a state party in Orissa, "Utkal Congress". He then did not look back and never joined the Congress till the end of his life.

Smt. Indira Gandhi wielded enormous personal power after her victory in Bangladesh war in 1971. Her popularity rose sky-high. She was very ruthless in dealing with those in the opposition parties. It was well nigh impossible to check the growing authoritarianism of Smt. Gandhi then unless all democratic opposition parties wedded to the parliamentary form of representative government were welded together to form a national democratic opposition to the ruling Congress party.

Once it so happened that some young men invited me and Biju Babu to their village in Cuttack district to address their club. We had a heart-to-heart talk there for the first time about the state of the nation existing then. Both of us agreed that the immediate formation of a national alternative of all opposition parties at the Centre would go a long way to save the country from the impending authoritarian rule of Smt. Indira Gandhi. Thanks to Biju Babu, he lost no time in getting the active cooperation of two former Chief Ministers (Sri Harekrushna Mahatab, Sri R.N. Singhdeo) in this regard. The net result of his efforts was the formation of Pragati Dal consisting of Swatantra Party (Sri R.N. Singhdeo), Utkal Congress (Sri Biju Patnaik) and the Samjukta Socialist Party (Sri Rabi Ray) formed in Orissa. The launching of Pragati Dal was bound to catch the imagination of the people in the State.

Biju Babu was an effective organiser par excellence. We both decided that serious efforts must be made to contact opposition leaders all over the country, so as to consolidate the democratic opposition parties as an alternative to the ruling Congress party at the Centre. As a first step towards this consolidation, I invited Biju Babu to an All India training camp of a prominent leader of Samjukta Socialist Party which took place at Jhadgram in West Bengal. Prominent among the Socialist leaders who attended this camp were the former Chief Minister of Bihar Sri Karpuri Thakur, Sri Rajnarayan and an eminent leader of tribals Sri Mama Baleswar Dayal. Biju Babu developed an instant rapport with all of them. His successful meeting with the socialist leaders at Jhadgram enabled him to rush immediately to Calcutta to meet Loknayak Jayaprakash Narayan to consult him and to get his blessings in this regard. Jayaprakashji did encourage him to proceed.

Biju Babu contributed his mite to form Lok Dal under the chairmanship of Choudhury Charan Singh when four other political parties such as Utkal Congress, Swantatra Party, Samjukta Socialist Party and Bharatiya Lok Dal decided to merge together. Choudhury Charan Singh and Biju Patnaik became President and Vice President of the Lok Dal respectively. Rajnarayan, myself, Sri Rajendra Narayan Singhdeo and Sri Piloo Mody among others were members of the national executive of the Lok Dal.

I was selected by Pragati Dal as a candidate to the Rajya Sabha from Orissa and won the election with an overwhelming majority. I also became the leader of the Lok Dal Parliamentary Party in the Rajya Sabha.

Smt. Gandhi could not tolerate the emergence of a national alternative, which was possible due to the combined efforts of Biju Patnaik and Charan Singh. She was so vindictive towards Biju Babu that she sent Income Tax Department officials to raid Biju Patnaik's residence (11, Aurangzeb Road, New

Delhi). The officers of the Income Tax Department returned empty handed. I raised this issue in Rajya Sabha and as a result the government cut a very sorry figure in the Upper House of Parliament. It was personally a great humiliation for Smt. Gandhi.

Biju Babu's residence in New Delhi became the nerve-centre of intense political activity, and opposition leaders were meeting frequently to discuss ways and means to form a national alternative. Both Biju Babu and myself became comrades-in-arms and left no stone unturned to build an All-India Opposition Party based on the twin concepts of egalitariansim and secularism.

There was a sudden qualitative change in the political scenario of the country when Justice J.M.L. Sinha, the Honourable Judge of Allahabad High Court, declared the election of Smt. Gandhi null and void. The Socialist leader Sri Rajnarayan emerged as the hero in the whole episode as it is he who filed the election petition against Indira Gandhi in the Allahabad High Court judgement. She got a stay from the Supreme Court against the judgement and continued in power. She declared emergency and got Loknayak Jayaprakash Narayan arrested the day he was to address a protest meeting in Delhi. A functioning democracy was immediately converted to a dictatorial regime. The country was plunged into darkness.

Biju Babu and myself were arrested in Delhi. Sidhartha Sankar Ray, the then Chief Minister of West Bengal, did not arrest P.C. Sen and Jyoti Basu who were former Chief Minister and Deputy Chief Minister of West Bengal respectively. Smt. Nandini Sathpathy, the then Chief Minister of Orissa, on the other hand did not spare the former Chief Ministers of Orissa Sarvashree Nabakrushna Choudhury, Harekrushna Mahatab in Orissa from putting them behind bars.

Both of us, Biju Babu and myself, were lodged in Haryana Jails- he was in Rohtak Jail and I in Ambala jail. He wrote a letter from Rohtak Jail to Charan Singh, President of Lok Dal. Some excerpts from the letter are as follows:

"I hope you are well. Irrespective of our incarceration, I have to admit that as a by-product things are looking up for the country. The major gain is a sense of discipline, which you and I hold vital for our national growth. The 2-point programme as an outline of socio-economic change is something we all want but is so difficult to implement as it covers the mental make-up of an entire people steeped in feudal prejudices which has to be broken with fanatical zeal. Rigid population control is the single factor, which would determine whether the graphs of investment and productivity could meet at a point of affluence, within a measurable period of time.

All these cannot even be dreamt of unless democratic freedom can be balanced with clear responsibilities. I am of the view that the Central government should be clothed with adequate powers in the statutes to regulate the planned growth of India. Without such powers planning cannot be meaningful.

The big question is whether the political apparatus (loose in the ruling party and looser in the opposition without total dedication), along with a self-serving bureaucracy is able to carry out even the basic outlines of the PM's programme unless the entire cross-section of the people-government, the administration, the business, the youth, the peasant and the worker in the field, mines and factories - are totally achievement-oriented; otherwise the nation would drift and become poorer as the population grows.

Is it possible to stop political quibblings for some time to get on with the task of nation-building at the grass-roots level? We have to admit that the opposition, instead of growing and responsible, has gone somewhat in the reverse direction. I am beginning to feel that perhaps I would have done better by engaging myself in some specific task which would have added to the Nation's assets however small, instead of breaking my head against the possibility of creating a truly great opposition party worthy of the nation.

Now that you are out, you would have a better view of the situation in the country. Could you please let me have your indications on what we should do, in the larger interest of the country?

I must say that I am enjoying young Sanjay's exhortation to his party workers. Either get to work or get out, the days of promotion by slogans or garlands are over! How refreshing. I do hope he does well. If his age-group can function effectively there would be some hope for the country. Our time is so little and limited".

It is a very significant letter that reflects the mental agony of Biju Patnaik while in jail. He was released on parole and made a speech in Orissa Vidhan Sabha on similar lines as he expressed in course of his letter written to the President of Lok Dal, Charan Singh. His stout defence in praise of the emergency measures initiated by Indira Gandhi's son Sanjay Gandhi, came as a rude shock to his innumerable admirers all over the country. He got back his mental composure after he was finally released from the jail.

Indira Gandhi had to order election 1977. Rajnarayan in Amethi in U.P. defeated her by a margin of 38,000 votes. Our efforts to build a real national alternative to the Congress at the Centre bore fruit when Morarji Bhai Desai became the Prime Minister of Janata Party government in 1977. Biju Babu was included in Morarji Bhai's first Cabinet and I was also included in the same some time later. Orissa for first time had two Cabinet Ministers in the Central Cabinet under the dispension of a non-Congress government at the Centre. We both continued as Cabinet ministers in Charan Singh's Cabinet also.

It is a tribute to the tireless efforts of Biju Babu and others of his ilk that the Janata Party was formed after the leaders came out from the jail in 1977. The struggle for democracy under the leadership of Loknayak Jayaprakash Narayan during the dark days of 1975-77 has aptly been called as the "**second freedom movement**". All those who are anxious to forge a third front as opposed to the policies of both the Congress and BJP in the present political scenerio of our country are bound to take a cue from the Janata experiment in 1977 of which Biju Babu was one of the architects.

He was a great Indian and a prodigious Oriya too. He dedicated his life to build a great egalitarian and democratic India. His life was a **saga of sacrifice and adventure**. Julian Huxley, the great zoologist of international fame and the brother of eminent world philosopher Alduous Huxley, speaking about Biju Patnaik, has rightly said;

"A memorable Indian whose adventures will surely fill a book".

Biju : A Paradoxical Personality

2

Sarat Kumar Kar

Biju Patnaik though now a house-hold name in Orissa yet there was a time when he was rather lesser known to Orissa and Odiyas but better known to the British Indian Rulers. As a dare-devil ace pilot of the British empire, he was being trusted the most from among the natives. Paradoxically, he was equally trusted and better known to the under-ground freedom-fighters like Netaji Subhash, Jayaprakash, Lohia, Aruna as their most daring patron of under-ground activities.

At last the cat was out of the bag when his art of camouflaging was detected and he was detained along with the top freedom fighters. Not as a political prisoner but as a most dangerous traitor of the British empire, he was chained hand and foot like an Andaman (*Kala Pani*) detenu. He was forced to drink urine when he asked for water in jail. One cannot imagine such misery and plight of a person who was enjoying his life with the choicest drink, dance, mirth and laughter as one of the ace pilots of the British empire.

The decision of the British to free India, at last, ended his jail life which otherwise would have ended his life like that of any other national martyr.

He came back to Orissa on the advice of the national leaders specially of Pandit Jawaharlal Nehru to strengthen the Indian National Congress in Orissa. He helped the then Orissa Congress leaders like Shri Biswanath Das, Dr. H.K. Mahtab and Shri Nabakrushna Choudhury in building the State of Orissa. In every important step of Orissa Government, he had a major role to play including the establishment of the first Industry in Orissa like O.T.M. Even great projects like the Hirakud Dam and Rourkela Steel Plant were granted to Orissa by Mr. Nehru due to his persuasive initiative and drive.

During the dawn of freedom he was entrusted with many epoch-making secret parlours and consultations by the then Prime Minister Mr. Nehru including Azad Kashmir aggression and the Nepal insurgency by the democrats. He was entrusted with the most adventurous task of rescuing a few important national leaders of Indonesia from the clutches of the Dutch and bring them to New Delhi for participation in an International Conference. This won him the most prestigious title of honour "BHUMI PUTRA" of Indonesia.

During the Indo-Chinese war, though he was the Chief Minister of Orissa, he virtually acted as the adviser of Prime Minister Nehru in response to his invitations, in all important matters relating to defence. He was sent to the U.S.A. as the Prime Minister's special envoy to discuss with the American military authority regarding the situation arising after the Sino-Indian war. Thus he was enjoying the utmost confidence of the first Prime Minister of India, in matters of administrative, diplomatic and defence strategies though he was not a member of his Cabinet. He was elected as the most popular leader of Orissa, and as its Chief Minister was entrusted with the task of building a new Orissa. In addition to that he was helping and advising the most powerful Prime Minister as and when needed by him. This evoked the jealousy of many national and state leaders and politicians. He was beginning to be the victim of a series of political anger from many quarters. But nevertheless his strength, stamina and will power as a Statesman helped him to withstand everything and created fear and respect for him among many leaders.

He was tall and physically well-built as a sportsman and since his young days was bestowed by nature with a strong will power and sportsman's spirit. This in politics made him taller than any compelling counterparts and adversaries in dealing with the issues and affairs of State and the Nation. But he is the tallest among Indian politicians probably with three exceptions (*i.e.* Mahatma Gandhi, Pandit Nehru and Netaji Subhash). The combination of Mr. M.K. Gandhi, Mr. Subhash Chandra Bose and Mr. Jawaharlal Nehru, can be termed as a three-in-one combination.

He liked Mahatma Gandhi, who was a humanitarian, benevolent and a broad visionary with a mission to raise the poor, the neglected, the women communities, the untouchables and the unprivileged minority.

He was a daring, adventurous and ardent fighter for India's freedom with legendary skill like that of Netaji Subhash and even risked his life and career for that purpose.

He was an able administrator, advisor and a man full of vision to build the nation with a statesman-like zeal and ability like that of Nehru. In fact, he was extremely close to him and co-shared his ideas in building a modern India. Nehru had immense confidence in him for which he sent his daughter Indira and Biju together to execute some of his exclusive ideas concerning party and government into action. This enviable position and relation with Nehru cost him very dearly after Nehru's death.

So he had the requisite quality and charisma of Nehru which made him widely known in India and lovable in Orissa in spite of hostility and adverse propaganda against him by different parties having their self interests.

I have described the many unknown facts and legendary achievements of his career in many public meetings and have replied to the adverse comments of his adversaries and their prejudiced propaganda. But, precisely, in conclusion I have no hesitation to record that in his personality he combined the noble quality of Gandhi, the daring adventure of Subhash and the vision and statesmanship of Nehru. He is thus a colourful personality, a unity of three-in-one. Such a gem of an Indian, Biju Patnaik, who had been honoured by the Indonesian Government for his role in the Indonesian freedom struggle and honoured by the Russians for his services in the Second World War against the Nazis, has been conveniently forgotten by Indians.

I therefore have made a humble endeavour, through this article, to resuscitate this august name 'Biju Patnaik' to make the world aware of his dynamic and towering personality once again on his 84th birth anniversary.

The Way I Look Upon Biju Babu

3

Late Banka Bihari Das

Biju Babu is a very brave person. He never shirks to face any difficult situation nor does he escape from it like a coward. Whatever he thinks right, he speaks it, be it right or wrong from other's point of view.

Seeing this trait in his nature, many call him adventurous. In an underdeveloped and static state like Orissa, I have heard people say that he is brave and adventurous not only in economic matters but also at the mental level. So there is a clear line of demarcation between the brave and the adventurous. But what I appreciate most in his personality is the quality of being adventurous; but I do this not by praising him on his face but by firmly believing that the brave alone can do something positive and constructive for the society and conversely the coward is incapable of it.

For this reason Biju Babu is a controversial figure in Orissa politics. Any one who wants to create something cannot but come into the ambit of controversy. Some may support by flattering a man and some may oppose him out of ignorance. But only a few gifted with far sight may support or oppose a person for valid reasons. Very few belong to the latter category. A person or leader who does administration or politics with a view to being appreciated by all creates nothing, nor does he contribute anything to society. Hence the growth and development of personality takes place in the midst of criticism and controversy. The same thing happened in the life of Biju Patnaik. So those who maligned Biju Babu's personality when he was living had to change their opinions towards the end of his life or after his death.

Very often we have been in rival political parties in Orissa politics. In the legislative assembly also we were rivals. But only for a short period, we were together in one party. Therefore many think that we are trenchant critics of each other and others still believe that we are enemies of each other. I might be his critic, but was never his enemy; nor for that matter he was my enemy. Till the end, the bond of friendship and affection between both of us remained unsevered, like the ever-flowing (perennial stream) water of the river Saraswati. When in the opposition party he at times comes running to me or calls me to him by messengers, being confronted with a crisis of thought. At times we correspond through exchange of letters and this is the proof of our being intimate to each other.

The purpose of writing all this is to inspire Oriyas to evaluate aright one of their own leaders. The just and fair evaluation of a personality cannot be done in the midst of flatterers and blind supporters. This worthy son will be really honoured and worshipped, if the people of Orissa evaluate him properly and in a just manner. In appearance he is as tall, handsome, calm and serene as he is great and noble in his qualities.

In comparison with those who are currently very active in the politics and social affairs of Orissa, my relation with Biju Babu is pretty old. I became intimate with Biju Babu in the early part of 1945-46. He and I were imprisoned for August agitation and both got released from prison simultaneously and then I took up the responsibility of the State Congress party as its Assistant Secretary. At that time Biju Babu had no motor car of his own. He came to the Congress office, in those days, riding a green model Raleigh bicycle, to meet and talk to Mahatab Babu and Naba Krushna Choudhury and on those occasions he spent sometime talking to me. I still remember how Biju Babu became the primary member of the Congress on payment of four *annas* and registered his name in a Khata; and I was the person who used to write the names of persons who became Congress members on payment of four *anna* subscriptions. Though older in age, yet our friendship grew more and more intimate with the passage of time. But we have also quarrelled on many occasions and that was because of our stay in rival political parties and from that time I have got the real picture of his personality. How can I forget all these?

It will certainly be a book, if one writes the entire story of Biju Babu. How is it possible to incorporate all this information in such a small article like this? My health does not permit me to record all those reminiscences that crop up from the abysmal depth of memory like the various sequences of action that roll on one after another on the silver screen of a cinema. After all how can an endless story have an end? After all the voluminous life story of Biju Babu admits no end.

Life is ever mobile. With the flow of events various new experiences come up. These conceptual changes influence a man's activities. How can Biju Babu be an exception to this truth? When he became the Chief Minister of Orissa for the first time in 1961, he then visualised to bring up an underdeveloped and backward state like Orissa to the forefront as a developed and progressive state by rapid industrialisation with the proper and optimum utilisation of its natural resources. That was his dream of Orissa's future. Being enthused by this dream, Biju Babu marched ahead. And the rest was left behind.

But when he became Chief Minister for the second time in the nineties, a fundamental change in his attitude was perceptible. He laid emphasis on the development of the poor and the Adivasi communities and upliftment, especially the women community so that they could participate in the affairs of the contemporary society which is progressive as well as industrialised.

Basing on this line of thinking, he laid greater stress on one third women members to be elected as representatives from the Gram Panchayat to the Zilla Parisad level and provisions were made for reservation of seats for women. Along with this, provisions were also made to appoint elected women representatives as Chairperson or Vice Chairperson of those institutions.

During meetings, held before elections in the Adivasi dominated districts like Koraput, he used to listen seriously to the complaints and difficulties narrated by the Adivasi women and assured them to redress those difficulties by instructing the local and district administration to take steps immediately to solve their problems. After listening to their sorrows and difficulties, he was deeply touched at heart to realise how liquor has been the primary cause not only of their economic disaster but also for the loss of domestic peace and harmony. He made a novel arrangement when he assumed power as Chief Minister in 1991.

In the light of this new arrangement he appointed an illiterate though experienced Adivasi woman of Rayagada district as his private secretary. And whenever a problem arose he called them to Bhubaneswar and took their suggestions and opinions. Keeping in view the basic lowest wage of a labourer starting from the farm labourer to various other categories of workers, he suddenly announced that the basic minimum wage of a labourer will be fixed at Rs.25 per day. I still remember that the lowest minimum wage of a daily labourer then was Rs.10 or Rs.12 in the Adivasi dominated areas of Koraput district and Rs.15 to Rs.20 per day in the coastal belt of Orissa. Though the above-mentioned rates were the market rates of that time, the official rate then was Rs.12 per day.

This sudden double hike in the minimum wage of a daily labourer led to sharp criticism and strong resistance both within and outside the ministry. But Biju Babu in spite of strong opposition did not reverse his decision. As a result, it was implemented in all construction works of the government, though not in the private sector; but gradually under its impact, the minimum wage of a labourer outside was also revised.

The plight and suffering of Adivasi women affected and worried him very much. On their suggestion he banned traffic of country liquor in many areas. He advised Adivasi women to attack and demolish country liquor shops wherever they existed. Since this clandestine country liquor trafficing was going on with the connivance of the police and excise department, the Adivasi women who resisted it on the advice of Biju Babu had to suffer at the hands of the officials of local administration, yet at the same time Adivasi women resisting these illegal activities were also openly helped by local administration and thus it paid off good results. It is a matter of regret that in the plea of higher revenue collection, changes were introduced to reverse this policy of Biju Babu. What can be expected of those who are callous to the suffering and plight of the weaker section of the society!

From all these experiences, he realised that the entire machinery of the government is not able to run according to his instructions. The vested interest of the officers and outsiders together did not allow his dreams to transform into a reality. As such restless by temperament, he beacme more so, naturally, when he was not able to curb corruption and misuse of power for the benefit and progress of the poor, he being in power himself.

Being the Chief Minister himself, he encouraged the public to fight against corruption and vested interests. During emergency he, being a friend of Sri Jayaprakash Narayan, was imprisoned several times, but he always believed that the might of the people should be encouraged against the political might. Therefore, during his own government, if the machinery of administration went corrupt he called upon the people very openly, to strongly resist it and later justified his declaration. Everywhere, in different meetings and public gatherings, he very openly encouraged people to be strongly united and to attack corrupt officials and even beat them if need be. He advised people to just inform him over the telephone, after beating a corrupt officer. He assured the public that he would then see what happened. This was criticised in the newspapers and other media under the caption "Theory of thrashing". But he is not a person to easily withdraw what he has decided; he says that he has come to power for the people and if the administration does not run on right lines he pleads, "what can we expect from people?" Though such pronouncements, on the part of a Chief Minister, are not teneable from the legal point of view, yet he was obdurate enough, not to realise his mistake, such was his restlessness and discomfiture at the rampant corruption prevailing in society.

It is only possible in case of a person of towering personality like Biju Babu to erect permanent memorial by setting up Paradeep Port and Nilachal Highway on the one hand, and devise programmes for the welfare of the poor Adivasis on the other. He who was a man of exceptional talent has taken permanent leave of us. On the occasion of his death the massive crowd that had gathered at his residence cannot be easily believed unless seen with one's own eyes. At least during my life-time I haven't seen a greater tribute being paid by Oriyas to a departing Oriya. The noble and elevated honour that people of Orissa had given to Biju Babu on his death is a burning example of their affection, love and esteem for him. I take this opportunity to offer the wreath of my sincere, heartfelt and loving tributes to this great honourable soul of Orissa of whom we feel truly proud.

Biju : A Statesman

4

Bhagabat Prasad Mohanty

In public life two categories of persons come forward to render service to the people of a country or a state. The first category of persons may be called 'Politicians' while the second category which is superior to politicians may be termed as 'Statesmen'. Very few and limited persons can come under the second category of 'Statesmen'. For the sake of distinction, politicians' thinking is narrower than that of the 'Statesmen' who do have a broader and wider thinking. In my assessment Biju Patnaik can be called a 'Statesman' in the right sense who always concerned himself with the interest of the people and the future of the country. The other leaders who preceded Biju Patnaik and could be brought into this fold were Jawaharlal Nehru, Sardar Vallavbhai Patel, Dr. Rajendra Prasad and Lal Bahadur Sastri. Perhaps this was genuinely realised by Pandit Nehru who utilised his services many a time after independence.

If I remember correctly, when the Mandal Commission report was implemented two contradictory opinions emerged, one in favour and the other against the policy of reservation of seats for Scheduled Castes, Tribes and other backward down-trodden people in government services. It would not be out of place to mention here that way back in 1960-61 the then Prime Minister Pandit Jawaharlal Nehru wrote personal letters to almost all Chief Ministers expressing his reactions in this matter. He asserted the view that government services are meant for the interest of the people, not that of the servants. If the policy of reservation was implemented, he further insisted, India would ultimately emerge as a third rate country where development in the field of Science and Technology would remain a distant dream. When this question was deliberated in Orissa, Biju Patnaik reacted sharply by emphasising that there should be no reservation in the name of caste, class or community. This, he felt, was not exactly what social justice implied. In his opinion only two classes of people existed in a society, the poor and the rich. A thought of this nature can emanate only from 'Statesmen', not Politicians.

Biju Patnaik had a unique personality and so far as this singularity was concerned he was second to none in Orissa except perhaps Dr. Harekrushna Mahatab. After leaving the Congress he formed several regional political parties like Utkal Congress and Pragati Dal and ventured to challenge the dissemination of the Congress. His prolonged battle against the Congress bore fruit after a long 27 years (of quitting Congress) when he became a non-Congress Chief Minister in 1990. Biju Patnaik was perhaps the only state-level leader who posed a threat to Mrs. Indira Gandhi at the centre stage national politics.

As a Congress leader and Congress Chief Minister, he was instrumental in achieving two dream projects for Orissa. Paradeep Port and Daitari - Paradeep Port Express Highway covering a distance of 99 kilometers were two of the monumental accomplishments of Biju Patnaik for which he will always be venerated. Another milestone for which the entire credit goes to him was the construction of Hirakud Dam. No other leader of Orissa apart from Mahatab had contributed so much for the formation of Greater Orissa.

Biju Patnaik as a functioning administrator was very broad in his outlook and never bothered about narrow and petty matters. Throughout his life he fought for the people of Orissa and ruminated over his dear State Kalinga (now Orissa) and its progress.

I had the good fortune of contesting against Biju Patnaik in several National and State elections and a very rare trait I found with him during these encounters. During election campaigns he never descended to slender and trivial levels. He was very open and fair to his political rivals and contestants. Anybody who saw his funeral procession could find the difference between a Politician and Statesman. He always accepted successes and failures alike. For him, fighting for the cause of Orissa and its people were of the highest priority. He proved time and again that Orissa's leadership was not weak. Unlike other contemporary politicians, Biju Patnaik had a strong political will and this he amply demonstrated many a time while in power. One example can be cited here. When he raised the minimum daily wage of unskilled labourers from Rs.11 to Rs.25, he was widely ridiculed but the current rate of minimum wage is indicative of the foresight of the man whose primary concerns were the people and the State and their future.

Biju Patnaik : As I Know Him

5

Girija Bhusan Patnaik

It is very difficult to write one's reminiscences about a person who had become a legend during his life-time. It is because he refused to talk about himself as stories, legends were created around him. And many started eulogising him with stories, which were not facts. Nobody tried to write about his life with facts and verified facts and without taking the pains of verification, it was easy to write about him anything that would be pleasing. And to add to it, innumerable Kanutian Courtiers veered round to him to get his favours and they started creating stories themselves without caring for the historical veracity of them.

My writing may also suffer from the same lapses. My only confidence is that I have tried to verify my contentions, with his family members including my wife.

Biju Patnaik's father Laxminarayan Patnaik was also legendary. But he was not a freedom fighter. He was a leader of the Orissan Renaissance. He served as Munsif in the British government and after retirement became the Dewan of Parlakhemundi where ruling Raja K. C. Gajapatisingh Deo was the first Prime Minister of Orissa, after the first elections of 1937. He is remembered for his services for the development of Oriya language, for creation of the Orissa province.

He was a pioneer in many things including the creation of Banks and this pioneering spirit came in the genes of Biju Patnaik who pioneered many institutions, and organisations. Which of them succeeded or not including the governments he led or "safe guarded" as crisis manager is not the question. But they inspired others to follow in his footsteps.

Biju Patnaik was brave from his childhood, again a spirit imbibed from his father. He was beaten by the Police Surgent when he was a student at school. Returning home with bleeding wounds, he was confronted by his father with the first question whether he has retaliated or not. Not a word of solace or sorrow!

Biju grew up with bravery in his blood and sometimes with the spirit of bravado!

He broke the two legs of the Surgent next year while playing Hockey with the Surgent playing for the opposite side!

A plane landed in Kaliaboda where there was a landing ground. He went to see the plane and went very near to it with all the inquisitiveness of a child and was beaten by the Police guarding the plane. And he returned home with the promise that he will have a plane one-day, a dream which looked impossible then, in the mid-twenties.

How do we remember him? As the Chief Minister of Orissa twice, as a Minister in the Government of India, as the "crisis manager" of the Janata Government?

Two hundred years after history would have wiped out from memory names of many Chief Ministers, Central Ministers or possible crisis managers.

But by that time our children and grand children will read in their text books the valour and bravery of a person who in a span of two decades played his glorious role in turning the history of several countries including India.

Hardly or never in history will such epoch-making events will take place in such a short time and still less will be the chance for a person to play his role and have the imprint on all the events ranging from Europe to Indonesia.

Biju Patnaik was always reluctant to speak about his life, except when provoked or stirred. And he freely allowed the rumours to float around with a stoic mood.

He passed I.Sc. from the historic Ravenshaw College, where he is still remembered by his records in sports, which were unbroken for many years.

While in his third year, he left for Peshawar by cycle with two of his friends. One dropped out in the middle, the other completed the journey, but Biju Patnaik stayed back in Delhi to become a Pilot and to become the first (or second) 'C' class Pilot from Orissa.

He took up a job in a Private Airline but somehow or other sneaked into the Royal Air Force and started operating in Europe. Those were the dark days for mankind. Entire Europe has been run over by Nazi forces. Europe lay prostrate bleeding with a thousand wounds. In Stalingrad, (now the name of the city has been changed) the Red Army was holding the ground and the Nazi soldiers determined to evict them, so that they could march to Moscow, where Hitler and Stalin would address the May Day rally. The future was engulfed in bitter darkness. Stalingrad was encircled by the Nazi troops and a house-to-house bitter fight was on, unparalleled in history. The Nazi troops had encircled the city and the Red Army was in bad need of weapons. They were running out of weapons but how to supply them? How to sneak through the encirclement of the Nazi troops who have innumerable planes and cannons? The world watched with bated breath. The Nazis would have to retreat from Stalingrad otherwise the whole world would be under the Nazi boots.

And there was a young man, a Pilot who dared to sneak through Nazi encirclement and carried as many as 27 sorties with weapons, which helped the Red Army immensely.

The turn of events bothered everybody from the redoubtable Winston Churchill to Rabindranath Tagore, who even a few minutes before his eternal sleep enquired from Rani Mahalanavis, who was siting by his side about the events in Stalingrad and was happy to know that the Germans are retreating.

Biju Patnaik kept the event almost a secret till the 50th anniversary of the Second World War, when the representatives of the Allied Forces of USA, UK and Russia felicitated him.

Biju Patnaik became the Pilot, his personal Pilot of Lord Wavel, the then Viceroy of India.

These were the days of the Quit India movement (1942) and secret files, papers for British action were with Lord Wavel, in his Black Box, and the dare devil Biju Patnaik, passed them on to Gandhiji, a risk which involved the risk of life.

And not only that. He carried the legendary Aruna Asaf Ali in the cockpit of the plane and landed her as well as carried her again from place to place. Aruna was the most wanted person at that time and the British declared a sizable prize to catch her alive or dead.

Biju Patnaik was caught and was imprisoned in the Red Fort and then in the Delhi Central Jail. In the Red Fort he was not given any drinking water and a thirsty Biju Patnaik when he asked for water during the rounds of the Governor of Red Fort, Late Chandulal Madhabalal Trivedi, he was offered his urine to drink.

And the irony of history is that the same Chandulal became the Governor of Orissa, in which Legislative Assembly Biju Patnaik was a powerful MLA and his political Guru Dr. Harekrushna Mahatab was Prime Minister (from 1946 to 1950) of Orissa Province!

Biju Patnaik drew the attention of Pandit Jawaharlal Nehru and became very close to him. It is said that once Pandit Nehru asked Late Dr. Bidhan Chandra Ray, then Chief Minister, West Bengal, if he has met Biju Patnaik, on hearing from him that he has heard about him but had not met him, Nehru replied, "Meet him, I like such young men, forward-looking and brave, but not knowing where he will land you."

But Biju Patnaik landed in Srinagar Airport with the Pakistan Army (clad in local dress) only a few kms away from the Airport. It was when the Indian Airforce has expressed their inability to land in the Airport as the army has reached in a striking distance and an exasperated Pandit Nehru throwing his hands up in despair "Is Kashmir then lost for us forever?".

He landed in the Airport, took over the control tower and enabled the Indian Airforce to land thereafter. Kashmir was saved for India by Biju Patnaik. I doubt if history will be allowed to record this and had that been, Srinagar Airport would have been named after him.

Biju Patnaik had organised a flying club to train young Pilots. And he was on his way to Indonesia, when Pandit Nehru asked him to meet the National Leaders of Indonesia, Md. Hata, Soekorno and Shariahar with whom he had developed rapport. Biju Patnaik landed in Jakarta and soon found that the Dutch forces had invaded Indonesia with all their forces - Land, Naval, Air Forces to re-occupy Indonesia.

Biju Patnaik in his single engine plane flew out of Indonesia, by passing the invading Dutch Army with Hata in his plane dressed as his cook. He carried the "cook" to

Jawaharlal's room, to the surprise of many including Jawaharlal himself.

Whom did he carry? Was it Hata, Soekorno or Shariahar? It is he who said in a reception at Cuttack, that it was Hata.

He was offered an island and a plethora of presentation all of which he declined to accept. He was declared **Bhumiputra of Indonesia** and was assured that anytime he wished for anything he could ask for it and it would be given.

Biju Patnaik asked several years after. There was a War against Pakistan and the Indian Navy was playing havoc with the enemy. Pakistan, in shortage of Submarines requested a friendly Muslim country Indonesia for a fleet of Submarines, which was granted by the mercurial Soekorno. Getting the news, Prime Minister, Lal Bahadur Shastri, summoned and sent Biju Patnaik to Indonesia to request the Indonesian authorities to refrain from sending the Submarine fleet.

It was a cloudy night. A storm was brewing and lightning with thunder were reigning the sky, when Biju Patnaik reached Jakarta and sent information to President Soekorno to grant an audience immediately. Mrs. Soekorno was in labour pain and Soekorno was tense. He wanted to meet Biju next morning but undaunted Biju Patnaik wanted an immediate meeting. The wish of Bhumiputra was granted and Biju Patnaik met Soekorno with the request that the Submarine fleet be called back. But they have already sailed, must have reached Pakistan waters, but do you think this will matter much, was the question of Soekorno, which was met with the reply "I am Bhumiputra, I am making this request for my country and my people". The request was granted and the wireless message turned back the Submarine fleet. That night Soekorno's wife gave birth to a girl, whom Biju Patnaik christened **'Meghavati'**, looking at the stormy clouds raising their heads in the sky, and she is today a front-ranking leader of Indonesia.

Biju Patnaik was irresistible, irrepressible. A bitter struggle was on against the ruling Ranas of Nepal by the freedom fighters of Nepal, with whom the national leaders of India had very intimate relationship. But there was diplomatic relationship between India and Nepal. Once Pandit Nehru casually told Biju Patnaik to see if something could be done to help the fighting Nepali Congress and Lo! the next day as many as 15,000 guns were air dropped in Nepal. Obviously, some of them fell into the hands of the Ranasahi causing terrible embarrassment to the Government of India. Asked by Jawaharlal Nehru, Biju Patnaik's characteristic reply was: you told us to help them and the most effective way to help them is help them with guns to fight against the armed Ranasahi!

Biju Patnaik was a pilot when he used to fly Dakotas. He gave up his flying, round about 1947-48. And with the period, the type of planes, their modes of operation had undergone considerable and radical changes! I recall when a new Air Force Chief of India was appointed his acquaintance and experience in flying not only the number of planes but also ultramodern planes were considered. Biju Patnaik had none of the experience.

When he was the Chief Minister of Orissa, one day he was travelling in the Indian Airlines flight to Bhubaneswar from Calcutta and the plane went into the eyes of a brewing storm. The flight could not be controlled and the plane flew over to the seas, loosing its track. And the fuel was running out. Seeing the plight of the Pilot, Biju Patnaik ultimately took over the responsibility from the Pilot and flew back the plane from over the seas and landed safely at Bhubaneswar, though he had given up piloting a plane long ago and had not the experience of flying the Fokker Friendship.

Biju Patnaik came from an "economically and politically backward Orissa" to quote Mr. Hangen in his book

'After Nehru Who'! And he had all the background to groom himself elsewhere, particularly in Delhi. But he opted for Orissa with dreams to develop this backward area not only economically but also politically.

His first Chief Ministership is still remembered for the Fertilizers, MIG Factory, Express High way, Paradeep Port, etc. The Express High way changed the physical geography and economic geography of Kendrapada district and there are still hundreds of people in the area to stake their lives for Biju Patnaik.

His legacy, his dreams, had entered the hearts of the people which was reflected in the unprecedented mammoth gathering to pay him homage and also to elect his son Naveen and his party to power to fulfil the dreams of Biju Patnaik. Such an event, a person who is no more, whose last days were marked with disappointment and failures, his dreams crushing down yet with a hallowed legacy is rare. And that was Biju Patnaik.

It will take a thousand years or more for my dear motherland to give birth to a son like Biju Patnaik, who in a short span of two decades played a role ranging over continents, not only the country where he was born. He was international.

One day everybody has to go. Nobody is immortal. But he who lives in the memory of his people, he, whose name inspires people to be brave and to fight, does not die. He lives on amongst his people.

To quote Rudyard Kipling:

"When the great scorer comes to write
against your name,
He writes not whether you won or lost
but how you played the game".

How I Knew Biju Babu

6

Dr. Jogesh Rout

While studying I.Sc. in Ravenshaw College (1943-45) and M.B.B.S. in S.C.B. Medical College at Cuttack (1945-50), I used to read in daily newspapers about the valour and adventures of Biju Patnaik. In 1932, as a student of only 17 years, he ventured to travel the then long hazardous distance from Cuttack to Peshawar by bicycle. He was associated with the freedom movement of India. He was imprisoned for participating in Quit India Movement from 1942 to 45. Similarly, Dr. Shariar and Mr. Mahammad Hatta took part in freedom movement of their country Indonesia, which was then ruled by Dutch government. Jawaharlal Nehru discussed with senior leaders how to save these patriots of Indonesia. Biju Patnaik was then a great pilot. He came forward to rescue these leaders of Indonesia from Jakarta for consultation and again drop them back at their capital Jakarta, though plane service was not very well developed in those days. Biju Babu risked his life by piloting the plane himself and brought

Shariar and Hatta from Jakarta. Again he dropped them back at Jakarta; and for this act of bravery and courage, Biju Babu was conferred the highest honour of Indonesian government called "Bhumiputra" (Son of the soil) in 1993-94. This was widely published in national newspapers and he was called variously as 'Kalinga Hero' and 'Samanta Kharavella of Orissa', in memory of the victorious king of Orissa who invaded Bihar and Peshawar during 3rd century B.C.

He was elected uncontested to the Orissa Legislative Assembly in 1947 after the independence of India. He was again re-elected in 1952 to Orissa Assembly under Adult Franchise. He was keen to industrialise Orissa. He set up Orissa Textile Mills and Kalinga Tubes at Choudwar by raising public shares. He set up a research team for extracting petrol out of coal, which is still available abundantly in Talcher, and sent them to Paris for further research. He established Kalinga Trust for awarding annual prizes to the best innovative research scholars of the world. He was so generous in donating money to students, patients and the poor that he was called a great donor after the legendary mythological figure Karna of the *Mahabharat*.

We were both elected in 1957 to the Orissa Legislative Assembly on Congress tickets and came closer to each other for which he liked me and always called me Doctor instead of Jogesh. He was enquiring about me when anyone from Banki met him. Biju Babu was a chain smoker. As a Doctor, I pointed out the cumulative effect of smoking. Later on he did not smoke at all, when he suffered from heart ailments. He was a very tall man and a voracious eater. We both were ardent supporters of Dr. Hare Krushna Mahatab, the Congress Chief Minister of Orissa in 1957. During lunch hour of Orissa Assembly session he discussed many things with the Chief Minister, especially on how to run the minority government. At that time he took lunch in the Assembly retiring room of Dr. Mahatab and called me sometimes to have lunch with him. He used to take non-vegetarian diet and I found that he was eating more than 2 kg of boiled and baked meat at a time. I can give another instance of his voracious eating and kindness to a friend. The married son of the then Balamukunda Mishra of Banki was stabbed to death by an anti-social. He approached Biju Babu for a job for his widow daughter-in-law when the latter was the Chief Minister of Orissa from 1990-95. Biju Babu could not recognise him as they met after a long gap of years and remained indifferent to his requests. But when Balamukunda Mishra reminded him of their young age travel together from Cuttack to Konark via Nimapada, and the latter swallowing 17 eggs at Nimapada, Biju Babu recollected the past incidents and did not hesitate to embrace a commoner like Balamukunda Mishra. He asked Balamukunda to stay in his residence whenever he came to Bhubaneswar and donated Rs.1000 for his maintenance. Besides, Biju Babu telephoned Collector, Cuttack to rehabilitate the widow daughter-in-law of Mishra by giving her an employment. He took pleasure in taking various non-vegetarian dishes till his death, even at the cost of his heart trouble and having oxygen cylinder by his side. He pleasantly narrated another eating incident before me and how at Baripada he took boiled and baked meat wrapped in green leaves.

He was also a book-worm, though he left studies while he was reading B.Sc. in Ravenshaw College and became busy in multifarious activities. Yet he was reading various books at his leisure time. I was travelling frequently by plane when I was the President of National Federation of State Cooperative Banks and Director, NABARD from 1980 to 1989 and during travels I found Biju Babu purchasing 2 to 3 books from Airport stall and reading them calmly inside the plane. Biju Babu was also a wonderful athlete and was awarded many prizes as best athlete during his school and college career.

R.N. Singh Deo an ex-feudal king of Bolangir was the leader of Ganatantra party. He too was the leader of the opposition then with 51 MLAs including many ex-feudal kings, as against 56 MLAs of Congress. Dr. H.K. Mahatab formed a minority government in 1957 with the support of Jharkhanda MLAs who were controlled by Jaipal Singh the then Jharkhand leader of Bihar. The Ganatantra party created trouble in de-establishing the government taking advantage of the marginal strength of the Congress. The Ganatantra party persuaded some ruling Congress MLAs to join their party and hid them at the Bhubaneswar residence of Sundargarh king, who was an MLA of Ganatantra party. Biju Babu was bold enough to bring back these MLAs from the residence of Sundargarh king in order to save the Congress government. Dr. Mahatab realised that coalition with Jharkhanda may not continue further. So he wanted to stabilise his government by making coalition with the Ganatantra party and with the ultimate merger of the Ganatantra with the Congress he could sideline Biju Patnaik, as many Ganatantra leaders were allergic to Biju Babu's big brotherly attitude. Biju Babu lost the election of the President of Orissa Pradesh Congress to Banamali Patnaik at the connivance of Dr. Mahatab. Biju Babu who then was the pillar of Congress and the king maker in Orissa politics, could not forget this defeat. He was determined to take revenge and therefore organised Congress MLAs and leaders opposed to Dr. Mahatab's policy of appeasement to members of Ganatantra party, whose design was to perpetuate their feudal land policy. Sri Banamali Patnaik an ardent supporter of Dr. Mahatab was first axed and removed by a no confidence motion moved by Biju Patnaik. Biju Patnaik was then elected as the President of Orissa Pradesh Congress in place of Sri Banamali Patnaik. Dr. Mahatab then got another jolt when he was reduced to the status of a minority leader in Orissa Congress legislative party in February 1961, just before the budget session. As a result, he was forced to resign as Chief Minister at the direction of Biju Patnaik and Governor's rule was imposed. Fresh election was held under the leadership of Biju Babu in June 1961. I was strongly backing Dr. Mahatab in leadership contest. But Biju

Babu was liberal enough in giving me Congress ticket to fight the Assembly election. Later on Biju Babu took steps for the merger of some prominent communist and socialist leaders to consolidate the Congress party in Orissa. Biju Babu took great risk and inevitably the Congress came out successful with absolute majority for the first time without the help of Utkal Keshari Dr. Mahatab - the king of the past two Congress minority governments of 1952 and 1957. Biju Babu became Chief Minister in June 1961. The people of Orissa became mad to see their hero and waited day and night whenever he went on tour and due to this the Congress captured a large number of Lok Sabha seats of Orissa in 1962. He was eager for the development of Orissa even at times without observing rules and regulations and then he did not care for the criticism of his adversaries. He was very much anxious for the rapid irrigation of land, as, he felt, it was mainly responsible for increasing agricultural productivity. Keeping this in view, he brought the famous retired Chief Engineer Dr. Khosla as the Governor of Orissa to complete the second stage of Mahanadi Irrigation Projects at Tikkerapada to irrigate the then Puri, Cuttack and Dhenkanal districts, without caring for the criticism of submersion of a few riverine villages of Mahanadi. He could take any risk to raise the standard of living of farmers, even though at times his adventure might not be fruitful but he would not be discouraged. He directed Chief Engineer, Hirakud on 09.07.61 to close Hirakud embankment gates for restraining the flow of flood water in order to save the standing crop in Delta area of the Mahanadi and due to this Hirakud embankment was threatened to be over flowed by flood water. I met him on 10th July, 1961 to inaugurate my Banki College. He was over-perturbed and worried as Hitler of Germany was, during the fall of Berlin, inside his bunker in the Second World War and told me, "Doctor! Cuttack will be washed away". The inhabitants of Cuttack had become panic-stricken and left for higher places and to Bhubaneswar in large numbers. But because of his good intentions, God helped him. Hirakud embankment was narrowly saved and did not topple as there was no further rain in the catchment area of the Mahanadi. He took immediate steps for the air dropping of food packets in the low-lying flooded areas of Cuttack district. As I have seen many floods in the past, I told him not to be in a hurry but he told me that nobody would starve under Biju regime. He introduced many innovative schemes like Panchayat industries in each block for rural employment and installation of tube wells for drinking water facility at the door steps of rural women who were then going more than one km. for a bucket of dirty contagious open-well or pond water. At that time he had been ridiculed by his adversaries as a dreamer but later, during the last decade by installation of massive tube wells in each village for supply of pure drinking water, he could transform his long vision and far-sightedness into a reality. He was bold enough to establish a major port at Paradeep and an Express Highway from Daitary to Paradeep, even when it was not included in the 3rd Five Year Plan. I was the Agriculture Minister in 1977 and held an election meeting at Rajnagar in favour of the Lok Sabha candidate from the Congress against Biju Patnaik of Janata Party, but persons present in our election meeting pointed out to me, in a straight forward manner, the Express Highway, as if Biju Babu was sleeping there. It was then the best communication link with the inaccessible inland areas for rural people, in addition to the transport of iron ores from Daitary to Paradeep. Moreover we got large employment in Paradeep Port for which Biju Babu was elected by massive vote in Kendrapada Lok Sabha seat in 1977. During his short tenure as Chief Minister he was advisor to Nehruji, the then Prime Minister of India to meet the challenges of the Indo Chinese war in 1962. He himself piloted the Kalinga Air Plane and dropped food packets and other military items in difficult hilly terrains of North East provinces bordering China. Biju Babu forced Nehruji, the then Prime Minister of India, for an aeroplane factory at Sunabeda against the pressures of Maharastra government, for which, as a compromise formula, Aero Engineering Factory was established at Sunabeda and the production of the rest of the plane components was established at Nasik. An All India Congress session was held at Bhubaneswar during the first week of January, 1964 under the guidance and supervision of Biju Babu. Such a grand session was not held ever before in which I participated as a delegate. Everybody was praising the efficiency and organising ability of Biju Babu. Also on request of Biju Babu, Nehruji laid the foundation stone of Tikkerpara project before the said session. After the session Nehruji became ill and for this there was speculation as to who would succeed Nehruji. A book was published in New Delhi containing details of some top leaders of Congress including Biju Babu (as successor to Nehru) for their past achievements, adventures and abilities. Unfortunately the Chagla Commission ignored his efficiency and recommended his resignation for the administrative impropriety of some of his actions during his tenure as the Chief Minister of Orissa. At that time the morale of the Congress party was very high. Biju Babu gladly submitted his resignation with due respect to the Chagla Commission findings. But, his two loyal friends became Chief Ministers after his resignation, and under his leadership and guidance the two succeeding Congress Chief Ministers ruled Orissa till 1967 Orissa Assembly election. After the death of Nehru in June 1964 he sided with the veteran freedom fighter and strong man Morarjee Bhai in Prime Ministership contest against Lal Bahadur Sastri and subsequently after death of Sastriji in January 1965 against Smt. Indiraji the daughter of Jawaharlalji and for this he incurred the displeasure of Indiraji. Unfortunately he lost Patkura Assembly seat in 1967 due to the split of Congress vote to the candidate of the combined opposition including Jana Congress led by Dr. Mahatab. After his defeat he was not given any weight and responsibility in

Orissa Congress for which he left the Congress. But he remained undaunted and formed Utkal Congress in 1971 to fight Orissa Assembly elections. Sometimes his adventure cost him heavily as he contested four Assembly seats and one Lok Sabha seat at a time and lost all these seats. However 21 of his supporters belonging to Utakal Congress got elected to Orissa Legislative Assembly in 1971 for which he was again reckoned in Orissan politics. But afterwards, he was elected in a bye-election from Rajnagar Assembly seat. Anyhow the Assembly was dissolved in 1973. Under Pragati Dal banner, opposed to the Congress, he was elected in 1974. Biju Babu then did not come to the Congress again but remained as a front-line leader of non-Congress parties in Orissa. Biju Babu thereafter was not defeated in any subsequent Lok Sabha or Assembly elections till his death in 1996 (i.e. he won elections in 1977, 1980, 1984, 1989, 1990, 1995 and 1996). He again went to jail during 1975 when emergency was imposed by the then Prime Minister Indira Gandhi for opposing her policy to dishonour the Allahabad High Court verdict unseating her out of Prime Ministership. After Lok Sabha election in 1977, Indiraji was defeated and Congress became a minority party in Lok Sabha. Morarji Bhai formed the government and became Prime Minister of India with strong support of Biju Patnaik. Biju Babu became Industry Minister and prepared a project to set up an Aluminium factory at Damanjodi of Koraput district and at Angul. He became Chief Minister again during 1990-1995 and took initiative for Rayagada Koraput Railway project, widening of Bhubaneswar Cuttack Road and setting up of another steel plant at Daitary, etc. He always had a soft corner for farmers and the toiling masses. He extended old age pension to all rural people above 60 years. I told him that the cost will exceed our state budget. But he told me, "Doctor, we are elected by rural people but we are offering pension only to limited service holders". Let this poor aged rural people enjoy pension for a token amount of Rs. 100 per month and let us not mind for the pressure on the exchequer. So he ordered for the survey of the old age people in villages for extending pension-benefits.

Biju Babu had faced many ups and downs in politics but he never felt discouraged. He had a great, towering, and versatile personality to influence national leaders for which he was treated as a great son of Orissa. The people of Orissa have got immense love for him, which was observed by the huge gathering at his funeral procession from Bhubaneswar to Puri in 1997. Biju Babu will be remembered for ever by Orissan people and by our Nation for his multi-faceted achievements. The Government of India has rightly renamed Bhubaneswar Air-Port after him to commemorate his formative career, as a daring pilot.

Biju Patnaik : An Enigma

7

Gour Mohan Sarangi

Almost fifty years back in 1964, an article published in Far Eastern Economic Review in its issue dated January 9, 1964 carried Biju Patnaik as its centre story, a paragraph which read thus:

"During the War (Second World War) he became an air-ace. He did not join the Air Force which attracted numerous young Indian pilots, but became a dare devil transport pilot when the British commandeered all commercial planes into a sort of Air-Transport Command. He pioneered risky operations over the Himalayan Hump into Chiang's China and even made a long hop into war-torn Stalingrad. When the Dutch were at the throat of the infant Indonesian Republic, Biju Patnaik flew clandestine missions into Indonesia and brought Sjharir and Hatta for personal conference with Indian Prime Minister Nehru. Patnaik flew the Indonesian leaders out of the fighting Republic by landing in improvised air-strips and fuelling his plane with petrol left over in little-known Japanese war-time dumps".

Biju Patnaik's life has been one of challenge, adventure and controversy. During his school days he was beaten up by Police for getting into an aeroplane which had landed at Kila Maidan, Cuttack. There is also a story regarding his breaking the leg of an European Officer during a hockey match as a revenge at the Officer's assault on innocent Congress volunteers. On 1st May 1932, he along with two friends started a cycle journey from Jobra to Peshawar on a 4000 plus miles journey. The incident of dumping an English Commander at Rueta for calling him a "bloody Indian Pilot" had become a household story in the military circle in the 40's.

As a Pilot in Air Transport command flying sorties between China, Middle East and the Far East, he had earned the confidence of the British. Biju Patnaik took advantage of this during the 1942 Quit India Movement and worked underground with leaders like Jaya Prakash Narayan, Aruna Asaf Ali and others. His Delhi residence had become an "Absconders' Paradise" (as told by his daughter Gita Meheta). Biju Patnaik was arrested in January 1943 from his Delhi residence and kept in solitary confinement for a pretty long period. After being released on parole in 1945, he was directed to keep himself confined within twenty miles of his Cuttack residence 'Ananda Bhawan'. By that time his father Laxminarayan had died in 1941 and his mother Asha Devi had also died in 1942. During this period of stay at Cuttack he got an opportunity of visualizing a new, industrial and prosperous Orissa. He then set his eyes on Choudwar as by then he had already floated his first business concern B. Patnaik & Company.

Biju Patnaik promoted the first textile mill in Orissa - Orissa Textile Mill, Choudwar. Then came the first tube factory - Kalinga Tubes, the first refrigerator factory, the 'Electrolux' - all at Choudwar. He promoted the first Low Staff Furnace in India, Kalinga Iron Works at Barbil, Keonjhar. He had founded the Kalinga Foundation Trust, which established the Chair at

Post-Graduate Department of Geology in Utkal University and the International Kalinga Prize for Science by the UNESCO. The Trust also had provisions for grant of scholarships for hundreds of meritorious students in Orissa. In 1950, apart from Biju Patnaik, other top Orissa leaders who were associated with Kalinga Foundation Trust included Dr. H.K. Mahatab and Naba Krushna Choudhury.

After becoming the Chief Minister of Orissa in 1961 (elected from Choudwar but lost from Dhenkanal) he started a number of projects in Orissa which included Paradeep Port, Balimela Dam, Express Highway and Corporations like Orissa Mining Corporation and Industrial Development Corporation. For the spread of education a number of universities were also set up by him.

But controversy never leaves Biju Patnaik, be it his cycle journey, a hockey match, his marriage procession, his career as a pilot, as a promoter of industries or as a politician. Though he was a political desciple of Dr. Harekrushna Mahatab, he fell out with him and was the architect of the Congress victory in 1961. Memorandums were sent against Biju Patnaik alleging corruption charges against his ministry and this led to the formation of a cabinet sub-committee by Government of India. Biju Patnaik resigned under the Kamaraj Plan on 1963 Gandhi Jayanti Day handing over the reins to Biren Mitra. Later Sadasiv Tripathy was the Chief Minister after the resignation of Biren Mitra.

A Commission of enquiry headed by Justice H.R. Khanna was set up after the coalition government of R.N. Singh Deo's Swatantra and Dr. Mahatab's Jana Congress came to power in March 1967. The Commission was appointed on 26th October 1967 and the report submitted on 15th January 1969. Biju Patnaik was arraigned by the State government in about 36 allegations (out of a total 70). The Commission held that out of 36 allegations only five were substantiated either totally or in part and held that the allegations proved would bring the case against Biju Patnaik within the ambit of the words "committed various acts of... impropriety and abuse of powers". These were sale of Kalinga Iron Works, purchase of Tubular Process from Kalinga Tubes, Daya Bridge Contract, appointment of Sundergarh P.P. and reduction in premium of land leased to O.T.M., Choudwar.

The main allegation of the State government before the Khanna Commission was that Biju Patnaik was not a man of means before 1947 and his object of sponsoring big projects and Corporations was to make illicit money. The Commission however held otherwise and said that the wealth of Biju Patnaik as determined by the Wealth Tax Officer was 22 lakhs in 1961-62, 24 lakhs in 1962-63 and 26 lakhs in 1963-64 and this increase was mainly due to appreciation in the value of the shares held by Mr. Patnaik (esp. the shares of Kalinga Airlines).

Irresponsible statements often dragged Biju Patnaik into unnecessary controversies. The latest being his call to assault corrupt officers when he was Chief Minister in 1990 and his plea for a military rule in India for a short spell. Even way back in April 1963, he was alleged to have stated at a public meeting at Jharsuguda that he was the owner of ten crores of rupees and if he wants he can become the Prime Minister of India. He was also alleged to have stated that for Paradeep Port normal financial and administrative rules be suspended. Khanna Commission commented that direction, if any, on these lines could only be considered as the result of misguided zeal. Biju Patnaik was always a man in a hurry and his interest for developing Orissa to a vibrant State found expression in his letter dated 15.01.65 addressed to the Prime Minister where he had stated that "The people of Orissa should cease to be the hewers of wood and drawers of water and look for jobs as coolies in Calcutta and Assam Tea-gardens."

Justice Khanna while concluding, had remarked that Biju Patnaik had the halo of an adventurous past. He had daring, dash, doggedness, personality. To all this he had a touch of flamboyance — Biju Patnaik did commendable job in certain spheres by introducing an element of dynamism in the administration, and the work he did by translating the idea of a port at Paradeep into a living reality is bound to make an impact in the history of Orissa. But the Commission added that Biju Patnaik allowed such a way to the pecuniary and business interests of his companies in its dealings with the State government that within 2-3 years of his stewardship his public image became tarnished — The architect of victory in 1961, lost even his own election in 1967.

The defeat of the Congress in 1967 was the result of waves of scandalous propaganda launched by Swatantra-Jana Congress. Biju Patnaik lost Patkura election to a school teacher by a margin of more than fifteen thousand votes. The people of Patkura were so repentant that in all the subsequent ten elections thereafter they have been continuously electing Biju Babu's candidates from Patkura.

Not only hopes of Orissa were shattered with the fall of Biju Patnaik in 1967, but Biju Babu also lost the hope of a come-back. In 1971, he contested four Assembly and one Parliament election and lost all five. He however came back to Orissa Assembly in a bye-election from Rajnagar. His Utkal Congress had also a share in the State government with Biswanatha Dash as Chief Minister from 03.04.71 to 14.06.72. This ministry was however short-lived because of constant pressure from Utkal Congress members to return to the Congress and therefore Nandini Satapathy became the Chief Minister in June, 1972.

Biju Patnaik was however not taken back to the Congress. In March 1973, Nandini Satapathy's Congress candidates for Rajya Sabha got defeated and immediately thereafter Biju Patnaik paraded 72 M.L.As. before the then Governor B.D. Jatti at Raj Bhawan and demanded that he be invited to form the Government. But Jatti had perhaps contrary instructions and he instead, recommended for Presidents rule in Orissa. Aggrieved, Biju Patnaik went to the Orissa High Court for justice. Though the High Court passed adverse comments on the conduct of the Governor, it could not redress the wrong done to Biju Patnaik because the 'pleasure' of Governor was not "justiciable".

Twenty years later the full bench of the Supreme Court held otherwise in "S.R. Bomai vrs. Union of India" (A.I.R. - 94-SC-1918) where abundant light was thrown on controversial roles of State Governors inviting President's rule. But for Governor Jatti, Biju Patnaik would have been Chief Minister of Orissa in 1973.

Then came the emergency in June 1975 and Biju Patnaik was confined to jail along with Jaya Prakash Narayan, Morarji Desai and others. With elections in 1977, Biju Patnaik was in the centre stage of Janata Party and All India Politics. He was Union Minister of Steel & Mines from 1977-79. Thereafter he continued to be elected from Kendrapara Parliamentary Constituency in all the four elections of 1977, 1979, 1980, 1984 and 1985. In 1985 he was also elected to Orissa Assembly from Bhubaneswar Assembly Constituency. He resigned the Lok Sabha seat, retained the Assembly seat and was the leader of Opposition in Orissa Assembly from 1985-90. As Chairman of Public Accounts Committee and leader of Janata Dal he toured extensively throughout the State and as expected after the 1990 elections became the Chief Minister of Orissa again for the second time.

Chief Ministership in 1990 did not come to Biju Patnaik in a platter. He had toured extensively and the youth who were born after 1965 heard so many stories on Biju's adventurous past that they stood behind him as a soft rock. His work during the cyclone of 1971, the excesses of the Emergency, his single-handed effort in shifting the Interim Test Range from Baliapal, all stood him in good stead. During 1987, he had gone for his heart treatment to the U.S.A. for which a contribution of Rs.1.5 lakhs was received from the people of Orissa. A video cassette

"Juga Sarathi" on his life and achievements was prepared and shown throughout the State before the 1990 elections and the people believed that only Biju Patnaik could build a new Orissa, by throwing money, the administration and financial rules to the Bay of Bengal.

They were correct and it seems the Khanna Commission had no sobering effect on him. It was his second or third day in office after taking oath; the Chief Minister's Secretariat had not started functioning. Since I was his Private Secretary as leader of Opposition, I confined myself to work as P.S. to Chief Minister. At about 11 A.M. I was summoned to his room in the Forest Park office. A South Indian old man and his daughter in twenties were inside. Biju Babu asked me to find out a job for the girl who was a graduate in Hindustani Music within a day or two. When I fumbled - saying that the vacancy position and post sanction are to be first found out, he shouted and said that the Chief Minister's order has to be carried out, and the concerned Secretary or Director be accordingly intimated. The girl got the job the next day, though on an ad hoc basis. Administrative niceties were of no consequence to Biju Patnaik, neither in 1961 nor in 1990.

In the sixties, his idea of a Port at Paradeep was translated into reality and in the 1990's he was obsessed with the idea of a Second Steel Plant for Orissa. Two years later on 9th May 1992 came the 'Shilanyas' of the Steel Plant at Jakhapura, with an industrialist N.R.I. Swaraj Paul (Late Lion Swaraj Paul). Then came MESCO of J.K. Singh and Rita Singh. The Singh couple were frauds as later events proved and Swaraj Paul also backed out leaving only a 'Kadamba' as a bitter memory of Biju's aborted attempts. The second term of Biju Patnaik was remembered for some populist and controversial decisions like Property Statement of Ministers, sudden decision to raise daily wage to twenty five rupees, restriction on use of government vehicle, reservation of 1/3rd seats for ladies, setting of Special Courts and his call to assault corrupt officials.

About 10 cases of corruption were initiated by the Vigilance, after Biju Patnaik came to power. The much talked-about case of 'disproportionate assets' of the ex-Chief Minister Janaki Ballav Patnaik could not stand the scrutiny of the Courts as the Vigilance had not taken into account the income of his wife Jayanti Patnaik as an M.P. while computing his total income! That goes to the credit of State Vigilance. But they have succeeded in getting two ministers of J.B. Patnaik's cabinet convicted, Sarata Rout and Bata Krishna Jena who have appealed in the High Court of Orissa. Five cases are pending.

During the first year of his second term, there was a great controversy on his alleged call to the people of Orissa to assault corrupt officials. A public interest litigation was filed in the High Court of Orissa seeking an injunction in this regard. It was argued that such a public call violated the basic structure of our Constitution and was against the Rule of law. Orissa High Court called for and referred to the speech of the Chief Minister on the floor of the Orissa Legislative Assembly and came to the conclusion that the basic idea behind such a call was to install a fear psychosis in the mind of the Officers by making them aware that Government would not tolerate corruption. The Court held that "The storm has been well blown over, we part with the hope that such a storm would not be seen again". (AIR -92 Orissa - 10).

It was during his second term as Chief Minister that Biju Babu introduced Reservation for Ladies in the Local Bodies. When people had not heard of Rabri Devi of Bihar, Biju got one house wife of Bhubaneswar Kiran Bala Mangaraj as the Chairperson of Bhubaneswar Municipality even though many eyebrows were raised. He also introduced the two child norm for the Gram Panchayat and Municipal elections. The country is still to opt for Women's reservation, - Biju Babu had done it since 1990's.

Biju Patnaik had become the 'Bhumiputra' of Indonesia for his contribution to Indonesian freedom struggle. In a special function at Indonesia in 1950, Indonesia as a mark of gratitude donated a large area covering mines and buildings built by the Dutch which was donated by the Patnaik couple to the people of Indonesia. In 1965 when Pakistan attacked India, on the request of Prime Minister Lal Bahadur Sastri, Biju Patnaik and Gyan Patnaik went to Indonesia at their own cost. On the request of the Bhumiputra, President Sukarno issued orders for return journey of the Indonesian subrumines which were on their way to attack the Indian ports of Madras, Bombay and Vizag. On the occasion of 50 years of Indonesian Independence he was the guest of honour at Indonesian Capital where he was decorated as Bintang Jasa Uttam (first class star of decoration) on 17th August '95.

Many people know about his Indonesian escapades, but very few know why Russia decorated him with a jubilee medal in a special function at the Russian Embassy at Delhi on September 29, 1995. It was for his "Aid to Russia" during World War-II.

Biju Patniak would have been the President of Janata Dal when Bomai was forced to resign because of "Hawala" but because of his statement some months back that to curb the evils of political system the country needs a short spell of military rule. How would such a person become the President of 2nd largest party of India.

In 1996 Biju Patnaik had won from two parliamentary constituencies of Cuttack and Aska. This distinction had gone to two other politicians of the country Narasingha Rao, ex-Prime Minister and Bajpeyee who became Prime Minister later. Biju Patnaik could not become a Minister even when Deve Gowda became the Prime Minister because Orissa Government had started a vigilance case against him for the 18 cores scandal.

Before the Khanna Commission it was stated by the State Government that Biju Patnaik was not a man of much means before 1947. The same story was repeated by the State

Government in 1996, Vigilance Court at Bhubaneswar where Biju Patnaik had to go on bail on May 30, 1996. A news item in the Samaj dated 16.12.39 stated that "Captain Biju Patnaik marries the grand daughters of Ray Saheb Radhasyam Seth of Roulpindi on 06.12.39 and the grooms party all travelled in private aeroplanes - It was the first marriage in India where "Barat" travelled in planes. In late fifties and early fifties he was the owner of 12 aeroplanes, promotor of ten companies and who had two luxury suites reserved for him throughout the year in the Grand Hotel, Calcutta. And they had argued that Biju Patnaik was not a man of means before he plunged into politics.

It is said Biju Patnaik is a good promoter but a bad manager and this is true in respect of his business adventures as well as politics. Had he not forsaken business interests in favour of politics, he would have become another Tata or Birla of India. Biju Patnaik is a story of "riches to rags". It is because of politics that he had to sell Kalinga Tubes, O.T.M., Kalinga Iron Works and other business concerns to raise funds for politics; he also sold a portion of 3 Aurangazeb Road, his Delhi house.

A painful period for him was the eighteen crores scandal period. Biju Patnaik had two accounts in Allahabad Bank, Bhubaneswar, one in his name and the other in the name of the President, Janata Dal, Orissa. After being Chief Minister in 1990, even though Ashok Das became the President, Biju Patnaik was authorised to transact the party accounts. Such transactions of accounts by him created suspicions in certain quarters and his transparacy was in doubt. However, he was much above such suspicion and he was never after money for his personal gain.

In fact at no point of time the cash credits of Janata Dal exceeded 1.5 crores and at the time of departure of Biju Patnaik for Delhi on 28.03.97 (his last journey from Orissa) the party account had only 4.45 lakhs and his personal account had three thousand only. He left for Delhi with two fifty rupee notes in his pockets and left a new bundle of 50 rupees (50 thousands) with Kairati Mian for sundry payments to newspaper venders, milkman and others.

Here ends the story of a legendary figure of Orissa whose dead body came to Bhubaneswar on 18.04.97. There was an off-season car festival at Puri at the time of his funeral where all former Prime Ministers (except V.P. Singh for illness) were present. Biju Patnaik in death was more in demand than when he was alive. But controversy has not left Biju Patnaik even after his death, the dispute on Biju Legacy is still on.

The question as to why Biju Patnaik stayed at 9, Tyagraj Road instead of 3, Aurangjeb Road during his last days is also a controversy.

Biju Patnaik : A Profile

8

Dr. Pabak Kanungo

Perhaps no other leader occupied the imagination of the people of Orissa like Biju Patnaik: freedom fighter, pilot, industrialist, politician and philanthropist. He was Orissa's restless son and became a legendary hero. His ability to create confidence among people and inspire them was phenomenal. He had a remarkable capacity to transmit his cheerful strength to others. Biju was basically a secular man and was an instinctively nationalist as his hero Napoleon. Like Pandit Jawaharlal Nehru, he navigated by the four immutably fixed stars of his convictions—national unity, democracy, secularism and the end of imperialism. Sir Julian Huxley had described Biju Patnaik as a "remarkable Indian whose adventures would fill a book". In an obituary reference the prestigious magazine *The Economist* says, "It is worth writing about Biju Patnaik for at least two reasons. His long life can be read as something of a history of India back to the time when the country was run by the British. And he gave Indian politics a rare fresh of colour". *The Encyclopedia Britannica* described Biju as "Indian

Politician; who parlayed his fame as a World War-II aviator, anti-British freedom fighter and commercial airline entrepreneur into a political career, notably as Chief Minister of Orissa State, 1961-63 and 1990-95".

Bijoyananda (Biju) Patnaik was born in Cuttack, Orissa, on 5th March, 1916 to Laxminarayan Patnaik and Ashalata Devi. Although he was in judicial service, Laxminarayan was a great nationalist and a prominent leader of the Oriya Movement. He was closely associated with two architects of modern Orissa—Utkal Gourav Madhusudan Das and Utkalmani Gopabandhu Das. He was taking great pride in Orissa's cultural heritage. Biju inherited the qualities of fearlessness and love of Orissa from both his parents.

Biju had two brothers and one sister. His elder brother Sradhananda (Dr. George Patnaik) was a renowned dentist and his younger brother Jayananda (Siju) was a pilot and the only sister was Sukruti Patnaik. Biju, who was married to Gyan, has two sons and one daughter. His elder son Prem is an industrialist and second son Naveen is a writer-turned politician. His daughter Gita Mehta, who lives in New York, is admired as a novelist and as an author of books on the westernisation of India.

Biju had his early education in Mission Primary School and Mission (Christ Collegiate) School of Cuttack. In 1927 he joined the famous Ravenshaw Collegiate School, where Netaji Subhash Chandra Bose was once a student. In 1932 he passed matriculation with a first division and got admitted into the intermediate science class of the famous Ravenshaw College, Cuttack. From his days at the Ravenshaw Collegiate School, he was an accomplished sportsman and led the University teams in football, cricket, athletics and hockey. For three consecutive years he was the sports champion of Ravenshaw College.

Biju first saw Mahatma Gandhi in 1927 during the latter's 'Khadi Tour' of Orissa and came under his spell. The desire to defy British rule first awakened in him from his school days. He was assaulted by a British police officer as he tried to get a glimpse of the Mahatma, who was visiting Cuttack. He showed his penchant for the extraordinary at a very young age. Like his role model Napoleon, he seemed to have deleted the word 'impossible' from his dictionary.

Biju discontinued studies for a B.Sc. degree to undergo training as a pilot at the Aeronautic Training Institute of India and Delhi Flying Club. In fact, as a child Biju was fascinated by aeroplanes and from his school days, he had decided to make a career in flying. A small aeroplane had landed at Cuttack's Killa Fort, when he was a student of Mission School. Biju ran away from school to touch his dream object. But he was chased away by the security police. "At that time I had only seen pictures of aeroplanes in books"-he recalled later. His great pleasure was flying and his exploits as a pilot provided his career with a metaphor that endured from the frolics of his youth to his ambition to be a politician and industrialist. He was, everyone said, a high flyer. It is said that at his wedding to Gyan in 1939, guests arrived in Tiger Moths.

When the Second World War broke out Biju Patnaik joined the Royal Indian Air Force and along with British friends who, like him, had learnt the rudiments of flying at the Delhi Flying Club. When Japan entered the war in 1941, Biju Patnaik evacuated British families from the advancing invaders. He flew supplies to China and the Soviet Union. He pioneered risky operations across the Himalayas to help the Chinese revolutionaries in Chiang Kai Shek's China. He once flew all the way to Stalingrad on yet another mission. The British Government particularly appreciated his efforts to evacuate British families from Rangoon (Yangon) when the Japanese invaded Myanmar during World War-II.

As '*The Economist*' says—Biju Patnaik had a second loyalty. When he was 13, Biju had met and come under the spell of Mahatma Gandhi, the proponent of passive resistance to British rule. In the War he sought to satisfy both of his strongly held beliefs: the need to defeat Japan and to give India independence. While flying over Indian soldiers under the British Command he dropped bags of Gandhi's "Quit India" leaflets to them. But though he served the British, Biju Patnaik's loyalty was with the Indian freedom struggle. While on leave, he ferried independence leaders to secret meetings with their supporters. As head of the Air Transport Command of the RIAF, he sheltered in his house prominent fighters like Jaya Prakash Narayan, Ram Manohar Lohia and Aruna Asaf Ali. While flying the British to safety from Yangon, he also air-dropped leaflets supporting the cause of Netaji's Indian National Army. "When the British authority found out, they nearly got me shot for subversive activities. That was the time I was put behind bars during the Quit India Movement," Patnaik said later. Some of the hazardous flying missions that he undertook first with the RIAF and later with Indian National Airways earned him the sobriquet of a "daredevil".

Aruna Asaf Ali, who was one of the prominent fighters of the Quit India Movement has said—"Among the thousands who came forward to take up the challenge, Biju Patnaik was one of the most fearless, who mobilised his fellow pilots and inspired them to help the "Underground Directorate". But for their courage and fearlessness, we could never have succeeded in linking up with our comrades in Bombay, Calcutta, Madras and New Delhi. We also used the airlines for travelling incognito sometime".

But Biju Patnaik's scarcely concealed double-life could not last. Arrested on January 13, 1943, he was sentenced to two years imprisonment and lodged in Firozpur Fort Jail.

After his release from jail in 1945, Biju was elected to Orissa Assembly in 1946 from North Cuttack Constituency. Though more recognised as a politician, once he reminisced—"Flying is my first love and though it has dimmed with age, it still remains so". While his love for the country had his opposition to British rule made him plunge into Indian freedom struggle in a daring manner as a young man, Biju played a significant role in the Indonesian freedom movement. The same indomitable spirit had him fly to India the leaders of the Indonesian freedom struggle, despite the threat of his plane being shot down by the Dutch Colonial rulers. He became internationally known, when, under Nehru's instructions, he conducted sorties to Indonesia against Dutch threats.

In what can be aptly described as a drama in real life, Biju took off in an old fashioned dakota with wife Gyan for Jakarta (leaving behind their 14 day old son), where the rebel's headquarters was located. In Singapore, he received a message from the Dutch threatening to shoot down his aircraft if it entered Indonesian airspace. "Resurgent India does not recognise Dutch colonial sovereignty over the Indonesian people. If my aircraft is shot down, every Dutch plane flying across the Indian skies will be shot down in retaliation" was Biju's reply. He also dashed off a message to Prime Minister Nehru—"Take necessary steps should my aircraft be shot down". As the world watched him with admiration, the 32 year old ace pilot, landing on an improvised airstrip and using left over petrol from abandoned Japanese military dumps, eluded the Dutch to land in Jakarta and flew back to Delhi with Indonesian leaders Mohammad Hatta and Sultan Shariar for holding confabulations with Pandit Nehru and Sardar Patel.

Biju thereafter became a focal point of all activities relating to Indian support to the Indonesian freedom struggle. The wide publicity given to the exploit gave a boost to the cause of Indonesian independence. A grateful Indonesia twice decorated Biju Patnaik with its highest civilian honour 'Bhumi Putra' in return for the bravery the Indian leader had displayed at its hour of crisis. Biju Patnaik liked to tell the story of how he persuaded Sukarno to call his daughter, Meghawati (Goddess of the clouds). She is now the President of Indonesia. In 1996, on the occasion of that country's 50th independence day, Biju received, the "Bintang Jasu Utama"-Indonesia's highest national award.

Biju's daring-do continued even after Indian independence. He started his own airline, the Kalinga Airways and in 1947 carried soldiers into Kashmir, when it was threatened from across the newly created border sky. At great risk, he landed the first platoon of troops in Srinagar.

Biju Patnaik is considered as a pioneer of the industrial growth of Orissa and established a string of industries in mission. He set up the Kalinga Tubes, the first modern Textiles Mills at Choudwar, Orissa, the first Refrigerator factory at Jobra, Cuttack and a low shaft Furnace at Barbil. In 1951 he established the Kalinga Prize for the popularisation of science and entrusted the responsibility to the UNESCO.

Like a colossus, Biju strode Orissa's political arena for more than four decades. Whether in power or in the opposition, he was one of the most influential politicians of the country. It was while trying to build an industrial empire at Choudwar, just across River Mahanadi from Cuttack that he forayed into electoral politics. He won an Assembly election from North Cuttack Sadar seat in 1946 and set up Kalinga Tubes at Choudwar, his flagship industry and at one time Asia's largest pipe manufacturing plant. The resounding success in 1961 midterm poll established him as a superb party organiser and the brief period of his administrative stewardship built his image of a dynamic man who could electrify the people of the State with a sense of urgency and keep bureaucrats on their tiptoes.

Biju Patnaik had a brief tenure in office as he was 'Kamarajed' out in October 1963. But during this period he injected a rare dynamism into the administration and lifted the "featureless and futureless" people of Orissa out of the slough of despondency. He acutely felt that Orissa mirrors the paradox of all backward areas—poverty amidst potential plenty. Orissa has a wealth of natural resources and yet it is the poorest and most backward state of India. Therefore for him any plan for the development of these vast natural resources, which shall help transform poverty into plenty may well serve as a model for other similarly situated areas in India.

Within that short period during which he took the stewardship of the state administration, Biju Patnaik laid the blue print for Orissa's development and the State was on the threshold of a new era of industrial revolution. He not only accelerated the process of development but was able to locate a number of new industries in the State—the MIG factory at Sunabeda, Balimela Dam, Public Corporations, Panchayat Industries, the Express High Way and a lot many. His ambitious projects, which he named as "Decade of Destiny" was meant to elevate the State to a new height.

A towering personality and administrator, who meant business all the time, Biju could not tolerate red-tapisms. He would have a thing done immediately and not suffer any delay. Result - he was charged with administrative impropriety. To the officials his advice was, "be loyal to me not to the government but to the destinies of this State, to the prosperity of the people." There is a story that once when a speeding motor truck carrying stones for the Paradeep Port was stopped by a traffic policeman, the driver humorously replied that the speed suggested by the policeman would delay the port work by several years, when Biju Patnaik wanted everybody to work at top gear.

The importance that Biju attached to Orissa's industrial development was reflected in his speech which he delivered at the inauguration of the Orissa Planning Board on June 15, 1962. He had said—"A people cannot grow unless the industries were developed and established here". Calling upon the bureaucrats to change their work-style, Patnaik said, "In the new set-up, in the new adventure which we are going to embark upon, I would expect my officials to become thinkers and administrators in turn. I would expect them to collectively and willingly push the State towards the goal of prosperity. I would expect them to become leaders of men and not leaders of the longest notes on the files".

At the invitation of Biju Patnaik, internationally known Biologist, Scientist and Philosopher Prof. J.B.S. Haldane accepted the post of the Director of the Biomety and Genetics Laboratory at Bhubaneswar, which was set up by the Government of Orissa. Prof Haldane, who imparted to the Indian scientific scene a certain colour and character, became an Indian citizen in 1960 and devoted himself to assisting development of science in this rapidly developing country. He accepted Biju's offer because he (Biju) was 'capable of displaying great respect towards individuals whom he considered to be performing worthwhile work'. This genius died in Bhubaneswar on lst December, 1964.

After Biju Patnaik took the rein of the State administration, Orissa witnessed rapid strides in education. The period between 1961-67 is aptly described as the golden era in the history of education of the State. At his initiative the Regional College of Education was set up at Bhubaneswar, The Regional Engineering College at Rourkela was established. In 1961, the Orissa University of Agriculture and Technology was set up and during the Chief Ministership of Biren Mitra (when Biju was the chairman of the State Planning Board). Universities were established in Berhampur and Sambalpur. Thus Biju is responsible for the giant leap forward of education in Orissa. When Biju was in the Congress, his courage and defiance of the Central government during the Nehru era built his image among the people. When the Union government refused to construct the Paradeep Port, as the Chief Minister of Orissa he took upon himself to mobilise resources from within the State and built the Rs.14 crore Port when the Centre did not show much interest in the project. Patnaik's strong stand on the issue was vindicated when the Centre took over the Port after some years. Biju Patnaik proved his extraordinary organising ability by successfully holding the Congress Session in 1964 at Bhubaneswar. His dream was fulfilled when on 12th March 1966, the Paradeep Port was commissioned.

Biju Babu was all along trying to spread science education in the state and was of the view that the common man, with little or no education should have access to the latest scientific developments. In the Oriya daily 'The Kalinga' which he had started, there was a separate science section and he encouraged many eminent Oriya scientists or science popularisers to regularly write for common men.

A close confidant of Pandit Nehru, Biju enjoyed free access to Teen Murti Bhawan, the P.M's official residence. Nehru had entrusted him with the additional responsibilities of advising him on defence matters during the Chinese aggression and Patnaik was allotted an office near the P.M's office in North Block. Pandit Nehru had asked him to visit the United States as an Advisor to the Ministry of External Affairs and discuss sensitive defence issues with the U.S. administration. During his stay in Washington Biju gave interviews to 'Baltimore Sun' and 'Washington Post', in which he said that he had come to seek both ground-to-ground and air-to-air missiles along with radars, which could conceivably be tied to a network of the South East Asian Treaty Organisation (SEATO). US newspapers also portrayed the Orissa Chief Minister as the coming Defence Minister, who will replace Y B Chouhan. The opposition charged Biju Patnaik with 'impropriety of revealing defence secrets, including details of the strength of the Indian Army'. There was a furore in Parliament and even the Lok Sabha Speaker Sardar Hukum Singh ruled that—'it is not proper to disclose such information which is denied here'. But the Prime Minister strongly supported Biju and declared in the Parliament that whatever has been said by him to American newspapers 'did not harm us in any way'. This controversy highlighted how close Biju was to Pt. Nehru.

During the time Biren Mitra was Chief Minister, a

memorandum was submitted to the President of India by opposition parties making allegations of impropriety and abuse of office against Biju Patnaik, Biren Mitra and other ministers of Orissa. The Home Ministry referred the matter to the Central Bureau of Investigations for a preliminary enquiry. After the receipt of the report of the CBI, the Prime Minister Lal Bahadur Shastri constituted a Sub Committee of the Union Cabinet, which studied various allegations. In a letter to Biju Patnaik dated January 15, 1965 the Prime Minister said:

> "The Sub-Committee has given the finding that in the various transactions in which you were concerned, you had not personally derived any pecuniary benefits ...".

However, Shastriji pointed out, there still remains the question of improprieties to which the sub-committee has drawn attention. In reply to Shastri's letter Biju Patnaik drew his attention to the fact that the sub-committee have arrived at their conclusions based on "scrappy and disconnected informations" furnished to them. He said, "where corruption charges are not established, the next handle would be administrative impropriety, irregularity or indiscretion and would even be stretched to lack of judgement, wisdom, prudence, each succeeding one made to appear more heinous than the previous one". Appealing to P.M. to consider the reality, Biju Patnaik said—"As one who has the pride to serve the party and the people with some dedication, I can assure the P.M. that I don't seek any special consideration except common justice to uphold individual dignity and honour. If a combination of events and circumstances is deliberately created by a determined few, then the prospects of a fearless, free and democratic India are bleak indeed ! After Indira Gandhi took over as Prime Minister in 1966, Biju realised that he is not very comfortable in the Congress Party. In 1967 general election, the Congress Party suffered humiliating defeat in Orissa, as elsewhere and Patnaik was also defeated from a number of Assembly seats.

After the 1967 general elections the Congress government was replaced by the Swatantra-Jana Congress coalition and the new government set up the Khanna Commission to enquire into the charges of corruption and administrative impropriety levelled against Biju Patnaik and others. To the pleasant surprise of many Patnaik-admirers, although the commission found the charges of administrative impropriety true in some respects it made it clear that none was meant for individual benefit. It paid Biju Patnaik rich compliments. The Commission said:

> "The need of Orissa is of a leader of great calibre, inspired by the cause, dedicated, devoted and determined, who may arouse the enthusiasm which is so far dormant, of the masses, harness it to fruitful activity and thus pave the way to economic betterment and future prosperity. Biju Patnaik gave hope of that calibre. He had the halo of an adventurous past. He had daring, dash, doggedness and the advantage of youth, good physique and a tall imposing personality. To all these may be added a touch of flambuoyance. Biju Patnaik did commendable job in certain spheres by introducing an element of dynamism in the administration and the work he did by translating the idea of a Port at Paradeep into a living reality is bound to make an impact on the history of Orissa and its future development".

More than two decades later, when he returned for a five year rule as the Janata Dal C.M. in March 1990, Biju Patnaik would often recall the Khanna Commission's findings and said, "I will commit such improprieties even today if it helped Orissa to progress".

The Indian National Congress had split in 1969. In May, 1970 Biju Patnaik and his followers left the Congress (R) in protest against "naked bossism" and central imposition after he had been denied a ticket to Rajya Sabha by the Congress High Command; although his case was sponsored by the Provincial Congress Committee. In 1970 he resigned from the Congress Party and subsequently formed a regional party Utkal

Congress. In the 1971 election, no party came out with a clear majority. Biju Patnaik and the Swatantra leader R.N. Singh Deo joined hands. This came as a surprise to political observers, as Singh Deo was a bitter critic of Biju. And with the support of the Jharkhand Party, they formed a United Front. Biju successfully persuaded the 82 years old veteran politician Biswanath Das to become the Chief Minister, after his long spell of political retirement.

Utkal Congress and Swatantra Parties fought election under the banner of Pragati Party and the political combine fared well in the election. Biju was closely associated with the Lok Sangarsha Samiti of Jaya Prakash Narayan and organised the Orissa visit of J.P. in 1975. When Indira Gandhi declared emergency on 25-26 June, 1975, Biju was one of the first to be arrested under MISA and lodged in Rohtak Jail in Haryana. In the 1977 election, he was elected from Kendrapara to Lok Sabha and was inducted into the Morarji Desai government as Minister of Steel & Mines. In the 1980 election, he was again elected to the Lok Sabha. In 1985 he resigned from Parliament retaining his Assembly seat and became the leader of the opposition in the Orissa Assembly.

Biju's illustrious political career culminated in his party's resounding victory in the 1990 Assembly polls and he returned as Chief Minister for the second time on March 5, 1990. For the first time he completed the full term (1990-95). A Biju critic says that he functioned in an arbitrary and autocratic manner "I am the party and I am the government"—he used to say "Am I not enough ?" was his reaction when immediately after being sworn in as Chief Minister in 1990 he was asked, how long it would take for him to choose other members of the Cabinet. Biju had a painful feeling that in spite of being so rich in natural resources, Orissa has remained one of the poorest and most backward states in India. The quality of its administration has steadily deteriorated, to the disgust of the voters. Since bureaucrats are virtually unshakable in India, he suggested in a speech that disgruntled citizens should assault them. Biju was never comfortable with the Mandal Commission recommendation and did not hesitate to publicly air his stand against V.P. Singh's decision to implement the Mandal Commission. Although many pro-Mandal leaders of the Janata Dal were never happy with Patnaik for his views and style of functioning, they did not dare to do anything to displease the Grand Old Man of Orissa politics. Another point on which his critics find fault with him is that when he lost power in 1995 as in 1967 in the election that followed, he never attempted to build a second line of command in his party.

During the final term as Chief Minister (1990-95), he acted more as a statesman than the head of the government. He caused a turmoil when he threatened that Orissa would secede from the Indian Union if the Centre continued to neglect it. Prime Minister Chandra Sekhar took serious exception and demanded that Biju should clarify his position. Patnaik explained that Orissa should be given fiscal autonomy in a true federal structure to script its own economic development. He also floated the demand for full convertibility of the rupee.

The final phase of Biju's political career was perhaps an unhappy chapter to his long, chequered political career. Having been voted out of power from the State in 1995, he contested two Lok Sabha seats—Aska in Ganjam district and Cuttack Sadar. He won both the seats at a time when the Congress had swept the election in the State. People naturally expected that he would hold a centre-stage at the national politics. But to their dismay, they found that lesser elements within the party, including some who owed their political existence to him, were out to undermine his importance and every possible method to undermine their leader was adopted. To prevent him from joining the Union Cabinet, even graft cases were slapped on him.

Biju Patnaik was disillusioned over the brand of politics going on at the Centre. He was also unhappy over the constant bickering within his party. As a matter of fact, he was never comfortable with the Mandalisation of the Janata Dal and thought that the Dal claim about introducing social justice were suspect. Towards the end, he had become a convert to the ideas of having a broad-based, democratic coalition, which included the Congress.

A long, illustrious career came to an end on 17th April, 1997 when Biju Patnaik passed away at Delhi. His death was one of the worst tragedies that had ever happened to the State of Orissa and removed the greatest figure of our time at the very climax of his career. Grief and shock swept across Orissa as news of his death spread. It was perhaps a tryst with destiny that Patnaik was cremated at *Swargadwara*, Puri. He was to rest in peace close to the abode of his *Kalia* (Lord Jagannath). Though he was not religious in the traditional sense, he had a sentimental attachment to Lord Jagannath. While addressing public meetings in front of the Puri Jagannath Temple, he used to enter into a monologue with the Lord.

Adventure indeed! It is in his blood from boyhood. It is this love of adventure that goaded him to have a bicycle ride from Cuttack to Peshawar when he was a student and to change his profession of an aeronautical engineer to that of a pilot. It is this call of adventure that inspired him to undertake the risky jobs of flying the stranded Britishers in Burma to safety during the Second World War days and to carry on at the same time anti-British subversive activities which ultimately landed him into jail. In providing indispensable leadership, he emerged as the greatest political figure of his age. The story of his adventurous life still inspires the youth of Orissa.

Biju never flinched in his determination to develop the country and uplift the poor. "Never despair" was what he used to say to his supporters. Always he exhorted the people of the state to emulate the ideals of Kharavela. Timeless fortitude, persistence and respect for the common man made him a unique personality. He devoted his life to build a new era of progress and did it with a combination of skilled statesmanship and innovative spirit. He touched millions of Oriyas in a very personal way and earned his place in the home and hearts of a whole generation.

As the '*Hindustan Times*' editorially commented after his death—"It may not be an exaggeration to say that Biju Patnaik was the tallest among all the leaders from Orissa, who made their mark in national politics. A major reason why he acquired this status was undoubtedly his romantic, impulsive nature, which made him stand out even at a time when, with Nehru and J.P. at the height of their power and there was no dearth of colourful politicians in India".

People were fascinated by the considerable charm and the range of accomplishments of this Grand Old Man of Orissa, who led a full life. No matter what the challenges, he believed that the facts were only one part of reality—the other part was how you react to them and change them for the better. That he was a visionary can be underscored by an illustration—Way back in the sixties, when the licence raj permit was at its peak, Biju startled people by talking about liberalisation. He remained a votary of economic reform till the very end and had the courage of conviction to take on those who blindly aped this model or that. He was so clear about basic issues because he was not just a politician - an industrialist and a dare-devil that he was, he invested his life with an all-too rare elan.

According to a veteran journalist, there is no epithet that is not used about him. "Wily, volatile, flamboyant, dynamic, reckless, dare-devil, damn efficient" and what not ? Perhaps all these suit him in one context or the other. But in the jungle of attributes his essential human qualities, his deep love for his people, are often missed. Once Patnaik is deeply moved by the peoples' distress, he will move mountains to give succour. In October 1971, when the entire administration was benumbed by the rude shock of the killer cyclone and tidal wave that had flattened the coastal Orissa, it was Biju Patnaik who rose to the occasion. When Governments at the State and the Centre were busy doing maths on relief expenditure, Biju pressed into service a private aircraft and himself started dropping food packets to the marooned thousands who would have perished, but for this prompt step.

This stalwart was endowed with exceptional talent and courage. He had great interest in literature and was a voracious reader. Biju's life was one of the commanding events in the history of modern Orissa. He had an innate grasp of the Oriya temper and devoted his entire life in restoring optimisim among people. Perhaps that is why he enjoyed a long and largely unquestioned popularity among his people.

Biju was the architect of grand designs. Delivering Binod Kanungo Memorial Lecture on 'Orissa of my dream' on 27th January, 1992 at Bhubaneswar, instituted in memory of his dearest friend, encyclopedist and freedom fighter Binod Kanungo, he had said:

> "In my dream of the 21st century for the State, I would have young men and women who put the interest of the State before them. They will have pride in themselves, confidence, in themselves. They will not be at anybody's mercy, except their own selves. By their brain, intelligence and capacity, they will recapture the history of Kalinga. I would like my Orissa of the 21st century to have excellent artisans, superb craftsmen and sculptors, greatest musicians and poets ".

Tales and anecdotes about him are a legion. There is a story that Pt. Nehru once asked Dr. B. C. Roy—'Have you met a young man called Biju Patnaik'. "I have heard about him; but not yet met him", was the reply of the Bengal Chief Minister. Nehru said, "meet him sometime. I like such forward-looking, brave people. The only difficulty is that sometimes you don't know where he will land you".

Biju was known for his curt and sometimes self-defeating, off-the-cuff statements. He did not help his cause with impulsive comments about the need to beat up corrupt officials or about Orissa being forced to secede, if the Centre continued to neglect it. During his first tenure as Chief Minister (1961-63) he had told a public meeting—I spent rupees one crore to become Chief Minister. I will have to spend rupees ten crores to become Prime Minister. This statement created controversy. Similar were the remarks that he helped his party colleague, friend and former Chief Minister Biren Mitra earn Rs.6 lakhs in a single year through his Orissa Agency, which was doing business with the State government. Some of maverick Patnaik's utterances and actions during his second Chief Ministership were also typical of him. Sometimes he is painted as arrogant, but in reality at times his confidence merged into arrogance.

Despite being a big name in Indian politics, Biju Patnaik had seen hunger and poverty from close quarters in the mid-forties. He had once said-"I stayed in my father's house in Cuttack after being released from Jail in 1945. I did not even have Rs.2 to purchase milk for my children", he said. Biju, who was a chain smoker then, had to quit cigarette-smoking because of this.

A giant transference of energy had taken place between him and his people. He delighted the people by his youthfulness of spirit and body and the people were attracted to his spontaneity and utter freedom from pompousness. In the end, his great strength far outweighed his weakness. Therefore when he died, even his most partisan adversaries felt compelled to acknowledge the immensity of the man they had opposed.

Biju : The Lotus Eater (The Dreamer of Dreams)

9

Dr. Nishamani Kar

While going north-ward towards Chandrasekharpur in the posh Jayadev Vihar locality of Bhubaneswar, in the May-Fair Lagoon Cross, a pensive but prodigious statue draws our attention. It baffles us often; its right hand raised with the index finger pointing at the blue horizon and the eloquent eyes lost in the expanse of the limitless sky. Kudos to the sculptor, whose chisel has rightly captured the nuances of the feel and the dream of the erstwhile great son of Kalinga, Biju Patnaik, the name which speaks volumes about the larger-than-life dimension, a mere mortal can reach. His life-story gives the impression of the chivalrous knight of the medieval romance, the maverick persona, who had the urge to shape the destiny of millions. For him life was not'a tale/told by an idiot, full of sound and fury/Signifying nothing'; rather it proved to be 'a dome of many-coloured glass/With a white radiance of eternity'. Inevitably, he was a 'lotus-eater, the dreamer of dreams', the romantic hero, who could also rightly hear 'the still sad music of humanity'. Here, we can make an attempt to collect the strands of his multi-dimensional dream, which transcended the divisive, parochial loyalties based on race, religion, nationality, creed, class or ethnicity.

Biju was not guided by any dogma, nor could any creed enthuse him. He was charismatic. The values he cherished all through his eventful life were democracy, freedom of speech, the scientific temper and economic progress, which, he insisted, must seep down to the lowest rungs of the society. He was against the oppressive rule by the chosen elites and the occult obscurantism of the limited few. He stressed upon mitigating human suffering and ensuring positive social conditions, so that all people would have the opportunity to achieve happiness and fullness of life. He affirmed humanism as a realistic alternative to theologies of despair and ideologies of violence. He was a humanist to the core - progressive, adventurous, outgoing, creative and exuberant. As a humanist, he believed in the fullest realisation of the best and the noblest that one is capable of as a human being. In his scheme of analysis, an open and pluralistic society assures freedom and opportunity for the greatest number of people. For him democracy (of course, not of the type we do have now) posits the best guarantee of protecting human rights from authoritarian elites and repressive majorities. He was concerned with securing justice and fairness in society and with eliminating discrimination and intolerance. Such a bid for the 'brave new world' forced him to face the ever-more-perplexing riddles of the present-day political situation squarely. How much he succeeded or failed is none of our concern here, but our interest is to ascertain the courage of conviction he had to meet the challenges offered by his solicitude for men and society.

Nevertheless, Biju's love for the common man was typical. He was born with a silver spoon in his mouth and was groomed in the sophisticated domestics of his Munsif father (very few Oriyas were in such ranks during the Raj); but his heart was always craving for the people belonging to the lowest stratum of society. He knew pretty well that the average man is just not a pawn, but the basic tool in giving shape to the future of a society. All through his life, he dreamt of a prosperous and meaningful social setting, where everyone would get his due— 'each according to his need ...' . He stressed upon the growth of the individual, as he could rightly identify that everyone has a propensity to grow. Eventually after all, each individual should be groomed to play the intended role. He was not in favour of a limited number of vocal politicians, who only bash on spurious and simulated promises. He was not for a still limited number of armchair intellectuals either, who only revel in ineffectual and abortive contemplation. He was a pragmatic visionary, who wanted his dreams to be realised in action by all and sundry. On the occasion of the state-level Panchayati Raj Day celebration on March 05, 1993 (incidentally, his birth day), he declared in unequivocal terms:

> Some time ago, I had dreamt of a new India. In that India of my dreams, democracy should not have been the luxury of a few vocal and so-called intellectuals. I dreamt of an India where democracy should not be fully tuned towards election. It would be the medium to involve people intimately in every field. The village is the soul of India. In the India of my dreams, democracy would have sprouted from the village and spread out gradually to the higher echelons.[1] (free translation)

In the aforesaid statement Biju's disenchantment with the present-day politics and politicians is amply expressed. The luxurious and lavish life-style of our political and bureaucratic elites was anathema to him. As the Chief Minister during his second term, he was going to the office on a bicycle/ rickshaw without any security cover. As the Chairman of the Committee on Austerity Measures (he was so appointed by the Narasimha Rao government), he recommended certain realistic and timely measures, which were not palatable to the glib ganders - most of our political and bureaucratic masters. He also wanted the public to rise to the occasion and to tackle the corrupt officials. Obviously, there was wide-spread reaction against Biju's prescription, a comment that made the rounds then was that Biju had gone "quixotic". Incidentally, however, there was a grain of truth in his obsession for a clear, responsive and people-friendly administration. In Orissa, the land of his dreams, the workers were up in arms, but he trounced them boldly and gracefully. The editorial comment: 'Tremors in Orissa', by the *Statesman*,[2] was audaciously answered, through a letter written to the Chief Editor, a few lines of which we can cite here:

> Biju Patnaik has only one government vehicle at his service. There is no police cordon around him. There is no personal assistant in the residence, no telephone also, at the government-cost. He never conducts his tour in the company of security guards with a fleet of cars. He never takes salary and stays in his own home, built forty five years ago.[3] (free translation).

In fact, he was amply conscious of the tax-payers' money, which was (and even now, is) squandered away for a limited few. The political demagogues of our time speak volumes on cutting the expenditure, but in their personal lives they act contrary to the vouchsafed ideals. Biju, however, was made of a different mettle. He knew, 'example is better than precept' and, therefore, set the ideals for others to emulate. The bragging in the aforesaid statement gradually calmed down and later in an interview to the *Times of India*, he presented his cause in a very convincing manner:

> Hard decisions are a must. No development is possible without human sacrifice ... For any human development, there have been human sacrifices galore. So why do we shy away from paying a price for development?[4]

Biju was copiously conscious of our limitations. As a man blessed with extraordinary entrepreneurial ability and business acumen (he was one of the leading industrialists of India in the late 40s), he was in favour of rapid industrialisation and the growth of infrastructure. For him, rapid industrialisation was the only panacea to our endemic problems. The pilot-turned industrialist, Biju, was in favour of an unprecedented string of technological revolutions, which, he believed, must make room for the 'knowledge economy'. But, the industrialist-turned politician in him faced a different reality. Being a major participant in our journey from midnight to dawn, he could rightly identify our dubious distinction of hosting the largest number of the world's poor as well as illiterate masses. He contemplated on his earlier commitment and could recognise that mere creation of wealth would never solve our problems. The earlier parameter 'wealth is knowledge and knowledge is power' took the back-seat. He introspected: 'power for whom and to do what?' When he donned the mantle as the Chief Minister, he subscribed (typically in the Gandhian way) to the institutional solutions: community development, panchayatiraj, land reforms, and co-operatives with the intention of improving access of the poor to productive resources. He identified the target groups and championed the cause of area-based programmes; Orissa under his stewardship saw the proliferation of panchayat industries, digging of tube-wells and popularising massive tiled roof housing projects in the village sector. The present Finance Minister of India, Yashwant Sinha in the budget for 1999-2000, however, created numerous provisions for 'social development', especially in the rural sector, typically (should we say?) in the Bijuvian way.

Again, during Biju's first Chief Ministership, when he was told by the Centre about the resource crunch to finance the Paradeep Port Project, he spent money from the state exchequer (for which he had to face the Khanna Commission later) and sought the approval of Nehru (the then Prime

Minister) to seek foreign investment. Of course, such an occasion did not come and Government of India declared it as a major port. But in the 90s in course of our restructuring, we opened up our economy and sought substantial foreign investment. We are thus forced to subscribe to the remark: 'What Biju thinks today. India thinks decades after'.[5] Obviously, his clairvoyance saw through the cloud of our misdirected initiatives and the culture of hypocrisy and untruth. But in his rush for the upliftment of village and villagers, he did not reject the earlier call of Nehruvian propositions. Paradeep Port, HAL - Engine Manufacturing Unit, PPL, NALCO, Indravati Project, Hirakud Dam Project and many others could also see the light of the day under his direct supervision and initiative. Truly speaking, Biju presented the cause of a compromise between the Gandhian and Nehruvian models of social development.

The commitment to a meaningful cause was, however, of paramount importance. He wanted the youth to rededicate themselves to a worthwhile cause. Time and again, while addressing the youngsters, he would go nostalgic: as the leading pilot of Royal Air Force, how he was serving the underground activities (1942) spearheaded by Jayaprakash Narayan, Achyut Patvardhan and Aruna Asaf Ali; as the emissary of India how he brought the Indonesian rebel leaders like Dr. Shariar and Dr. Hatta to New Delhi for discussion in his Dacota plane at the teeth of strict surveillance of the harsh and cruel Dutch colonial masters; as the representative of Nehru how he convinced the US President to extend his helping hand to flout the cause of Chinese aggression and again, how he played the key figure in consolidating and uniting the despirited opposition against the unrelenting and autocratic regime in mid 70s! He was in the forefront all through, someone presenting the cause of a courageous, fearless and undaunted spirit tuned to set things right. Most of us, of course, stumble to see through his dreams - his Promethean craving to serve humanity. Rightly, he chose the youth to be his forerunners to receive the mantle from him. While presenting the Binod Kanungo Memorial National lecture (1992) he asserted:

> In my dream of 21st century for the State, I would have young men and women who put the interest of the State before them. They will have pride in themselves, confidence in themselves. They will not be at anybody's mercy, except their own selves. By their brain, intelligence and capacity, they will recapture the history of Kalinga.[6]

In another instance, while addressing women and girl-students in a seminar on August 8, 1993 he stressed, in distinct and laconic terms, that so long as there is no development of women, it would be futile to expect the development of the nation. Today we remain vociferous in the name of women empowerment, but Biju could feel the same way almost a decade back and wanted women to be the source of extraordinary strength, power and courage. He asserted thus:

> Do not waste yourselves away into the 21st century. Make the 21st century a standard-bearer for your strength of mind to meet all kinds of challenges, specially the challenges of your own society. It's a very hard task, a very difficult task. But you, my daughters, my daughter's daughters, cultivate great confidence in you. Wherever you may be, light a lamp as I have lighted here and remove the darkness from the society where you live. If you have done this, you have done a great service to yourself, to the society and to the nation...[7]

Here, Biju Patnaik sounds like a visionary with the never-ending urge to lead kindly light. It is interesting to note how a man of patriotic adventure during his youth responds to the sublime reckoning in his twilight years. Nevertheless, the lofty ideals he cherished all through remained instrumental in firing the imagination of the youngsters. His mission and message, his ambition and speculation are exemplary. He is truly a legendary personality, an apocryphal being, who defies our comprehension to set him in any particular mould. He is truly an 'individual', not a ' type' who remains the apple of every vigilant eye, even after his death. Aruna Asaf Ali commented thus: "My admiration for men like Biju Patnaik and his courageous comrades remains undiminished even today".[8]

Biju is neither here nor there. He is just not'the other'. He is a dreamer and thinker moulded into one, a pro-active actor on the Indian stage of the 40s and after. He has foregrounded his dreams before taking any concerted effort to meet the desired end. His dream of a prosperous and resurgent Kalinga is yet to be fully realised. Orissan society was his artefact and he dedicated his life to give it a covetable shape. He failed at some fronts, but success could not elude him thoroughly. A failed sculptor no doubt, but a sculptor nonetheless, a vendor of dreams who clamours almost in the Yeatsian way: 'Don't trample on my dreams/I live on them".

References

1. 'Panchayatiraj 0' Mo Swapnara Bharatbarsa', *Mo Swapnara Odisha*, Bhubaneswar: I & P.R. Department, 1994, p. 33.
2. *Statesman*, June 11, 1993.
3. 'Mora Moha Bhanga Hoi Nahin, Karana Mora Moha Nathila', *op.cit, Mo Swapnara Odisha*, p. 13.
4. *Times of India*, June 13, 1993.
5. Natabara Khuntia,'Biju Tanka Samaya Tharu Kei Dashandi Agare', *Biju Cetana*, (ed.) Ashok Samantrai, Bhubaneswar: Biju Sena, 1999, p.14.
6. *Orissa Review*, Vol. XLVIII No. 9, April, 1992, p.l.
7. *Ibid.*, Vol. L No. 2, September, 1993, p.3.
8. 'Biju Patnaik: A Veritable Dare-devil Freedom Fighter', *Ananya*, (ed.) Guru Mohanty, Cuttack: Biju Patnaik Jayanti Committee, 1990, p. 206.

Biju Patnaik : As People Remember (10)

Prof. J K Patnaik

A nation recognises and remembers its heroes on many counts. There are heroes who provide the people with inspiration and technique to fight, and others who idealise themselves with valour and ultimate sacrifice. There may be another category of heroes who remain unsung, perhaps not because they are unnoticed but preferred not to be noticed. All these classifications can be very rarely associated with one person, except perhaps Biju Patnaik, who, with his versatility, could ascend to the pinnacle of glory. Biju Patnaik inspired people, fought with a sense of dedication but still did not like to be adored. He was dynamic, reckless, wily, flamboyant, volatile, irrepressible and was so tenacious that when an enquiry commission raised eyebrows at some irregularities committed during his Chief Ministership, declared unequivocally that he would commit a thousand such irregularities for the development of his State.

Politics is a game of power and power is an irresistable temptation. When a politician gets blinded by this allurment he invariably lands himself in an ocean of confusion from which he has no escape. Biju Patnaik was an exception who considered politics as a hobby. That was perhaps why he had neither any repentance nor remorse for the temporary setbacks that came his way during a long span of more than four decades. He accepted laurels and depredations alike, appreciated reasoned discussions and civilised debates and above all ignited the spirit of Oriya compatriots.

For him the sky was not even the limit. His aspirations ejected him to such a height that his detractors envied him helplessly. He had the natural gift to lead and hold sway over everybody around him.

Biju Patnaik excelled in every field that he entered during his life time. In his adolescence he dreamt to be a pilot and he became one, one whose services were very often requisitioned by none other than Jawaharlal Nehru during and after the struggle for independence. His adventurous trip to Indonesia and dared-evil stunts at Srinagar shall always remain imprinted in the minds of the people who reminisce about him. In recognition of his singular contribution during the Indonesian struggle for liberation, he was bestowed with the title "Bhumiputra" which is a rare distinction for an Indian to earn, especially from a foreign country. It would be of interest to note here that when the Government of Indonesia, after her independence, handed over a document containing some gifts worth crores to Biju Patnaik, he returned the same to President Sukarno as a token of India's goodwill for the Indonesian people. Can a person ever conceive of such a noble gesture? This was the uniqueness of Biju Patnaik.

After independence and before his entry into State politics, Biju Patnaik had tried his luck in business. He was perhaps the first successful industrialist in Orissa whose pioneering work subsequently attracted many other prospective businessmen into this field. He chalked out the road map for the second generation industrialists who considered him a beacon. However, his interest in business could not suppress his predilection for politics. He found politics to be more fascinating and thus a politician was inducted into the State politics who at a later stage was to bring glory for the entire State and its citizens. He was a politician of a different kind who had ascendancy over all his adversaries. Unlike the modern-day politicians, Biju Patnaik had no animosity towards his political opponents. He loved his friends and foes alike and surprisingly was disdainful of sycophants.

Biju Patnaik was a proud Indian who had unfailing faith in democratic institutions. In spite of his vast popularity he could not keep himself within the fold of power. Somehow political power always seemed to elude him. During a chequered and transparent political career of forty odd years he could become Chief Minister of Orissa only on two occasions. Once for a period of 30 months and then a full five-year term. During post emergency period he was deeply involved in the national politics where he assumed the role of a Kingmaker. He was Union Minister twice for a brief period of less than 3 years. All this should not be compared with his spartan quality of leadership. He was an entirely different kind of leader who had something special in him.

Like many contemporaries Biju Patnaik loved his State dearly. It pained him always to find his beloved Orissa considered to be one of the poorest of the States. He always strove to elevate the stature of Orissa at the national level. His guileless affection for his State was manifest to all who knew him closely. The name "Kalinga" (ancient name of Orissa) was highlighted both at the national and international level by this worthy son of Orissa who named everything of which he was either the founder or institutor after his beloved homeland. Kalinga Prize, Kalinga Airlines, Kalinga Foundation Trust, Kalinga Tubes, Kalinga Iron Works were some of the organisations and institutions which were solely of his making. Biju Patnaik was a man of versatility, if ever there was one. He can be regarded as a person who opened the door to an entirely different vista of legend and statistical lore.

No one knows what place history will give this man a hundred years hence but an honest historian would find it very difficult to omit Biju Patnaik from his most glittering pages. The niche carved out by Biju Patnaik in Orissa politics will remain the envy of many who aspire to plunge into the perilous game of politics. His dream of seeing a prosperous Orissa was never fulfilled but the hope within him never died out until he breathed his last. Perhaps the word complacence was not there in his dictionary. He was, and always had been, a fighter. He was a marvel, and no less.

Biju Patnaik's character was cast in a different dye whose patriotism was exceptional. He was one of India's most talented and formidable personalities. As a person he was kind and generous, as a pilot bold and daring, as a politician astute and enigmatic, as an industrialist prosperous and flourishing and, above all, a philanthropist par excellence. His raw nationalism will always be fondly remembered by posterity.

One thing unique about Biju Patnaik was his unfailing faith in the younger generation. He believed that rising responsibility in the youth was the key to a better and brighter future. But this was not to be. He was always anguished to find degeneration amongst the youth. His forceful personality and strongly held opinions will always remain a source of inspiration for the generations to come. A live wire and high flying politician like Biju Patnaik deserves his genuine place in the annals of history and, if posterity gives him his rightful place in the history of India, at least his soul will rest in peace.

Biju Patnaik : The Colossal Leader of Orissa

11

Dr. Debadatta Mohanty

No historian would ever attain success in writing the political history of Orissa, from the days of the Quit India Movement till the present time without writing a whole chapter on Biju Patnaik's most colourful, adventurous, political, economic and social activities of varied dimension.[1]

Bijayananda Patnaik, Son of Smt. Ashalata and Sri Laxmi Narayan Patnaik, better known as Biju Patnaik, as he is endearingly called by his older and younger friends alike, has always been a man of exceptional courage, bravery, unbounded enthusiasm and strong determination with no sentimentality. While he takes up a matter he does not leave it without solving that. "His risk taking ability and adventurous spirit brought him to the forefront in every activity he took up, whether it was studies or sports or any other matter".[2] His political life was full of ups and downs, bright and dark like a revolving light house. His was a much talked-about, remarkable, towering personality either in the Congress or in opposition. He commanded overwhelming support from the Orissa electorate as a leader of the Congress in 1961, Utkal Congress in 1971 and as a Janata leader in 1977. When Congress could obtain 20 Lok Sabha seats out of 21, it was Biju Patnaik alone, who retained the Lok Sabha seat of Kendrapara in 1980. At the same time, the main target of the Fourth General Election (1967) in Orissa was Biju Patnaik. He was a much-hated person in electioneering. One of the most important tasks before the Swatantra-Jana Congress Government was to set up a Commission of Enquiry against Biju Patnaik and his associates on the charges of corruption and misuse of powers by which he became a more powerful man. One report of the Commission was "administrative impropriety, not financial corruption."

He contributed a lot to the political leadership in Orissa and played a vital role in nation building, State building, opposition building and social activities for the people of Orissa. It was his spirit of adventure which led Biju Patnaik into politics as well.[3]

Nation Building

The final struggle against the British rule in India was launched in August 1942 and many youngmen and women from all parts of India joined it. As a true nationalist, Biju joined the Quit India Movement, being inspired by the call "Do or Die" of Mahatma Gandhi. Aruna Asaf Ali, one of the fore-front socialist leaders of India, praising the heroic deals of Biju Patnaik, writes: "Among the thousands, who came forward to take up the challenge, Biju Patnaik, Chief Pilot of the Dalmian - Jain Airways, was one of the most fearless (and veritable dare devil), who mobilised his fellow pilots and inspired them to help the 'Underground Directorate' consisting of Jayaprakash, Achyut Patwardhan, Ram Manohar Lohia and some others like myself". But for their courage and fearlessness, we could never have succeeded in linking up with our Comrades in Bombay, Calcutta, Madras and New Delhi. We also used the airlines for travelling incognito sometimes. For instance, when Rajgopalachari wanted to meet and dissuade us from carrying out our plans of underground resistance, Patnaik himself flew Rajaji from Madras to New Delhi to meet J.P. and Directorate, sometimes in Dec-January 1942-43.... My admiration for a man like Biju Patnaik and his courageous Comrades remains undiminished even today."[4]

His participation in August Movement put him behind bars on 13th January 1943 in Ferozepur. After his release in 1945, he played an active role in State politics.

He played a vital role not only in the freedom movement of India, but also outside. His dare-devil character, which can be marked from school days, as a social worker in flood relief work with Pandit Gopabandhu and his cycle expedition from Cuttack to Peshawar, has helped him to bring international repute and to gain confidence of national leadership and thus became a trusted man of Pt. Nehru.

The Indian leadership, particularly Pandit Nehru, was very much sympathetic to the Indonesian freedom struggle because of the traditional link between India and Indonesia. Indonesia was under Dutch administration from 1816. During the Second World War in 1941, it came under Japanese control. She declared her independence on August 17, 1945, two days after the Japanese collapse in the War. The Dutch government tried to keep Indonesia again under her control and started attack. Dr. Soekarno, the President and Dr. Sultan Shahrir, the Prime Minister (14.11.45 to 27.06.47) of the new government started to mobilise world opinion in their favour. During this period, the Indonesian government had established close relationship and trade link with India. Pandit Nehru was the Prime Minister as well as the Foreign Minister of the Interim Government. In July 1946, a Trade Agreement was signed between these two-an infant and a baby to be born-countries, by which Indonesia would supply 40,00,000 tonnes of rice in exchange of textile, Ore, agricultural goods and others. Besides,

Pandit Nehru called Dr. Shahrir as a special invitee to the first Inter-Asia Conference on 23rd March 1947, attended by leaders of twenty-two Asian countries. Though Kinggadjti Agreement was signed on 25th March 1947, to end the Dutch hostility on Indonesia, the Dutch continued the attack. A massive attack was launched on 21st July 1947. President Soekarno consulted and directed Dr. Shharir to go abroad to mobilise international public opinion. But he along with his Cabinet colleagues were kept under surveillance. Being informed of this, Pandit Nehru asked Biju Patnaik to take up the task of freeing them from Dutch control as Panditji was aware of his adventurous and courageous background and knowledge in aeronautics and piloting. Biju Patnaik flew to Java and brought Dr. Sultan Shharir and Mohmmed Hatta by his own Dacota to Singapore on 24th July 1947. Dr. Shharir addressed a Press Conference at Singapore on their freedom struggle and Dutch oppression and returned the same day to New Delhi to have consultation with Pandit Nehru. Pandit Nehru issued a Press Statement denouncing Dutch oppression that, "It is an astounding thing which the new spirit of Asia will not tolerate. No European country, whatever it may be, has any business to set its army in Asia, against the people of Asia, and when it does so, Asia will not tolerate it."[5] On 28th July, Nehru declined Dutch air traffic over Indian territory. On 30th July, India and Australia raised the issue in Security Council and called upon the U.N.O. to take action, under Chapter VI of the U.N. Charter.[6] For this noble and heroic deed, Biju Patnaik was awarded "Bhumi Putra", the highest Indonesian Award, a rare distinction granted to a foreigner.

Just after a few months, in the same year, he played another remarkable role in the Kashmir Operation of 1947. After India got a dominion status, the Princely States became independent. Maharaja Hari Singh of Jammu & Kashmir wanted to retain his sovereignty. But Kashmir was attacked by Pakistani soldiers on 22nd October. In the meantime, Pakistan had already occupied a portion of Jammu & Kashmir territory which is at present known as Azad Kashmir and continued to march towards Srinagar. There was no time to send troops by road and the only possible course open was to drop the troops from air. But it was also highly risky and hazardous for several reasons. First, the valley has great elevations. Secondly, its landscape is dangerous for flying. Thirdly, at that time the Indian planes had neither de-icing equipment nor were they provided with oxygen system, which is a must for high altitude flying. And most important was, nobody knew whether Srinagar Airport had gone under Pakistan control or continued to be under Indian possession. At this critical juncture, against all adversities, Biju Patnaik was able to land the first platoon of troops at Srinagar Airport on 27th October 1947 at 10 A.M.[7]

During the early part of his political career, though he had no visible presence in national politics, he acted as 'the P.M.'s hatchet-man', filling in as defence adviser to Nehru during the Indo-China War. Samarendra Kundu, ex-M.P. and socialist leader of Orissa writes, "He had occupied one of the highest places in the Defence Ministry during the Chinese aggression and earned a special recognition from Nehru".[8] He was sent as a special envoy of Pt. Nehru to the U.S.A. to mobilise and get international support in favour of India. During this time, he was also instrumental in raising the B.S.F. and C.R.P.F. as an alternative to the Indian military force. In 1965, when War broke out between India and Pakistan, Biju Patnaik was asked to fly to Indonesia to dissuade President Soekarno from sending the Indonesian Fleet in aid of Pakistan.

His dare-devil activities, dynamism and personality made him a notable leader of both the State and the Nation.

Leadership

Linderman described a leader as "an individual whose rationalization, judgements and feelings are accepted (responded to) by the group as the basis of belief and action."[9] If we place Biju Babu in this model, he will surpass almost all leaders of the State, barring Kulabrudha Madhusudan or Utkalmani Gopabandhu Dash, and a few Oriyas saw him as a "Saviour".[10] For Bernard, "Any person who is more than ordinarily efficient in carrying psychological attitude to others, and who is this effective in conditioning collective response, may be called a leader."[11] For Allport, leadership is an inter-personal process. "Leadership means the direct, face-to-face contact between the leader and follower; it is personal control."[12] The social activities and personality of Biju Patnaik, from his school and college days developed his power of command as well as fellow-feeling among his followers. According to Bogardus "A leader is a person who exerts special influence over a number of people."[13] Excepting Madhusudan and Gopabandhu, Biju Patnaik was the other leader who thought for Oriyas. His relief work during the flood and cyclone, his social activities have kept a place for him in the heart of Oriyas. "Leadership is an interpersonal influence exercised in situations and directed through goal or goals."[14] So, a leader must have a sense of purpose and direction. The main purpose of Biju Patnaik was to give Orissa a proper place in the industrial map of India and recognition in the whole world. Before him, Kulabruddha Madhusudan Das thought of highlighting Orissa before the people of the world. His Kalinga Award gave Orissa world (international) recognition.

Different authors find different qualities for evolving a leadership scale.[15] A leader should be friendly and affectionate. Decisiveness, intelligence and integrity are qualities which should be an integral part of his character. To be more specific, at the State level the leader functions as an organiser, as a mobiliser, as a decision maker. He should initiate and expedite in implementing specific development programmes. In these respects, among the Chief Ministers of Orissa, Dr. Mahatab, Biju Patnaik and J.B. Patnaik came to the fore-front. They have faced many ups and downs, rise and fall, victory and defeat in their political career. However, among these three, Biju Patnaik was the most dynamic, dashing and dare-devil type. Towards the end of the sixties, his personality was compared with that of a sphinx by C. Rajgopalachari.[16] Either as a pilot or as a politician, always he was a path finder, not a follower, never a conventional traveller. "For a politician to come to power, it would have been 'Matching Dynamics' but for an entrepreneur like Biju Patnaik, it was "Dynamics of Conquest."[17] He took the leadership of the Orissa Congress Party in 1961 and became the youngest Chief Minister of Orissa. He had a strong determination to take Oriyas into the national mainstream, either as an entrepreneur or as a leader.

State Building

After his release from jail in 1945, he actively participated in politics. He contested from Cuttack Town Constituency in 1946, in spite of opposition from a group of senior politicians of the State. But the other group led by Dr. Mahatab strongly put forth the candidature of Biju Patnaik, visualising his courage, bravery and dynamism. At last with the whole-hearted support of the Congress leadership of Dr. Mahatab and Laxmi Narayan Sahoo, he got elected. It was the foundation of his legislative career. Since then, he had always been in the State political system, either in the Assembly or as a Member of Parliament or in any Party hierarchy. Prof. Samar Guha writes, "Biju Patnaik is not known as an eminent orator or a debator of exceptional talent, but he has an amazing aptitude to go straight into the core of a political problem and tackle it with any metaphysics of politics, and is gifted with an innate capability to easily understand its practical implications."[18]

In the First and Second General Elections of 1951-52 and 1957; the Indian National Congress could not get a clear-cut majority in the State Legislature. In the First General Election, out of 140 seats, the Congress could get 68, Ganatantra Parishad-81, Socialist-10, Communist-7, Forward

Block-1 and Independents-23. In February 1952 the Congress government was formed under the Chief Ministership of Nabakrushna Choudhury with the support of some independent members. But due to internal faction which became intense inside the Orissa Congress, the Government had to resign on 19th October, 1956 and Dr. Mahatab formed a new ministry, which continued till the Second General Election, i.e. February 1957. In the Second General Election of 1957, no party could get a clear majority. The party position in the State Legislature was, Congress-56, Ganatantra Parishad-51, P.S.P.-11, Communist-9, Independent and others-13. Dr. Mahatab formed the Government with the support of Jharkhand and Independents, but the Government could not continue and was bound to resign. The Mahatab Ministry of 1957 was formed by political horse-trading, causing political defection. Sunit Ghosh in his book "Orissa in Turmoil" writes, "the second legislature was one of the murkiest in Orissa's political history - a period that witnessed intense politicking and furious horse-trading". The ministry enjoyed favour from its supporters through regular payments.[19] F.G. Bailey observed, "The ministry showed disproportionate tenderness to even the least of its supporters."[20] In May 1959, the first coalition Government was formed in Orissa, under the Chief Ministership of Dr. Mahatab.

Biju Patnaik played the key role to bring about a coalition between Dr. Mahatab and R.N. Singh Deo, the Maharaja of Patna and the leader of Ganatantra Parishad. Both of them were arch political rivals. Ideologically both the parties differ too. The Congress is a cadre-based, national party which stands for democratic socialism since 30's, whereas the Ganatantra Parishad was a regional party of ex-princes and landlords, having rightist inclination and a party of reaction.

The reasons of Biju Patnaik playing a role as the principal negotiator between Dr. Mahatab and Patna Maharaja to form a coalition ministry was two-fold. First, he wanted to tarnish the image of the Parishad as the main opposition and second to expose Dr. Mahatab as a power monger. The Congress High Command, though it was doubtful and suspicious of the coalition, extended its support. Even some prominent members of the G.P., who were against this doubtful political move of Dr. Mahatab, remained quiet. It is said, Biju Patnaik influenced Pandit Nehru and Congress Party at Delhi in the pretext that the coalition would protect the interest of Orissa and build the future of the Congress Party in the State. Even Pandit Nehru declared that the Parishad was the natural representative of the tribal people of Orissa. F.G. Bailey remarks, "The Congress had at least the sacrifice of all its principles and ideologies by joining hands with its avowed adversaries just for the sake of remaining in power even though it had no majority either in the Assembly or in the electorate."[21]

Biju Patnaik, who had played a crucial role in the formation of the coalition, made a more tactical move to dissolve it. Biju Patnaik took over the P.C.C. leadership in January 1961 and directed the legislative wing to resign from the coalition, which was materialised a month latter. It is alleged that a faction of Congress leaders, under the leadership of Biju Patnaik wanted to destroy the coalition when the Government did not agree to their proposal for establishing industries in the ex-princely States. The proposal ran as follows:

"In order to build up the Congress organisation on a strong basis and to be able to secure a large number of seats in the next General Election, the Congress organisations should be based upon some definite industrial programme. Each district particularly in ex-State areas should have at least one industry, which is to be run by Congressmen and through these industries Congressmen would come into contact with the people and then exercise their influence over them."[22]

Dr. Mahatab the Chief Minister has admitted before the then Finance Minister, who was a member of the Parishad that, it was very difficult on his part to continue in office "in view of the pressure tactics of certain groups in the Congress for their own gains."[23] Myron Weiver has observed, "Groupism in a ruling party is inevitable and the Congress party in India was no exception to this rule."[24]

Political instability in the State, like its existence in many other States of India, has broadly followed two patterns.[25] First as no party could get a clear majority, coalitions have been formed and having failed to satisfy the claims of the partners, the Government had collapsed and President's rule had been imposed. Secondly, the Congress ministry in the State has been unable to get support within the party, which may be due to factionalism; resulting in the resignation of the Chief Ministers. Shri Choudhury and Dr. Mahatab were the victims of the second.

The emergence of Biju Patnaik helped in improving the electoral fate of the party. The Congress party which could not obtain a clear-cut majority, under the saintly Chief Minister Shri Choudhury and now under tactful, shrewd Dr. Mahatab; had spectacular, and unprecedented success under the dynamic leadership of Biju Patnaik. "Patnaik with his youth-fulness, organising ability, good campaigning strategies and as a successful fund-raiser landed the Congress electioneering in a new phase."[26] He was able to erase the badname of the Congress for its "Political Opportunism."

Dr. S.C. Dash in an article had summed up the reasons behind the Congress success (82 seats in the House of 140). Out of six factors, one was "The personality of Biju Patnaik, who was an ace-pilot, who had some daring exploits to his credit at the time of the Indonesian struggle for Independence, who had started an industrial empire at Choudwar even from scratch and who had developed the reputation of a wonder-man, had a magnetism for the common people, who thought of experimenting with the youth leadership after a boring leadership of one man for about fifteen years."[27]

The Presidential election 1969 reveals that a group of Congressmen acted in defiance of Biju Patnaik. He was no longer the undisputed leader of the Congress in Orissa. He tried to be a member of the Congress Working Committee but failed. In Rajya Sabha election, he tried his best to get the Congress nomination and got the support of the State Legislature Party. But the Congress Parliamentary Board rejected the recommendation of the Orissa Congress.[28] The Congress Party set up Narayan Patro as the official candidate, who was defeated. The Party High Command charged Biju Patnaik for sabotaging and made him responsible for the defeat of the Party candidate. Hence, he resigned from the Congress on 6th April 1970.

For a decade from 1961 to 1970, the Orissa Congress was completely under the control of Biju Patnaik. During this period, the Party was in power as well as in opposition. Though in the Fourth General Election, the Congress lost the election, his grip over the Party continued, till 1970, when factionalism again played a vital role in State politics.

On 16th and 17th May 1970, the Utkal Pradesh Congress Committee took the decision to free itself from the AICC and functioned as an independent State level party, namely "Utkal Congress" in protest against the "naked bossism" of Indira Gandhi,[29] for the greater interest of the people of Orissa[30] and continued as a force to reckon within the State politics. Since then, all political battle in Orissa have been fought between Biju Patnaik and Indira Gandhi and after Indira's death Biju Patnaik and Rajiv Gandhi.

Upon the failure of the Congress ministry in February 1973, Biju Patnaik demanded to form an alternate government, under the banner of Pragati Dal, but was not allowed. The then Governor of Orissa, B.D. Jatti, on 1st March 1973, recommended President's rule and the dissolution of Orissa

Legislature. He wrote, "Taking the views of Dr. Mahatab and taking into consideration the letters which I have received from two members of the Legislative Assembly within a few hours after they claimed to have majority indicates that the present strength of Orissa Pragati Legislative Party may not remain steady and is likely to change under other pressures.... In view of the above facts, after a careful consideration of the political situation in the State, I am satisfied that no party or parties with any substantial majority can form a stable government. It will be better to obtain a fresh mandate from the people.... I, therefore, recommend the President to take over the administration of this State under Article 356 of the Constitution of India and the Orissa Legislative Assembly be dissolved."[31]

The Honourable Orissa High Court, while dismissing the case of Biju Patnaik and others vrs. the State of Orissa (O.J.C. No.334 of 1973) due to lack of jurisdiction observed that, "The Governor is not concerned whether the ministry could be stable in future. If the Ministry which would have been formed by the leader of the opposition would have fallen afterwards, the Governor would have been justified to recommend the President's rule if at that time no other person was in a position to form an alternative ministry by having majority support."[32] Hence this is what Dr. S.N. Mishra has observed, "the Governor of Orissa, instead of acting as the constitutional head functioned as the political head."[33] On this issue, the Governor protected the interest of the Congress Party.

For the upliftment and to give Orissa a proper place in the industrial map of India, he followed the path of Kulabruddha Madhusudan Das, who believed that the development of Orissa and Oriyas is only possible through industrialisation. He established B. Patnaik & Co. with two partners, Biju Patnaik - 45%, Pratap Singh, son of the industrialist Sankar Lal - 45% and Bhubananda Das with 10% share. Subsequently he established Orissa Textile Mill, Kalinga Tubes at Choudwar,

Kalinga Industries, Barbil, Kalinga Airlines, Kalinga Refrigeration, Cuttack and Kalinga Publication. For the establishment of these industries, he was influenced by Manubhai Shah, another great entrepreneur, who subsequently became the Union Minister for Commerce. In a reply to his father, he would have told, he had established these industries not for personal gain, but for the development of Orissa and its people. Later on, during his administration or through his initiative, the Mig Factory at Sunabeda, Balimela Dam, the Cement Factory at Bargarh, Sponge Iron at Palaspanga, Samal Barrage, Mahanadi Barrage, etc., were established. He started a minor port at Paradeep with nineteen crores from the Contingency grant of Orissa government which subsequently, with the blessing of Pt. Nehru, became a major Port of the country.

Surendra Mohan, an eminent socialist of India, writes, "Biju Patnaik led Orissa's industrialisation by his own drive and entrepreneurial capacity in the 50's and through his administration in the State in the 60's."[34] Even Banamali Das, a reputed State Legislator, leftist leader and critic of Biju Patnaik writes, "He built up so many institutions and organisations... Panchayat industries and a host of other things of national importance. Nothing he named after himself and nothing, I think, he could retain for himself. His love for India is synonymous with his love for Kalinga, the ancient name of modern Orissa; I would, therefore, be wrong to picture him as the prodigal son of Orissa alone. His thoughts, deeds and dreams cover the whole of the country. The Country as a whole very badly needs the outstanding creative faculties and talents of Biju Patnaik and his like for its rapid transformation from the colonial status to one of dynamism and modernism."[35]

"The Patnaik period in Orissa politics marked the era of development. He was both a dreamer and planner. He wanted Orissa to be industrially developed and to shed away its backwardness. For that he injected a new dynamism into policy-making and a visible transformation was seen in administration."[36] He wanted to lift the people of Orissa out of the 'Slough of despondence' with his great pull with the Central leadership and particularly his connection with Prime Minister Nehru; he established a number of prestigious and eye-catching projects and institutions like Sunabeda Mig, Talcher Thermal, Balimela Hydro-Electric Project, the Paradeep Port, Defence Air Field at Charbatia, R.E.C. Rourkela and Express Highway (N.H.5A) connecting the iron ore areas of Tomka-Daitari with Paradeep Port.

Moreover, to increase the revenue of the State, he created some new Corporations like Forest Corporation, Orissa Mining Corporation, Orissa Construction Corporation, etc., during his tenure.

Orissa is predominantly a State consisting of villages. To boost the rural economy, he initiated the novel idea of Panchayat Industries and got the approval from the Planning Commission. Under this scheme, seven Sugar Mills, twenty tile-making units, ten carpentry units, ten small foundries, a paper mill and factories based on agricultural products were established in a single year. He had an idea to industrialise each block in due course, to utilise the available resources and to generate employment for the rural people. To increase zeal and enthusiasm for industrialisation at the block level, prize money amounting to Rupees Twenty Five Thousand to One Lakh was floated. Cooperative Bank and other financing institutions were directed to finance the Panchayat Industries. Besides, three revenue divisions of the State declared an award of one crore each to the best Panchayat Samiti for its achievement in the field of industrial development. Hence, he was the fore-runner of the Garibi Hatao Programme in rural Orissa.

The State Planning Board was his brain child. It became a trend setter for other states as well for their planned development. With the assistance and guidance of Governor A.N. Khosla, a reputed irrigation engineer of India, a Ten-Year Plan for integrated development for the river basins of Orissa, known as 'Decade of Destiny' was drafted. To conclude, "The Patnaik era heralded the period of economic development".[37]

Moreover, he brought a "new revolution" in the educational development of Orissa. The Regional Engineering College, Rourkela, Regional College of Education, Bhubaneswar, Sainik School, Bhubaneswar, University Engineering College, Burla, Medical College, Berhampur, Orissa University of Agriculture & Technology, Bhubaneswar and Industrial Training Institutes at different places and government Science Colleges in backward tribal districts were established during his period of administration or by his initiative and insistence. Moreover, he also raised a number of Government scholarships for meritorious students and personnel and that has helped many students to carry out their studies in India and abroad. Sunit Ghosh writes, "I came across many Oriya students working happily abroad who acknowledge with much gratitude to have received his help directly and indirectly".[38] .Though his first Chief Ministership was for a short period, Prof. N.R. Mohanty writes, "The Patnaik ministry tried to give a new lease of life to the declining image of the Congress Party in the State. His enchanting slogans, his vigour and zeal made people hopeful amidst prolonged stagnation and widespread frustration."[39]

He successfully organised AICC at Bhubaneswar in January 1964, where Pandit Nehru declared a planned economy, a change of social structure and curb of socio-economic disparity as the motto of the Congress. More important was the laying of the foundation stone of Tikarpara Dam, which could not be materialised due to the opposition from the people of Baud and Sonepur, as a portion of these two districts was to be sub merged and due to political opposition.

Opposition Building

In the seventies, he advocated opposition unity and consistently tried for it. He vehemently opposed emergency and was jailed. He took the leadership of Janata Party and, like the result of mid-term election 1961, gave it an unprecedented victory in the Parliamentary and State Assembly elections. The Party secured a threatening majority of 110 seats out of 147. In 1980 and 1985 General Elections, he was the only opposition leader of the State, who could win from Kendrapada constituency against Congress backed by pro-Indira wave.

He took the most active role in Opposition merger, which ended Congress rule at the Centre. "Ever since 1974, there has perhaps been no opposition conclave connected with the possible merger of parties, which Biju Patnaik had not attended. Some even call him 'merger specialist'.[40] "Most people think that the Haryana Boss, Devi Lal, was the most active man behind the division of the three opposition parties and the Jana Morcha to merge into a new party. But ... it was the political adventure from Orissa, Biju Patnaik, who did most of the ground work for the merger. Incidentally, his residence was not only a rendezvous for opposition politicians, but also the place, where the final merger decision was announced, ..."[41]

Fore-Runner of Kamaraj Plan

To get rid of "unmanageable Chief Ministers and intriguing Central Ministers,"[42] Nehru conceived a new political strategy, known as the Kamaraj Plan in August 1963. Sadasivan writes, "In asserting his para-charismatic authority against the growing opposition to his leadership, Nehru devised the

Kamaraj Plan, by which he secured from the Party the exit of those leaders, who lacked his confidence."[43] Though Biju Patnaik had not lost the confidence of Pandit Nehru, he decided to step down under the Kamaraj Plan for the interest of the party. It is said that, the Kamaraj Plan was initiated by Biju Patnaik. Morarji Desai in his autobiography has written, "Jawaharlal went to Kashmir in May or June 1963, after the Lok Sabha had been adjourned. Biju Patnaik met him there. Patnaik later told to Morarji about the talks, he had with Nehru, Prime Minister that he had suggested to him a plan which was very much like what was later known as the 'Kamaraj Plan'. In fact, the Kamaraj Plan was started by Biju Patnaik, it was unknown to the public."[44]

Social Activities

He was a social worker from the very school days. He joined relief operations with Utkalmani Gopabandhu Dash and showed his bravery to pick up the umbrella of Gopabandhu from a highly flooded river. In 1960 he took personal care and supervision for the air dropping of relief in coastal flood-affected areas, for which he had requisitioned Dakota helicopters. Though he was not Chief Minister in the early eighties, the relief goods arranged by Biju Patnaik were dropped earlier, before the government relief reached the flood-affected areas of Kendrapara district.

Always he thought for Kalinga and its inhabitants. He named his iron pie factory as Kalinga Tubes, Airline as Kalinga Airlines and he instituted an International Kalinga Prize to popularise science. It is monitored by the UNESCO, which brings international repute for Orissa. But he was not parochial, an Oriya chauvinist. His personal family relationship was far far from narrowness, for which he had been criticised by his opponents. In a leaflet distributed by the Congress Party in its election campaign in Kendrapara, it had been propagated that,

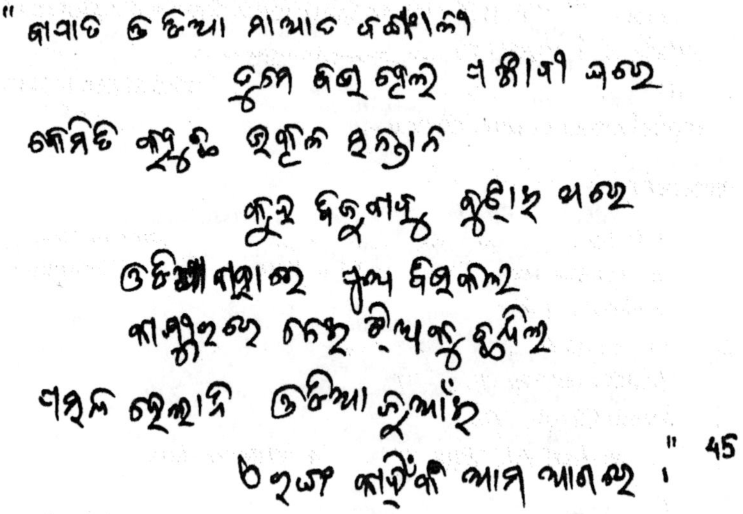

But, on the other hand, it shows how he was broad-minded and above narrow feelings. He has distinguished himself as a courageous volunteer, a champion of sports, particularly in the field of foot ball, hockey and Pole vault. An aeronautical engineer, navigator, an air-pilot, industrialist and an eminent freedom fighter and above all a crowning statesman of national and international repute. A rare celebrity indeed!"[46]

In the messages to the Oriyas in 1994 as the Chief Minister, he said, "There was a time when the Kalinga empire extended from the Ganges to the Godavari and the sons of Orissa knew no defeat. Valorous warriors like Kharabela and Kapilendra Deva could elevate the pride of Oriyas through conquests. The Oriya merchants had to brave the rivers and the seas to establish commercial trade links with Java, Sumatra, Bali, Borneo and many other South-East Asian countries and made the Kalinga Empire affluent. The epoch also witnessed a galaxy of architectural marvels at Puri, Konark and Bhubaneswar. "Oriyas used to lead in all spheres such as dance, music, art and craft, literature and the pursuit of philosophy and science."[47] "We will have to think today for the development of Orissa ... I appeal to my brothers and sisters of my State... to join hands to rebuild Orissa by carrying forward my stream of thought and course of action."[48]

References

1. A.P. Shastry *"Biju Patnaik's Place in Orissa's Political History"* in Ananya (ed), Cuttack: Biju Patnaik Jayanti Committee, Nimasahi, p.213.
2. Er. A. Mohapatra *"Biju Patnaik: Our Super Entrepreneur"* in Ananya (ed) *op.cit*, p.185.
3. Sumit Ghosh, *"Reach for the Sky"*, *op.cit*, p.230.
4. Aruna Asaf Ali *"Biju Patnaik: A veritable dare devil"*, *op.cit*, p.205.
5. For detail. see Keesings Contemporary Archives, 1947-48.
6. *Ibid.*
7. Seventh Lok Sabha, *Who is Who*, 1980.
8. Samarendra Kundu *"Felicitation of the Birthday"* in Ananya (ed) *op.cit*, p.240.
9. Linderman, E.C., *Social Discovery*, New York: New Republic Pub. Co., 1954.
10. Ranajit Mohanty, Bar-at-Law *"Oriyas See a Saviour"* in Ananya (ed) p.212.
11. Bernard, L.L., *Introduction to Social Psychology,* New York: Henry Holt & Co., 1925, p.520.
12. Allport, J.H., *Social Psychology,* Boston: Houghton Mifflin Co., 1924, p.419.
13. Borgardus, B.S., *Leaders & Leadership*, New York: D. Appleton Century Co., 1934, p.3.
14. Robert Taunenbaum & F. Nassarik (eds) *"Leadership Frame of Reference" in Leadership Organisation*, New York: Mc Graw Hill Book Co. Inc., 1961, p.24.
15. Tread, Ordway, *The Art of Leadership*, New York: Mc Graw Hill Book Co. Inc., 1935, p.5.

Sanderson Dwight, *Leadership for a Rural Life*, New York: Associated Press, 1947, p.48.

16. Surendra Mohanty *"Durbara Adamita"* in Ananya (ed) *op.cit.* p.1.
17. Er. A. Mohapatra, *"Biju Patnaik: Our Super Entrepreneur"*, *op.cit*, p.189.
18. Prof. Samar Guha, Ex-M.P. *"A Man of Patriotic Adventure"*, *op.cit,* p.177.
19. Ghosh, S., *Oriya in Turmoil*, Calcutta:1978, p.105.
20. Bailey, F.G., *Political & Social Change in Orissa in 1959*, Barkley, 1961, p.93.
21. *Ibid.*
22. P.K. Deo, *"My Humble Contribution"*; Bhawanipatna: G.P. Orissa, 1961, p.334.
    Quoted by Mishra, R.N., *Regionalism and State Politics in India,* New Delhi: Ashish, 1984, p.203.
23. *Ibid.*
24. Quoted by Mishra, S.N., *Party Politics and Electoral Choice in an Indian State,* Delhi: Ajanta Publications, 1989, p.244.
25. Weiner, Myron (ed), *State Politics in India* (N.J. Princeton Univ. Press, 1968, p.21-26.
26. Mishra, S.N., *op.cit,* p.60.
27. *Ibid*, p.62.
28. The Hindustan Times, New Delhi, dt. 16.05.70.
29. Sunit Ghosh, *"Reach for the Sky"* in Ananya (ed) *op.cit* p.230.
30. The Amrit Bazar Patrika, dt. 17.05.70.
31. Quoted in Routray N., *Smruti O Anubhuti*, Cuttack: Grantha Mandir, 1986, p.572.
32. *Ibid*, pp.573-74.
33. Mishra, S.N., *Op.cit.*, p.6.
34. Surendra Mohan, *"Sri Biju Patnaik"* in Ananya (ed) *op.cit*, p.183.
35. Banamali Das, *"Symbol of Creative Actions, Thought and Dreams"*, in Ananya, *op.cit.*, p.238.
36. S.N. Mishra, *"Election & Political Development in Orissa"* in Padhi A.P. (ed), *Indian State Politics*, New Delhi, B.R. Publications, 1985, p.71.
37. *Op.cit*, p.72.

38. Sunit Ghosh, *"Reach for the Sky" op.cit.*, p.241.
39. Manoranjan Mohanty & S.N. Mishra, *"Orissa: Politics of Stagnalism"* in Narain I (ed) *State Politics in India*, New Delhi, Meenakshi, 1976, p.246.
40. Janardan Thakur, *"Biju Patnaik: The Merger Man,* in Ananya (ed), p.208.
41. *Ibid.*
42. Mishra S.N., *Party Politics and Electoral Choice in an Indian State*, *op.cit.*, p.76.
43. Sadasivan, S.N., *Party & Democracy in India*, New Delhi, 1976, p.274.
44. Quoted by George Patnaik, *"Biju Tankapani Piladinoo"* in Ananya, *op.cit*, p.11.
45. From the original leaflet distributed by Congress Party during the election campaign under the heading *"Kaiphiyat"* printed at Ashok Press, Kendrapara.
46. D.C. Das *"Biju Patnaik: The Vision of a Patriot"* The Orissa Review, Vol.I, No.9, April, 1994, p.7.
47. The Orissa Review, April, 1994.
48. The Orissa Review, January, 1994.

Biju Patnaik and the Indian Federal System

12

Prof. Swadesh Kumar Ghosh

Federalism as a political arrangement has been fashionable both in the east and the west. It is a complex and cumbersome system and at the heart of it lies a paradox "unity in diversity" which is at once a threat and a promise. The basic conditions of federalism is plurality, its fundamental tendency is harmonization and its regulative principle is solidarity. Thus, 'Federalism combines a desire of the people for a union which will provide unity, solidarity, harmony, safety and security and a desire for retaining the identity of their independent culture, ethnicity, language, religion and rights[1]. Federalism as a mechanism of state organisation became 'essential and indispensable' in a pluralist society like India designed to preserve and promote unity in diversity which is the essence of Indian culture and civilisation.

In a federal system where there is division of powers and resources between the Centre and the States, conflicts and tensions between the two are inevitable[2]. As a matter of fact, it is very difficult to find a frictionless and tension-free federation in any part of the world. In the Indian political system also centre-state conflicts continue to arise and at times disturb the harmony of the federal relationship[3].

Political scientists who have examined the dynamics of federalism and centre-state relations in India have come to realise that one of the important causes of centre-state conflicts and tensions in the Indian federal system is the unfortunate neglect of an area or state by the Central Government. As has been rightly said, "The Indian constitution provides for safeguarding small nationalities and a balanced, social, cultural and economic development of different areas. But the centre's indifference to the development of certain regions has created imbalances. Some areas are well-developed with adequate infrastructure while others are way behind. This indeed explains the growth of regional parties in the states because their problems have not been tackled by the national parties and the aspirations of the people have not been fulfilled.[4]

Rightly or wrongly when the people of a state feel that the centre neglects their state and ignores its development, they pin their faith on certain leaders who in their opinion can safeguard the interest of their state and fight for their rights. One such leader on whom the people of Orissa put their trust without almost any reservation was Biju Patnaik. As regards his commitment to Orissa and its people, it has been very aptly said, "Biju Patnaik has spoken, written, raged, threatened and fought most of his life for a single cause - the betterment of his fellow brethren. The economic plight of the Oriyas has been his single-most concern and there has never been a dilution on this count. He is fretful to relieve his people out of the spectre of economic deprivation perpetrated through neglect and indifference.[5]

Hence, Biju was almost uncompromising when it was a question of Orissa's development or the betterment of his people. In fact, he had always the guts and conviction to quarrel and fight with the central authorities, if so required, for the sake of Orissa and its development. It may be noted that Biju Patnaik almost fought a royal battle for the establishment of the MIG factory at Sunabeda in the tribal district of Koraput and got it established during his first term of Chief Ministership from 23.6.1961 to 2.10.1963. As has been said, "He then almost quarrelled with Pandit Nehru on this point. Biju went up to the extent of sounding a note of caution to Nehru that if the MIG factory was not set up in Orissa he was going to resign from Chief Ministership. It clicked, Koraput got the MIG factory along with Nasik and Lucknow.[6] The extent to which Biju could go to fight against central neglect and apathy towards Orissa was evident from one of his most controversial statements during his second term as Chief Minister (1990-95) when Chandrasekhar with the outside support of the Congress ruled at the Centre. That controversial statement which almost created a hue and cry across the country putting his nationalist credentials to question in certain circles was that 'Orissa may consider seceding from the Indian Union if the Centre continued with its step-motherly and apathetic attitude towards Orissa.[7]

It will not be out of place to record the views of George Fernandes on Biju's astounding call for secession if the Centre continued to neglect his State. In the view of Geroge Fernandes, Biju was not taken in proper perspective for his aforesaid exuberant remark. As he defended him in a press conference on May 29, 1993 "... it was a Biju only echoing his frustrations and those of his people who are shackled by economic exploitation and under-development. When a great patriot like Biju who had staked his life during the freedom struggle said something for the plight of his people one ought to go to the root of the problem of economic injustice."[8] Biju's remark even though unfortunate smacked of no real intention of secession or separation by Oriyas and it would simply be unjust and improper to read anything anti-national in Biju's mindset.

In his quest to understand Biju and his mindset in the light of his aforesaid remark it has been rightly observed: "The disgusting economic disparities and abominable concentration of economic power in a few selected houses, selected hands have built up into an explosive situation. The terrorist outfits in Jammu & Kashmir and Punjab and the insurgent activities in the north-eastern areas of the country are bean evidence of the growing unrest and discontentment of the people especially the youth, of those areas. Political parties and leaders of the country have to take appropriate lessons in economics and micro-development, so that the regional unrest and insurgencies that have raised their head for decades past be suitably tackled. Biju's warning is surely for contemplation by the national leaders and thinkers."[9]

Biju's remark, it may be submitted, was never prompted by any anti-national design; on the other hand, it was a mere reflection of his frustration and angst that in the existing federal system of financial subordination of the states to the centre neither rapid nor equitable development of all states has been made possible.

When Biju Patnaik talked of Orissa seceding from the Indian Union, his mind was really working for the autonomy of the states in the Indian Federal System and more particularly what he wanted was financial autonomy for all the states. That he put topmost priority on financial autonomy is evident from his proclaimed view that "Orissa should secede from India if it was not granted financial autonomy."[10] Like Biswanth Dash, he did not want that the states due to excessive financial subordination should be treated as Charity boys of the North Block of the Central Secretariat.

However, this demand for financial autonomy which Biju brought to the centre-stage of politics during his second term of Chief Ministership (1990-95) was not born all on a sudden. It was in fact a virtual continuation of his own demand since the 1970s and of course that of the state autonomy activists for the last many years. It may be noted that the Utkal Congress of Biju Babu which was born in 1970 virtually demanded this financial autonomy. As has been said, the Utkal Congress advocated the State's claim for a greater share of Central resources and started a vigorous campaign for Orissa's economic development. Biju made public accusation against the Central Government for its tardiness in allotting resources for urgent development projects in the State. The Utkal Congress raised the slogan that Orissa can no longer be a colony of India... the Utkal Congress demanded more economic power and freedom for the State to remove Orissa's centuries-old backwardness and poverty.[11]

On 26th December 1973, Biju Patnaik, the leader of the Pragati Party at the time, is reported to have said... "the states should have concurrent economic powers and that since the people of India" lived in the states and not in the archives of New Delhi there should be some decentralisation of economic authority by making the states more responsible and more responsive to meet the problems of their own areas. Before long the Bharatiya Kranti Dal leader Charan Singh called for greater autonomy for the states in financial matters.[12]

When Biju Patnaik demanded the grant of financial autonomy for Orissa, he was virtually making a demand for the grant of financial autonomy for all the states in the Indian Federal System. As has been aptly said, "when Biju fights for Orissa, in essence he fights for the states. It has been his constant refrain in the last four years that the State governments should have financial autonomy. If the centre would continue to neglect the state's interest the county will break up.[13] Biju sought to explain his concept of financial autonomy when he said, 'his demand was for separation of the financial powers so that with my own resources I will deal with money wherever it is from for the state's development as the centre has no fund'.[14]

Biju loved Orissa with every fibre of his being. That Orissa should remain poor and backward in spite of its rich natural resources was unbearable to his sensitive self. He was then at the fag end of his life; in spite of his undying spirit of youth and dynamism time was running out for him; he also met with hindrances at the central level to actualise his plan of a second steel plant or get the vital rail links laid in the State. This frustrating experience made him a more determined advocate of state autonomy. Clamouring for changes in the constitution in regard to centre-state relations in general and financial relations in particular he said : "Let the Centre keep the army but must grant fiscal independence to States ... We will have to make a vigorous campaign for the fiscal autonomy and if necessary the constitution must be amended.[15]

To strengthen the demand for financial autonomy for states, Biju Patnaik did not hesitate to candidly expose the Centre's antipathy to Orissa's development as an example to show how in the existing federal system the Centre holds the key to a State's development. In fact he listed the areas in which the Centre has ignored his state's plea. Those areas were: permission for an integrated steel plant, development of railway projects, and deepening of Paradeep port. In Biju's view "had these projects been through, about two lakhs unemployed youths in the State could have been provided jobs". He was frustrated because all his sincere efforts to set up the steel plant yielded little response from the centre.[16]

Biju Patnaik's concept of state autonomy was beautifully explained in his letter to the Prime Minister of India. Reiterating his demand for fiscal autonomy to the states he maintained in his letter that the Central apparatus should limit its responsibility to defence, foreign affairs, currency and the like, while the states should be left free to do their own planning, development and ability to negotiate with finance world and to put to use their tremendous natural potential inside their boundaries. He said further: "Thirty years back when I became the Chief Minister of Orissa I had proposed this to the then Prime Minister Pandit Nehru who readily agreed that India should be a federal country with appropriate authority to the states. But the arrogance and love of the central authority held sway and today we have the spectre of strong fissiparous tendencies. How many more warnings do we require to set our house in order"?[17]

Biju Patnaik's aforesaid letter to the Prime Minister of India contains the kernel of his philosophy of federalism. It may be said here that Biju's views on federalism were not those of an ivory-tower political scientist but the outpourings of a veteran politician and those of an active participant in India's federal system who had the unique privilege of enjoying power both at the State and Central level. It may be noted here that Biju was the Chief Minister of Orissa from 23.6.1961 to 2.10.1963, Cabinet Minister for Steel & Mines from 1977 to 1979, Union Minister for Steel, Mines and Coal from July 1979 to January 1980, and Chief Minister of Orissa again from 5.3.90 to 15.3.95. What is particularly interesting and also accords weight to his views on federalism in India is that he was the Congress Chief Minister in the 1960s and the non-Congress Chief Minister in the 1990s and interacted with the Central government as a key functionary in India's federal system for a period of more than seven years as Chief Minister.

Analysing Biju's view on the working of India's federal system and centre-state relations, it has been rightly said "Biju's federal thesis would hinge on two vital points : one, states having natural and human resources have not been allowed their full play under the existing federal structure, and, secondly, the concentration of power in the Centre has resulted in fissiparous tendencies". "It was Punjab and Assam yesterday; it could be Orissa some day...", Biju would argue.[18]

Biju's call for autonomy to the states was not meant only for public consumption to be harped on for a while and forgotten thereafter. He meant business and demanded the Constitution of a Constituent Assembly to redefine parts of the constitution dealing with centre-state relationship and devolution of power to curb the fissiparous tendencies in the country. He said that for forty five years we have tested a pattern of government, it is time we now call it "United States of India."[19]

As has been said, Biju loved Orissa with every fibre of his being. That Orissa should remain poor and backward in spite of a vast resource back-up of minerals, forests, agricultural potency and well-developed skill profile of labour ever pinched his inner-most self. He realised that lack of infrastructure in railways, road communication and power constituted the greatest stumbling blocs to Orissa's prosperity and development. So when the Tenth Finance Commission headed by K.C. Pant visited Orissa in January 1994, he brought out a strong case for Orissa to be treated as a "special category state" which alone could help Orissa to be at par 'with other developed states in the country.' Biju's reasoning as has been said, 'would go this way once the State is declared a 'special category state' it would attract proper treatment both by the Finance Commission and the Planning Commission.[20] This was however not the only occasion when he articulated this demand for Orissa to be treated as a 'special category state'. As a matter of fact, he had been doing it for years now.

Biju Patnaik in his second term as Orissa's Chief Minister delivered two important speeches which have their bearing on Indian Federalism. Those two speeches were :One, at the 18th meeting of the Eastern Zonal Council held on the 21st September, 1991 at Bhubaneswar and the other, at the meeting of the National Development Council on December

23, 1991. These two speeches which breathe his outlook and vision on the management of a federal polity brings him out as a far-sighted thinker and statesman.

Biju Babu made one important suggestion at the 18th meeting of the Eastern Zonal Council held on the 21st September, 1991 at Bhubaneswar with regard to the strategy to be adopted for containing extremism in the eastern states and the role of the Government of India vis -a-vis this problem.

The rise of extremist activity in some parts of Orissa and Bihar engaged his mind and attention. His serious probe into this extremist activity made him convinced that it would be wrong to equate it with terrorist activity elsewhere. Wishing that extremist activity in states like Bihar and Orissa does not convert to terrorist activity, Biju Patnaik said: "The last point concerns a matter that must be attended to at once if we must as we should avoid a situation obtaining in states where terrorist activity is pronounced.[21]

Biju Patnaik who made a serious probe into extremist activity in the eastern states like Orissa sought to explain its rise, growth, and its nature. He rightly said, "It must be understood that the headway extremism made in this part of the country is because of deprivation. It is not extremism produced by fundamentalism or ethnic chauvinism. This extremism is seen as a response to inequality, exploitation and poverty. These factors have to be alleviated if extremism has to be contained.[22]

Biju possessed the maturity of a statesman and he rightly suggested that extremism in the eastern states caused by poverty, inequality and deprivation should not be treated as a law-and-order problem. In his view this extremism could be more successfully faced when our political system, our system of governance tries to establish an egalitarian, exploitation-free and equitable social order which guarantees the barest minimum to one and all.

To deal with this extremist activity, Biju made another well thought-out suggestion bearing on the ideal of co-operative federalism which seeks cooperation of both the centre and the state on several matters of common interest. It is essentially a mechanism making for a two-way movement of influence. It ensures that the states are not entirely on the receiving end.[23]

Biju's well-thought-out suggestion was to the effect that the Central government should assist those extremism-affected states in implementing a special programme of economic development to eradicate poverty and deprivation.

Biju Patnaik's speech delivered at the meeting of the National Development Council on December 23, 1991 appears to be a brilliant piece of political literature dealing with his views on federalism and nation building in India.

The suggestions made in the aforesaid speech in the interest of Indian federalism and its future display the vision of a far-sighted statesman and thinker. Those ideas have an importance of its own particularly because of the fact that those were made out in the aftermath of the break-up of the Soviet federation in the 1990s when it got divided into a number of sovereign and independent states. It may be said that the Soviet Federal system was based on the communist principle of democratic centralism in which centralism rather than democracy was the most pervasive reality. It may be said that imposition of this centralism was possibly one of the important causes of resentment and dissatisfaction of the units of Soviet federalism and that at the earliest opportunity those units got themselves free from the bondage of an inhibiting central authority.

Reflecting possibly upon this excessive dose of centralisation in the Soviet federal system which largely accounted for its break-up, Biju Patnaik said:

> "The Soviet Union is now paying the price not only of doctrinaire economics but also of failure to manage a federal polity."[24]

Biju, as a well-wisher of the Indian federal system, doesn't want that the Indian federation should go the Soviet way and we would be forced to lose our Indian identity. In his words, he was for a new technique of political management which inspires in every Indian the faith that his Indian identity will remain unaffected by the area he lives in, the language he speaks and the religion he professes.[25] What Biju Patnaik conveys to us is that we should learn from the fate of the Soviet federation which broke up under the excessive weight of centralisation.

Biju Patnaik rightly realised that regional disparity in the matter of development may be a cause of discontent and tension among different states and "may weaken our integral nationhood."[26]

Giving a note of caution that uneven economic development and economic disparity among different states in the Indian federal system may endanger the unity and integrity of the Indian nation he said, "I would ... therefore submit that equitable regional development should be assigned as high a priority as macro-level planning policies. If we fail to do so, growth would have been highly disparate among the states of the Indian Union at the end of the Eighth Plan. It will be difficult to convince the people of the states where growth was slow relative to some other states that no injustice has been done to them. I am by no means suggesting that growth rate can be totally independent of natural endowments, but if investment on exploitation of natural endowments is insufficient or if benefits of development do not accrue to some people because communication to their areas is under-developed or because the production infrastructure is not comparable to what is available in developed states, can we in the long run, hold the country together?".[27]

Biju who wanted equitable regional development to be accorded high priority was specially concerned about the development of under-developed states. He was of the opinion that Government of India should give special attention to those states. As he said, "I fully appreciate that the Government of India may not be able to fully meet the needs of under-developed states. The quantum of special assistance which should be over and above the normal central assistance will naturally be small but what is important is that this principle is accepted and some critical projects identified for special funding.[28]

Biju seems to have realised like other advocates of state autonomy that it is not proper to make the states financially dependent on the Centre while they are performing the functions of rural development and implementation of five-year plans. Over and above, Biju must have been convinced that 'if states are assigned separate resources of finance then it will be convenient for them to perform developmental functions speeding.[29]

Hence, Biju favoured that a state should have the freedom to arrange funds even from abroad to bring about rapid development. As he said, "It is also necessary that state governments are allowed to mobilise within the parameters of national policy external resources. I am trying to do so in areas of mineral development and energy production."[30]

Biju Patnaik's views on Indian federalism even though it has nothing profound or original that could satisfy a theoretician on federalism or a political scientist, yet his views have a pragmatic and far-sighted perception. His warning that uneven economic development and regional disparity may open the flood gates of extremism and let loose forces of disintegration could hardly be ignored by the well-wishers of Indian Federal System. Though Biju Babu loved Orissa with every fibre of his being and put over-ridding focus on Orissa and its development, he was far from rank regionalism and pungent provincialism. As has been said : His love for his own native state has never stood in the way of his love for the country at large and his regionalism is not opposed to nationalism. He has some traits of Utkal Gourava Madhusudan Das, the maker of modern Orissa who awakened the Oriya race from their deep slumber in the first decade of 19th century. Some of his critics also go to the extent of saying that he talks much and does things impulsively, disregarding the means. But history shows that whatever works done by him on the impulse of the moment are not ciphers but monuments to posterity. As Sri Aurobindo puts it, "action is thought manifested". There can be no action without thought and no success without a dream.[31]

In his speech "Orissa of my dreams on first Binod Kanungo Memorial Lecture delivered on 27.01.1992 at Bhubaneswar he said, "I have been told that I should project the Orissa of my dreams. What would I dream? As Tagore said "When you dream, dream big, it is only by dreaming big things that big tasks are accomplished..." In India, today we have no social harmony, no religious tolerance, no caste tolerance. Certainly we cannot grow with all these divisions. In my dream of Orissa, there should be harmony, broad-mindedness, greater tolerance all-round and fellow feelings from neighbour to neigbour. We all together can make our State such that the whole world would say that Orissa is our dream land.[32]

References

1. Dr. Sharada Rath, Regionalism in Indian Federation: A Conceptual Analysis. *Orissa Political Science Journal*, Vol. VII, 1986-87, p. 23.
2. Dr.B.L. Fadia, *Indian Government and Politics*, Sahitya Bhawan Publications, Agra 1996, p. 283.
3. S.L. Sikri, *Indian Government and Politics*, Kalyani Publishers, New Delhi 1989, p. 274.
4. K.P. Padhy, Regionalism and national integration: its broad imperatives - *Orissa Political Science Journal*, Vol. VIII 1988-89, p. 60.

5. Bhaskar Parichha "*Biju Patnaik: A Political Biography*, Har-Anand Publications, New Delhi, 1995, p. 18.

6. *Ibid*, p. 67.

7. Hullasa Behera, *Biju Patnaik: The Legendary pilot and Live-wire politician*, Faridabad, Haryana, 1998, p. 16.

8. Bhaskar Parichha, *op. cit.* p. 96.

9. Hullasa Behera, *op. cit.* p.16.

10. *Sun Times*, March 30, 1991.

11. J.K. Mohapatra & K.L. Mishra, *Utkal Congress Govt and Politics in Orissa*. Ed. B.B. Jena and J.K. Boral, Print House India, Lucknow 1988, p. 268.

12. B.L. Fadia, *op. cit.* p. 290.

13. Bhasker Parichha, *Biju Patnaik: A Political Biography*, *op. cit.* p. 96.

14. *Sun Times*, March 30, 1991.

15. *Ibid.,* April 3, 1991.

16. *Ibid.,* April 3, 1991.

17. *Ibid.,* April 4, 1991.

18. Bhaskar Parichha *op. Cit.*, p. 97.

19. *Sun Times*, April 19, 1991.

20. Bhaskar Parichha, *op.cit.*, p. 95.

21. Speech of Chief Minister of Orissa Biju Patnaik at the 18th meeting of the Eastern Zonal Council held on 21.9.1991 at Bhubaneswar, *Orissa Review,* Oct. 1991, p. 2.

22. *Ibid*, p. 2.

23. K.R. Bombwall, *The Foundation of Indian Federalism*, p. 82.

24. Address by Sri Biju Patnaik, Chief Minister of Orissa at the meeting of National Development Council, Dec. - 23, 1991. *Orissa Review* p. I.

25. *Ibid*, p. I.

26. *Ibid*, p. I.
27. *Ibid*, p. I.
28. *Ibid*, p. 3.
29. B.L. Fadia, *Indian Govt and Politics, op.cit.*, p. 295.
30. Address of Biju Patnaik at National Development Council, Dec. 23, 1991. *op.cit* p.3.
31. Biju Patnaik, A Concept by B. Sukla, "*Ananya*", Published by Biju Patnaik Jayanti Committee, 1990, p. 235.
32. Biju Patnaik - Orissa of my dreams First Binod Kanungo Memorial Lecture delivered on 27.1.1992 at Bhubaneswar, *Orissa Review*, April 1992, p. I.

[The author acknowledges, with gratitude, the help and advice of Dr. Sridhar Ch. Sahoo, Reader in Political Science, S.C.S. College, Puri.]

Biju and the Media

13

Guru Kalyan Mohapatra

The Indian press has a long history of more than two hundred years. Look at the history: an Anglo Indian James Augustus Hicky brought out the first news-paper in India in 1780, known as 'Bengal Gazette', also known as 'Hicky's Gazette'. The history of journalism in Orissa has also got a glorious and meaningful past. The Christian missionaries have been bragging as they launched the first Oriya 'Gyanaruna' in 1849. In the year 1837, the missionaries established the 'Mission Press' (first printing press) in Balasore and Cuttack. Really, Reverend Laccy brought out this first magazine 'Gyanaruna' for propagating Christian ideas, but this could not survive long. Again Laccy brought out another Oriya magazine 'Prabodh Chardrika' in 1856. Of course, the Oriya stalwarts like Biswanath Kar (the editor of 'Utkal Dipika'), Nilamani Bidyaratna (the editor of 'Sambalpur Hetaisaani'), Brajabandhu Mishra, Damodar Mishra Padyalankar took the reins and played the meaningful role in nourishing and nurturing the press during its infancy. Raja Sudhala Deb and Krishna Chandra Gajapati also proved to be zealous patrons during that period. After enjoying a halcyon period since independence, journalism in Orissa had to pass through a critical juncture in the eighties in the last century.

When I entered into journalism in that critical phase, the Congress was ruling both at the Centre and the State. I vividly marked during the Congress regime that slanderous stories, suspecting Biju Patnaik's loyalty to Orissa were sent to the press. He seemed never puzzled at it. In 1980, I joined the Eastern Times', an English weekly at the behest of Bhatruhari Mahatab and Dr. Harekrushna Mahatab. No doubt, I was a student leader, known for my writings during those days. Dr Mahatab's literary personality and Biju Babu's invincible spirit inspired me to choose the profession, inevitably the source of my bread and butter now.

In an article Dr. Mahatab once wrote: "I mention all these factors which are overlooked when comparison is made between Orissa and other states on an all-India level not only with regard to the profession of journalism, but to other professions as well. The scope of journalism as a profession is limited in Orissa. Even then news papers have to be run as they are now a part of the life of the society. All the limitations of the economic and social conditions have to be overcome. In fact, they are being overcome by those who are on the field. But it is gradually becoming difficult to overcome the difficulties created by political considerations of the ruling authorities."

The aforesaid statement of Dr. Mahatab enthused me. I was equally curious to see through the slanderous stories against Biju. Dr. Mahatab's words and Biju's enigmatic and adventurous spirit influenced me a lot and I jumped at the offer from 'Eastern Times'. I came to the limelight when one of my investigative news stories appeared in the 'Eastern Times'. This front-page story: "Untold story of Indira Gram, Is Prime Minister Taking for a Ride?" attacted everyone's attention. Indira Gandhi was the Prime Minister and she was coming to

Orissa to inaugurate the Indira Gram near Ollatpur in Cuttack district. J.B. Patnaik was then the Chief Minister who was looking after the Prime Minister's programme in Orissa. The Chief Minister seemed flummoxed in my story, but, on the contrary, as heard from others, Biju Patnaik spoke highly of my attempt.

By and by I came in contact with Biju Babu, who was a towering personality in opposition in the State. I observed him thoroughly from close quarters. His style of functioning was intriguing: he would ask you the news first, if the news annoys him he would rebuke you. I was well aware of his approach and, therefore, never took his spankings seriously. Those were rather blessings in my long way to journalism.

My close observation of Biju Babu puts me in a fix, whether he was a friend or a foe to the press. We all know that he had established one Oriya news paper called 'Kalinga'. Rebel poet late Manmohan Mishra was its first editor and the writer late Surendra Mohanty was his successor. Surendra Mohanty admitted time and again (I have heard him speaking many a time) that Biju had never interfered in editorial freedom. However, he was reluctant to patronise the said newspaper, which met a premature end, in spite of the fact that it was in popular demand. Many eminent persons of the state insisted upon him not to discontinue the newspaper, but he never listened to them and stood firm in his own decision.

I take this opportunity to corroborate some interesting facts that I have heard from my uncle Nityananda Mohapatra. In 1961 Biju headed the state of Orissa as the Chief Minister and at that time, he had some misgivings against the then newspapers. It was because he had the feeling that some newspapers of the State were misusing their power and freedom. Thus, the 'Press Bill' (1962) was tabled in the Legislative Assembly. Nityananda Mohapatra (an independent member of Orissa Legislative Assembly, then and a minister, later) objected to the Bill wth the argument that the Bill once made an Act would be misused and it would also snatch away the freedom of the press. The Bill was, of course, passed smoothly because of the majority game on the floors of the Assembly. But one thing to be noted is that Biju had duly honoured the opinion of the opposition and he had never applied such an act against anybody; no news paper had been penalised so far on the basis of such an act. This is, perhaps, Biju's philosophy of life. He had stood non-commital; accolades and slanders could not affect his long innings in public life. He was a man of action-a 'Karma Yogi'. In his obsession for a clean, responsive polity tuned towards rapid development, he had given many remarks, unpalatable and also, at times, funny. The press was always after him, but he was not. It has been observed for long that the leaders across the world have remained very cautious, measured and, at times, tight-lipped in their interaction with the press. On the contrary, Biju had always been his natural self all through his public life, spanning almost six decades. When the newspapers had come forward to write about him or about his style of functioning, he had shown no inclination to go through and record his reaction. To sum up, he was never publicity-conscious.

In our quantum jump from print media to the electronic media, there had been a sea-change in our modes and manners. But Biju has remained undeterred - as if the earlier conviction predominated in his psyche. I vividly recollect a TV programme that came my way a few years back. Biju was found narrating his life-story to a group of young school-going kids. In the said programme he was found to be very humorous, vivacious and lively. Anyone, who has an opportunity to view the programme, must be forced to enjoy the programme vicariously.

In fine, Biju's relationship with the press is typical, which owes our interest. It is to be analysed with care. Biju has remained enigmatic, and so is his relationship with others, especially with the media.

Biju Patnaik and Women Empowerment

14

Dr. Srinibas Pathi

Biju Patnaik was a versatile genius. He was a living legend of his times. He belonged to that dare-devil genre of patriots who shirked no challenge to respond to any call of adventure for the cause of our country. And he also went far beyond the geographical boundary of India and directly participated in the freedom struggle of Indonesia against the Dutch which later on crowned him with that country's highest civilian honour, i.e., the Bhumiputra. Biju Patnaik, who has been very active in numerous fields of our socio-economic and political life, possessed a unique personality which might be described as larger than life. He was all in one - Freedom Fighter, Pilot, Politician, Industrialist, Entrepreneur, Diplomat, Chief Minister, opposition Leader, Union Cabinet Minister, Newspaper Owner, Visionary Leader and the Darling of the Mass.

Biju Babu was generous to the neck and was quite open-minded and pragmatic towards everything and everybody. He was brutally frank and outspoken which often landed him into trouble and complications. Perhaps this was the single-most important reason for his not becoming the Prime Minister of India in spite of having all the requisite qualifications. Few of his contemporary politicians could match the political acumen of Biju Babu.

Bjayananda, the second child of Laxminarayan Patnaik and Ashalata Devi, was born on 5th March, 1916. He spent his childhood at Anand Bhawan in Cuttack. His ancestral place was Rasolkonda (Bhanjanagar), a part of the then Madras Presidency. He had two brothers and one sister. Laxminarayan was a judicial officer under Bihar-Orissa province. Biju was brave, fearless and adventurous from childhood. There are numerous stories regarding his daring activities in school and college. While he was a student of first year science in Ravenshaw College, Cuttack, he went to Peshawar (now in Pakistan) in 1932 on a bicycle covering a distance of thousands of kms. Biju and two of his friends braved inclement weather, forests, rough terrain and many odds to reach Peshawar and even Biju had to fight with a Royal Bengal Tiger on the way! He introduced pole vault game in Orissa and was its reigning champion for a long time.

Biju Babu joined the Indian National Air Ways, a constituent of British Royal Air Force in the Indian sub-continent. He was not meant to serve the imperialist power. As per the suggestions of Netaji Subhas Chandra Bose and Loknayak Jaya Prakash Narain, Biju used the British plane to carry Indian freedom fighters during the Quit-India Movement to different parts of the country under the most difficult flying conditions and used to land in unorthodox grounds. During this period, he came in to close personal contact with leaders like Achyut Patwardhan, Ram Manohar Lohia, Ashoka Mehta, Aruna Asaf Ali, etc. Soon, he was sacked from the Air Force Service and was imprisoned on 13th January, 1943. He was put in different jails in Punjab and Orissa. After his release, he set up B. Patnaik & Company, one of the pioneering business concerns in pre-independence period.

Biju Babu became the Chief Minister of Orissa in 1961. He was the main organiser of the AICC Session in Bhubaneswar in 1964 wherein the famous resolution on 'democratic socialism' was adopted. During the next two decades, Biju Babu remained one of the most prominent leaders of the non-Congress parties and political formations that resulted in the rise of the Janata Party which assumed power at the Centre in 1977 following the black days of national emergency (1975-77) and in turn putting an end to thirty years of uninterrupted Congress rule. Biju Babu became the Union Minister for Steel and Mines. During 1980-90, he was designated as the unofficial national crisis manager in Indian politics by the media. Be it the issue of Rama Krushna Hegde's Chief Ministership in Karnataka or Vishwanath Pratap Singh's Prime Ministership that depended upon the peculiar support of the BJP on the right and the Left Front on the left, Biju Babu was always ready to mediate. And, in fact, Biju has visited New Delhi twelve times to sustain the V.P. Singh ministry for eleven months.

In 1990, the people of Orissa gave a massive mandate to Biju Babu in the Assembly elections. Under his leadership, the Janata Dal got 123 seats in a house of 147 and the outgoing ruling party Congress-I got only ten seats. Biju Babu became the Chief Minister of Orissa for the second time. In 1996, after the fall of the 13-day old BJP government led by Atal Bihari Vajpayee, the United Front, supported by the Congress-I from outside, assumed power at the Centre under the Prime Ministership of H.D. Deve Gowda and Indra Kumar Gujaral in succession. Biju Babu was a sure entrant into the Union Cabinet. But due to treacherous designs and unpardonable backbiting by a few of his own partymen, Biju Babu was not included in the ministry. He was admitted to Escorts Hospital, New Delhi on 30th March, 1997 and he breathed his last on 17th April, 1997. But like all great personalities, the man who succumbed to heart failure, continues to live in the hearts of millions of people.

Biju Patnaik was instrumental in the establishment of a large number of institutions and organisations that include, among others, the Orissa Textile Mills, Kalinga Tubes, Kalinga Industries, Kalinga Airlines, Kalinga Publications, Kalinga Refrigeration, Paradeep Port and Express Highway, Orissa Industrial Development Corporation, Ferrochrome Plant in Jaipur Road, Cement Factory at Bargarh, Sponge Iron Factory at Barbil, Regional Engineering College at Rourkela, Sainik School in Bhubaneswar, Panchayat Industries throughout Orissa, Balimela Dam, Mig Factory at Sunabeda, Thermal Power Plant at Talcher, Charbatia Air Base, Orissa Flying Club, CRP Centre, Radio Training Centre in Ravenshaw College, Medical College in Berhampur, Engineering College in Burla, Regional College of Education in Bhubaneswar (now renamed as Regional Institute of Education under the NCERT, New Delhi), Orissa University of Agriculture and Technology in Bhubaneswar, Tikarpara Multipurpose Dam, Mahanadi Barrage, Samal Barrage, Indravati Dam, NALCO and hundreds of educational institutions for girls and weaker sections of the society. Biju Patnaik has set up the Kalinga Foundation Trust in 1951 which in collaboration with the UNESCO has instituted the annual Kalinga Prize for the popularisation of science in the world through study, research and writings.

Biju Babu was a pioneer in many fields. He was nostalgic about the ancient Kingdom of Kalinga under Emperor Kharavela, the legendary Oriya King and warrior. He wanted to develop Orissa through the promotion of agriculture, education and industrialisation. It is a pity that most of the political leaders from Orissa do not have any clout in New Delhi due to a number of personal, political and circumstantial reasons. But Biju Babu was a class apart. He was always at the centre-stage of both national and state politics, a position he hardly exploited to achieve petty personal gains. When V P Singh resigned as the Prime Minister, Rajiv Gandhi, the then President of the Congress-I went to Biju Babu's Aurangzeb

Road residence in New Delhi alongwith his Doon-mate Naveen (the younger son of Biju Babu) to persuade him to form an alternative government at the Centre with the outside support of the Congress-I. Biju Babu turned down the offer which was gladly accepted by the Balia - strongman turned Bhondsi-Baba, an epitome of the highest opportunism in Indian politics.

Before going into the issue of Biju Patnaik's contribution to the cause of women empowerment, it is pertinent to discuss the notion of women empowerment per se. To empower means to give somebody the power or authority to act. So, this term is often used in the context of improvement of status, position and authority of some individual, group or community at large. Women empowerment has gained momentum throughout the world as a corollary of the feminist movement or feminism. Because women have not received their due or genuine place in most of the societies and have been the victims of male chauvinism and social stigma, feminism grew as a reaction or backlash. The situation often gets more complicated as in most of the cases the role of women is either eulogised or underestimated; but seldom appreciated in its proper perspective. It may be kept in mind that notions like feminism, gender and women empowerment should not be studied and analysed in isolation. Rather these ideas need to be located within the overall structural context and social dynamics both in macro- and micro-levels. The need of the hour is not to portray women either as victims or as martyrs; but to contextualize the discourse on empowerment. This has to be related to the theories of social movement, state and development.

Today, many writers have proved that the biological determinism or conventional wisdom of portraying women as the weaker sex is not based on facts or scientific truth. Women's biological, genetic and physical make-up makes them not only men's equal but their superior in many cases. The only issue is that adequate opportunity should be provided to women to prove their worth. Women constitute the bulk of the work force and they also contribute more than half of the wealth of nations. But, at the same time, race, ethnicity and social class shape the working conditions and wages of women which are very often hostile, improper and inappropriate.

The Human Development Reports published by the UNDP during the past few years almost as an annual ritual have presented many negative features regarding the status of women inside the member states of the U.N. In most cases, women are engaged in economic activities; but in return, they are either unpaid or under-rated. More importantly, women put in more labour and are engaged in various types of productive endeavours.

Coming to the situation in India, women with varied cultural, social, economic, political and linguistic backgrounds constitute nearly half of the population. But they all share one common cause - as they, irrespective of these variations, work as productive members of the society, with or without recognition and reward. Women sustain the family; shape the people's and society's fate; and share the bulk of life's burden. Social attitude, deprivation, unemployment, poverty and lack of opportunity only add to the precarious condition of women in India.

A number of social, economic, political, cultural and psychological indicators may be taken into account while analysing the status of women in India which include, among others: centuries - old tradition, belief systems and norms relating to girls and women and their role; education and literacy among women (again it may further be subdivided into urban and rural settings); employment, unemployment and under-employment of women; low and inequal wage and compensation and gender discrimination at the work-place; female infanticide and maternal morality rate; sex ratio; property and inheritance rights and privileges of women; plight of widows, destitute women, disabled and mentally challenged women; women's age at marriage; social evils like dowry, sati and oppressions like physical and mental torture and all kinds of violence and atrocities on women; and, last but not least, political participation of women and their role in the decision-making process.

Many religious, cultural and social reform movements have tried to ameliorate the condition of women in India and to bring them at par with men. Raja Rammohan Roy, Iswar Chandra Vidyasagar, Gopabandhu Das, Madhusudan Das and many other individual reformers and thinkers have tried to do their bit in this respect in modern times. Mahatma Gandhi, the Father of the Nation, was of the view that we should not compromise in the matter of women's rights. To call women the weaker sex is man's injustice to woman. If by strength is meant moral power, then woman is immeasurably man's superior. It is needless to mention here that women participated in large numbers in the freedom struggle including the Gandhian programmes like Satyagraha, picketing, bare-foot march and many other direct action programmes at par with men in different parts of India.

After independence, the Constitution of India was adopted and it guarantees equality, fraternity, justice and liberty to all men and women. Article 14 of the Constitution of India says that the State shall not deny to any person equality before law or the equal protection of the laws. Article 15 prohibits discrimination on grounds of religion, race, caste, sex or place of birth; wherein Clause-3 states that nothing in this article shall prevent the State from making any special provision for women and children. Article 16 (Cl.2) provides that no citizen shall on grounds only of religion, race, caste, sex, descent, place of birth, residence or any of them, be ineligible for, or discriminated against, in respect of any employment or office under the State. Article 19 states that all citizens shall have the right to freedom of speech and expression and other rights. Besides these fundamental rights, the directive principles of

State policy as given in Part-IV of the Constitution also provides a number of provisions for ensuring equality of men and women. Article 39 states that the State shall, in particular, direct its policy towards securing that the citizen, men and women equally, have the right to an adequate means of livelihood; equal pay for equal work for both men and women; and the health and strength of workers, men and women and the tender age of children are not abused. Article 42 provides that the State shall make provision for securing just and human conditions of work and for maternal relief.

During the British regime, a number of social laws were promulgated in India that affected the status, position and role of women in pre-independence era which include among others, the Sati System Regularisation Act of 1829; the Hindu Widow's Remarriage Act of 1856; the Indian Penal Code of 1860 (relevant provisions relating to award of punishment for various crimes against women); Special Marriage Act of 1872; the Married Women's Property Act of 1974; the Civil Procedure Code of 1908; the Child Marriage Restraint Act of 1929; and the Hindu Widow's Right on Property Act of 1937. These laws and a few such other Acts were the result of a number of socio-religious and cultural movements that were organised by social reformers and enlightened individuals and groups in different parts of India.

In the post-independence era, a number of Acts have been adopted in India that affect women and their position vis-a-vis men. Such Acts include, among others, the Hindu Marriage Act of 1955 (as amended in 1976); the Hindu Succession Act of 1956 (as amended in 1986); the Hindu adoption and Maintenance Act of 1956; the Dowry Prohibition Act of 1962 (as amended in 1984 and 1986); the Maternity Benefit Act of 1961 (as amended in 1976); the Medical Termination of Pregnancy Act of 1971; the Equal Remuneration Act of 1976; the Family Courts Act of 1984; the Sati (Prevention) Act of 1987; the 73rd Constitution Amendment

Act of 1993; and the 74th Constitution Amendment Act of 1993. These laws have been enacted by the Parliament of India in tune with the provisions of the Constitution of India, popular demands, agitation by feminist groups, and legal necessities. But there is a perceptible gap between the cup and the lip. A vast majority of women in India who are illiterate and who live in the rural areas still remain completely unaware of most of these laws and their relevant provisions which are only pious words and philosophical pronouncements as presented in the bulky law books.

However, the declaration of the decade 1976-85 as the Women's Decade by the United Nations brought about a change in the perception of the position and status of women and the issue of gender equality throughout the world including India. Successive U.N. conferences on Women and Development, including the one held in Beijing, have emphasised on gender equality, gender equity, women participation in development and women empowerment.

To conclude this theoretical discussion, it may be pointed out that women empowerment would be possible through a number of ways and means including those of a change in the mind-set of both men and women in all walks of our socio-economic and cultural life, better primary health care including reproductive health and reduction of maternal mortality rate; expansion of women's literacy, education (including technical and professional education); access of women to ownership of land and property; access of women (mainly rural and urban slum dwellers) to micro credit and marketing facilities; organisation of women's self help groups and cooperatives for self-empowerment and gainful productive endeavours; and adequate and proper participation of women in the decision-making process including the local, state and national level governance. Besides the government, the civil society including grass-roots level women organisations should play a more positive and pro-active role for awareness generation among women throughout India.

Now, it is pertinent to discuss the contribution of Biju Patnaik to women empowerment. As education (including literacy) is the main key to social development and women empowerment, Biju Babu was instrumental in setting up a large number of girls' high schools, women's colleges, women polytechniques and women B.Ed colleges throughout Orissa including a good number of such institutions in the tribal dominated areas. During his tenure as the Chief Minister, a large number of SC and ST girls students were provided with scholarship. Several concessions were declared by Biju Babu for the privately managed but government-aided girls high schools and women's colleges. He gave particular emphasis to science education, skill development and vocational training of girls. During the International Women's Week (01 March to 08 March, 1994), mass awareness camps were organised by the State Social Welfare Board to spread the message of equality, empowerment and entrepreneurship of women. Biju Babu himself participated in a State level Workshop on Women and Science and Technology, a pioneering step in the post-independence era in the State.

After education, next comes employment. Biju Babu took a decision to raise the upper age limit by five years for women candidates for various State government jobs and for appearing at various written examinations and interviews in connection with recruitment. And he did not stop at that. He went on to announce 30 percent reservation for women in all categories of government recruitment. Biju Babu's government decided to take over the management of all the government-aided primary, middle and high schools which benefited thousands of lady teachers. Moreover, he took a revolutionary step by making a policy decision that all the posts of primary school teachers in Orissa henceforth shall be reserved for qualified women candidates.

Biju Babu took a policy decision in 1994 to set up a Sabai Grass Development Corporation. Sabai grass is used by women belonging to SCs and STs to produce household items including ropes and rope-products. Often these poor women are exploited by the middle men and unscrupulous traders. It was decided that the Corporation would provide improved varieties of Sabai seeds and necessary implement to women engaged in this cultivation and trade. The Corporation would organise technical training to women for skill development and better production. Marketing of the products would also be taken care of by the Corporation. It was decided that the State government and "Youth-Ending-Hunger", an international voluntary agency, would jointly operationalise the Corporation.

With a view to implementing the National Plan for women's development, the Government of Orissa under the Chief Ministership of Biju Babu established the Orissa Women Development Cooperative Corporation (Orissa Mahila Vikash Samavaya Nigam) in 1991 which is currently working as the apex State level women's cooperative body. It is a joint endeavour by the Government of India, the Government of Orissa and a number of Women's Organisations. Its main aims and objectives are as follows: first, to integrate all the development plans for women at State, district, block, gram panchayat and village levels; second, to build women as a healthy social and economic force for nation building and to facilitate their individual and collective efforts; third, to train women entrepreneurs for individual, cooperative and joint enterprises; fourth, to provide margin money to women for availing loans from banks and other financial institutions; fifth, to set up a State level marketing network for the products manufactured by women; and, finally, to create a conginial environment and awareness for the implementation of women development programmes.

This Corporation has completed a decade of its existence and is working as the nodal agency to coordinate and monitor various women development plans. Some of the major activities that are being undertaken by the corporation include income generation schemes for women groups, social training programmes, marketing assistance to women, organisation of women self-help groups, the notion of gender equality within the development paradigm, and, organising meetings of women entrepreneurs.

Another interesting area of operation of the Corporation is its financial assistance and easy loan facilities to various women groups, educational institutions and NGOs to open 'Women Study Circles' to impart examination-oriented coaching to women candidates appearing in different competitive examinations.

Biju Babu was the first leader in India to take very bold steps in regard to grass-roots level democracy. It was during his first tenure as the Chief Minister in early 1960s that he restructured the rural and urban local bodies and brought in suitable amendments to the existing Acts of 1948, 1959 and 1960. But during his second term as the Chief Minister on 5th March, 1990 which is eventually celebrated as the Panchayati Raj Day every year, he announced that for the first time in the history of independent India, women will be given 33 p.c. reservation in the three-tier Panchayati Raj Institutions. And true to his word, he saw to it that the Orissa Zilla Parishad Act of 1991 and the Gram Panchayat Samiti Amendment Act of 1992 were passed by the Orissa Assembly that provided for 33 p.c. of reservation for women including SC and ST women. So, for the first time, more than twenty eight thousand women were elected to various Gram Panchayats, Panchayat Samities and Zilla Parishads. It was further provided that one third of the Zilla Parishads would have exclusively women Chairpersons. In the case of the Panchayat Samities and the Gram Panchayats, one of the two office-bearers, i.e. Chairperson or Vice-Chairperson in the case of the Samiti and Sarpanch or Naib-Sarpanch in the case of Gram Panchayat must be a woman.

Empowerment of women and political participation would be meaningless without proper awareness and orientation of the women concerned. So, Biju Babu saw to it that all the elected women representatives of the PRIs should receive adequate political and administrative training. Many of them now receive training with the help of the State Institute of Rural Development, the Orissa Women Development Cooperative Corporation and many other NGOs working in different parts of Orissa.

It may be pointed out that Biju Babu's policies on reservation for women were followed by many other State governments in India that culminated in the 73rd and 74th Amendment Acts to the Constitution of India which provided for similar provisions for rural and urban local bodies respectively.

Biju Babu established the State Commission for Women in Orissa in line with the National Commission for Women, another step towards highlighting the cause of women and protection of the rights and privileges of women. The Commission performs a number of functions including study of the economic, educational and health situation of women; compilation of information on instances of offences against women; preparation of reports on the status of women, and, investigation into matters relating to women, etc. Dr. (Mrs.) Ranu Mishra was the first Chairperson of the SCW in Orissa who was succeeded by Prof. Lopamudra Mohanty. Incidentally, Mrs. Jayanti Patnaik, former M.P. from Orissa, was the first Chairperson of the National Commission for Women in India.

Biju Babu wanted women to excel in all fields. Incidentally, his daughter Geeta Mehta is an internationally acclaimed writer. Biju Babu always encouraged girls to participate in national and international sports including adventure sports and mountaineering. In fact, he was instrumental in the inclusion of an Oriya girl in the Kalinga

Bali Yatra, an expedition through the ancient sea-route (from Orissa to Indonesian island like Java, Bali and Sumatra) to commemorate legendary 'Boita Yatra' by Oriya 'Sadhavas' (Sea-bound international traders)..

Biju Babu was concerned with very little things of life. Once he came to know that very few women officials of the government have been allotted government accommodation in the capital city of Bhubaneswar, thanks to the manouvres of their male colleagues. He immediately made a circular that thirty percent of the government quarters shall be kept reserved for women employees.

At times, Biju Babu behaved so strangely that his associates and security personnel had to run to him only to be scolded and ordered to keep mum. While visiting the tribal areas (incidentally about twenty five percent of Orissa's population is tribal) he would drop in at some tribal hamlet and would start talking to the old tribal ladies and enquire about the development programmes and their needs. Biju Babu was perhaps the only Chief Minister of an Indian state who 'appointed' five tribal ladies as his 'unofficial advisors' on prohibition, sustainable development, literacy and implementation of different anti-poverty programmes. He even told these lady advisers that they would have power at par with 'police' and they are free to communicate with the Chief Minister without any hesitation. Incidentally one of the ladies, Mrs. Sumani Jhadiani has been recommended for the national "Stree Shakti" award by the Government of Orissa in 2001, the year of women empowerment in "India".

Biju Babu was a legend during his life-time and his legacy continues to inspire millions of his followers. Numerous stories are told and retold by the people from all walks of life about the life, work, achievements and adventures of Biju Babu. He passed away in New Delhi and his mortal remains were brought to his Bhubaneswar residence 'Naveen Niwas' on the way to Swargadwar in Puri. A lone old lady was standing at a little distance from the crowd. She tried in vain to push her way through the throng of onlookers and admirers just to have a glimpse at Biju Babu on the way to his last journey. A Doordarshan cameraman covering the event could record the opinion of the old lady who in her feeble voice said that Biju was both my father and son. At times, he would call me mother and at some other times, he would address me as daughter. This lady resides in a slum near Bhubaneswar Air Port, now renamed as Biju Patnaik Air Port.

Biju Patnaik's contribution to the cause of women empowerment in India reminds us the famous sayings from the Rig Veda wherein a woman boldly declares that she is like the flag of the nation. Nobody should treat her simplicity and tolerance as her weakness. She is capable enough to shape the destiny of not only the family, but also the entire nation.

Bibliography

1. Prof. Samar Guha, *'A Man of Patriotic Adventure'*, Ananya, Cuttack: B.P.B.D.C. Committee, 1990, pp.177-81.
2. Surendra Mohan, *'Shri Biju Patnaik'*, 1990, pp.182-84.
3. Aruna Asaf Ali, *'Biju Patnaik: A Veritable dare-devil Freedom Fighter'*, 1990, pp.205-07
4. Janardan Thakur, *'Biju Patnaik: The Merger Man'*, 1990, pp.208-12.
5. J.E. Leewellyn, *The Legacy of Women's Uplift in India,* New Delhi: Sage, 1998.
6. U. Kalpagam, *Labour and Gender*, New Delhi: Sage, 1994.
7. Sangeetha Purushothaman, *The Empowerment of Women in India,* New Delhi: Sage, 1998.
8. Kiran Devendra, *Changing Status of Women in India,* New Delhi: Vikash, 1994.
9. F.E. Stifling, *Women in Politics: Forms and Processes,* New Delhi: Har Anand Publications Pvt. Ltd., 1993.
10. L. Nicholson, edt., *Feminism/postmodernism,* New York: Routledge, 1990.

11. R.W. Connell, *Gender and Power*, Oxford: Polity Press, 1987.
12. Maithreyi Krishnaraj, *Women and Development: The Indian Experience*, Pune: Shubhad Saraswat Prakashan, 1988.
13. Mrinal Pandey, *'Gender, Poverty and Caste on a Pilgrimage'*, Mainstream, New Delhi, Vol.30, No.24, April 04, 1994.
14. Najma Heptullah, *'Global Action Against Gender Discrimination'*, Yojana, New Delhi, Vol.37, No.10, June 15, 1993.
15. Ram Ahuja, *The Rights of Women: A Feminist Perspective,* Jaipur: Rawat Publications, 1992.
16. M.K. Gandhi, *Young India*, February 26, 1918.
17. *The Constitution of India,* New Delhi, 1950.
18. P.D. Saikia, *Indian Rural Women*, Delhi: Mittal Publications, 1986.
19. R.K. Tandon, *Women in Modern India,* Delhi: I.P. Distributors, 1998.
20. N.V. Varghese, *'Women and Work: An Examination of the Female Marginalisation Thesis in the Indian Context',* The Indian Journal of Labour Economics, Vol.34, No.3, July-Sept., 1991.
21. S. Mehartaj Begum, *'Women Rights and Rural Employment',* Kurukshetra, New Delhi: Ministry of Rural Dev., Govt. of India, Vol.48, No.7, April 2000, pp.60-64.
22. Robert D Putnam, *Making Democracy Work*, Princeton: Princeton Univ. Press, 1993.
23. P.K. Mishra, edt. *CWS Newsletter*, Bhubaneswar: Centre for Women's Studies & Development Programmes, Utakl University, Vol.1, No.2, December 1996.
24. *Annual Report*, Orissa Women Development Cooperative Corporation, Bhubaneswar, 1993.
25. Madhusmita Mishra, *'Women and Media: The Indian Scenario',* Sharada Rath, et al, edt, *Women in India: A Search for Identity,* New Delhi: Anmol Publications Pvt. Ltd., 1999, pp.107-13.
26. *The National Commission for Women Act*, New Delhi, (No.20, 1990), The Act came into force on 31 January, 1992.
27. *The Orissa State Commission for Women Act, 1993,* The Act came into force on 7 October, 1994.

Biju Patnaik : The Yogi of Orissan Development

15

Dr. Jugal K Misra

Wilfred Stone, in his book, "Caves and the Mountains" (1977) has explained, in no uncertain terms, the essential/paradigmatic difference between a 'Yogi' and a commissar. In his considered opinion a 'Yogi' is not a commissar. Studied against this backdrop, Biju Patnaik, the 'Yogi' of the Orissan Development, is a 'Yogi' in the sense of the term. He is a Yogi because of his— (a) tremendous power to sacrifice, (b) messianic zeal to suffer for the multitude, and (c) faith in Lord Jagannath, the Guardian Angel of the Oriyas.

Smitten by the bug of poverty in plenty, Biju Patinaik, the fiery petrel, tried his best to nurture Orissa in such a manner that she could be industrially buttressed so as to occupy a place of pride in the pantheon of industrial powers.

Making the best use of his precocity, Biju Patnaik, the massive monument of individual talent, harnessed his knowledge of living history, complex scientific technology and material management to the hilt. Encouraged by the catalytic influence of Jawaharlal Nehru, he bloomed forth as a top-notch statesman, totally devoted to Orissan Development.

His first flash in politics exhibits his enormous exuberance. He forgot that he was a pilot and flew as a politician. His path, however, was not strewn with roses. It was the time of nasty politics of washing the dirty linen in public. With his acumen and accomplishment in the Indonesian operation, Biju Patnaik was endeared to Nehru, much to the chagrin and envy of many top-ranking leaders and politicians of the time. Many even grudged his natural position in the centre court of Indian politics. When Welles Hangen, American journalist-writer, in his magnum opus "After Nehru who ?" predicted that Biju was a force to reckon with in the post-Nehru wrangle for the Prime Minister's job, he incited the Biju baiters to misprize him.

The basic stand of Biju Patnaik's thinking which in reality provided the foundation for his ideas on Orissan development, and was thus integral to his model of development, was the fact that Biju Patnaik believed from the beginning that industries would constitute modern temples for the social and economic revival of the state. While focusing on the urgent need to restructure the inequitable socio-economic set-up in the state, he had also emphasized on the human values of a free society, the freedom and dignity of the individual. It is this which explains the fact that he ardently advocated the cause of mixed economy as the most suitable one in the context of Orissan devleopment.

Biju Patnaik's plan was mostly aimed at the long-term requirement of the state and in this context he said : "Planning over the past decades has taught us the lesson that the process of development is a continuous one and the time does not have a stop at the end of every five year period."[1]

The quintessence of Biju Patnaik's strategy in this respect is best expressed in his own words:

"Produce more power from water and coal, take it to villages, set up suitable industries at every stage, the village, the group of villages and the region and organise technical schools not in isolation but as integral parts of the industrial fabric on the one hand and the educational stream on the other. Improvements in transport and communication and other items of economic and social overheads will of course have to be dovetailed into the above patterns. These measures will set in train the process of replacement of the costly human and bullock power and the relaxation of the present unrelenting pressure of population on land. A higher rate of productivity per capita in industry as well as agriculture is our aim. For, it is only through higher productivity and larger production that our people can reach the promised land."[2]

In planning the industrial prosperity of the State, Biju Patnaik pointed out to base the industries primarily on agricultural produce and industries, the output of which would assist for more agricultural produce. It was necessary in the context of the rice-based economy of the State. Accordingly, the approach required involved:

— high priority to the development of agriculture through expansion of irrigation and use of fertiliser;

— diversification of agriculture increasing the acreage of cultivation of commercial crops; and

— greater emphasis on agro-based and forest-based industry.

As a result of the above, attention was given to the improvement of obsolete techniques and the change of uneconomic cropping pattern. Power tillers, tractors, sprayers were provided. The change in cropping pattern included the double cropping programme and the spread of cash crops, and for this decision was taken to step up lift irrigation through cooperative societies of cultivators.

The rural industrialisation programme, conceived by him, was for making each Panchayat Samiti and Gram Panchayat head quarters a nucleus for the development of rural industries. Under the Panchayat Industries Programme (PIP), the industries were meant for processing agricultural produces and for providing better skills and improved "equipments to the local artisans and workers. This small scale industry programme envisaged location of hulling; grinding Mills and expeller units, tile factories, cold storages and many agro-based and forest-based industries. This programme was meant to suffice the purpose of regional dispersion and sectoral diversification of industries.

Besides, Biju Patnaik emphasized on mineral-based industries followed by metal-based ones. Owing to the rich mineral deposits in the state,[3] he considered mineral-based industries as the vanguard.

One important point of economic importance to the State is mineral raisings the utilisation of which is of social significance for its over-all development. With a view to developing the economy of the State, it was necessary to increase the exploitation and export of iron-ore and other minerals through Paradeep Port. Attributing the growth of Kolkata to the port system, Biju Patnaik cherished the idea that Paradeep Port could be the greatest single factor for priming the pump of economic development. Once it is built Mahanadi would play a very important part in ordinary boat movement and small vessel movement which would go towards additional traffic and income of the port, he believed. The Daitary Paradeep Expressway which is the indispensable ancillary project of the port project was envisaged and executed simultaneously. The hinterland of Paradeep Port, spread over parts of Jajpur, Keonjhar and Sundargarh districts, abounds with iron ore. Exploration and expropriation of iron ore to Japan, South Korea and other countries through this port becomes an all-

Orissa affair leading to the employment of the tribals, generation of income to them and to the State through royalty and earnings in foreign exchange. The Expressway running through parts of Keonjhar, Jajpur and Kedrapara districts serve as a vital communication link in these parts. Daitary mines would be connected with Paradeep and Paradeep would be connected with Cuttack by a major road, and the major road in turn would be connected with the national highway through the system. It would assist the growth of hundreds of smaller and medium factories all around that area alongside the road.

Biju Patnaik emphasized the need for tapping power resources from every possible area with an eye to generate maximum power at minimum costs. With regard to the methods and procedures, the generation of power to be linked with the transmission systems along with package plants to enable every Panchayat headquarters to receive power and plan out the industries to consume this power.

Realising the importance of technical education simultaneously, Biju Patnaik was of the view that the message of science and technology had to be taken to the very heart of rural Orissa. The young men and women should be put through purposeful and intensive courses of education not merely with a technical bias but with a large measure of technical content, and stressed that that had to begin at the very beginning, i.e., at the primary level and built up through the secondary and higher secondary stages to the tertiary level.

As it has been realised later on, the experiment of Panchayat industries failed to provide tangible results. One of the reasons for its failure was due to the promoters themselves who did not have that capacity of doggedly pursuing the objective without which no industry big or small could ever survive. But the most important reason was the lack of infrastructural support. Even one argument is given that the "industrial policy of the State tends to succeed better in an environment of growth of regional capital and genuine surplus being generated in agriculture".[4] In Orissa, however, the agricultural scenario being equally depressing, such a surplus is not available. The growth of regional capital is either conspicuous by its absence or negligible enough. This is in great contrast to what happens in Andhra Pradesh, a neighbouring state of Orissa. The growth of regional capital in Andhra Pradesh arising mostly out of agricultural surplus was largely responsible for the growth of the film industry up to 1971-72. Thereafter, its flow started financing the growth of other industries as well. Such a phenomenon is yet to emerge in Orissa.

Even for the development of agriculture, as a priority area, heavy investment is also required. This view has been well corroborated by the findings of the Reserve Bank of India (RBI) Committee and the Planning Commission Study Group.[5]

In this context, it is apt to mention that "Orissa's natural endowments have not merited positive central action to develop it as a 'growth pole' in the country. The Central Policy in the past years has made the economy of the state dependent on the neighbouring 'growth poles' - one part belonging to the Calcutta 'growth pole' and the other part belonging to the Southern 'growth poles" at Hyderabad and Madras and the economy has crippled."[6]

Hence the export potential of the State of Orissa is extremely negligible. The vicinity of Kolkata with a relatively developed manufacturing base and trading organisations constantly tends to overshadow the local manufactures in the state by dumping. The requirements of the state for manufacturing products are largely met by suppliers and agents representing farms from outside the state. Even the elementary requirements of the state such as banana and eggs mostly come from the neighbouring Andhra Pradesh. Most of the sundry requirements used also come from Kolkata market.

Thus in spite of rich natural resources, the people of Orissa have to suffer. Explaining this paradox Prof. Rajkrishna[7] observes: "Accidents of politics and *laissez-faire* economics concentrated early investment in particular regions... Areas with a high initial rate of capital formation continue to have a growing infrastructure base and a pool of skills and surpluses for investment. They not only have ample resources of their own but also a steady inflow of labour and capital from low investment regions. In the low investment regions, on the other hand, the vicious circle of insufficient infrastructure, income and market growth and the exports of skills and surpluses set in. Policy-makers can break this vicious circle in the background regions only with the deliberate and massive 'investment push' of the same magnitude as the luckier regions received in the past."

So without infrastructural development which requires substantial investment, the all-round development of Orissa will be a difficult task. In this context, Biju Patnaik's urge for 'financial autonomy for the States' needs to be understood.

Over the years the planning process in India has not only strengthened the phenomenon of financial centralisation but also has revealed another kind of imbalance: this being the unevenness in their levels and rates of economic development among the different states. It is evident from the relative infrastructural development index of Orissa which is 97.00 in 1993-94 compared to 144.00 for Tamil Nadu and 122.4 for Gujarat. So the State has failed to make any significant levels of investment in the infrastructure sector which has seriously limited its prospects for attracting private investment in the post-liberalisation era.

The macro-economic profile of Orissa[8] thus presents a grim picture. Nearly 48.6 per cent of the people of the State live below the poverty line according to the estimates of the Planning Commission. The gap between the per capita income of the state and the national average has substantially increased. In terms of human development also Orissa continues to lag behind the national average. The Human Development Index (HDI), a combined measure of achievement in education, health status and quality of living of the population, is estimated at 0.373 for Orissa compared to the national average at 0.428. Literacy rate at 49.1 per cent is lower than the national average and far below those of some states like Kerala. In fact the mortality rate of 96 per 1000 reflects the inadequacy of prime health care facilities in Orissa.

The magnitude of debt is simply unsustainable for a state like Orissa whose resource base is weak. The debt to GSDP ratio has increased from 28.52 per cent in 1985-86 to 33.83 per cent in 1995-96. This high debt burden has become an impediment to poverty-alleviation programmes in Orissa.

As a result of all these, the state is in a vicious circle of mounting revenue deficit necessitating large scale borrowing from year to year which again leads to higher borrowings and still higher doses of borrowing to meet the interest burden of the past borrowings.

In the backdrop of the above scenario, Biju Patnaik's demand for 'equitable regional development' at the meeting of the National Development Council on 23.12.1991 seems to be in tune with the interest of the people of Orissa at large. One thing he made it clear: the constitution gives precedence to the objective of maximising the economic welfare of the masses over that of maximising the economic returns of the national resources.

When seen in the context of the unfavourable treatment meted out constantly by the successive Finance Commissions of Govt. of India to Orissa, the veracity of Biju Patnaik's statement can be ascertained. No doubt, there has been a declining trend of central transfer to the states but Orissa has been incapacitated to the degree of being maimed. The relative share of Orissa declined from 5.21% under the award of the

Ninth Finance Commission to 4.28% under the award of the Tenth Finance Commission and has marginally increased to 4.78% under the award of the Eleventh Finance Commission. The relative share of Orissa with comparative position which is shown in the table below, indicates that states like Andhra Pradesh, Madhya Pradesh, Bihar, Assam and Uttar Pradesh have been benefited by the recommendations of successive Finance Commissions.

Table- 1

States	Relative Share of Population		Relative Share of Geographical area	Relative Share Under			
	1971	1991		8th FC	9th FC	10th FC	11th FC
Andhra	7.94%	7.86%	8.37%	7.33%	6.83%	7.98%	7.14%
M.P.	7.60%	7.82%	13.49%	7.48%	7.40%	7.10%	8.06%
Bihar	10.28%	10.21%	5.29%	10.67%	10.54%	10.88%	13.04%
West Bengal	8.09%	8.04%	2.70%	8.72%	6.99%	6.61 %	8.11 %
Assam	2.73%	2.65%	2.39%	4.07%	3.73%	3.69%	3.05%
Uttar Pradesh	16.12%	16.44%	8.96%	15.44%	16.46%	15.95%	18.08%
Rajasthan	4.70%	5.20%	10.41%	4.24%	6.15%	5.03%	5.42%
Orissa	4.00%	3.76%	4.74%	4.84%	5.21%	4.28%	4.78%

Source: White Paper on Orissa State Finance by Finance Deptt, Govt of Orissa, dated March 29th, 2001.

The precarious economic condition of the State naturally impelled Biju Patnaik to suggest umpteen austerity measures in administration. Very judiciously he stressed on the need for readjustments across several areas of government finance, improvement in the management of public expenditure, and comprehensive civil service delivery through increased accountability, integrity and productivity of the civil service. The necessity of reforms and the magnitude of his mental agony for the sordid state of economic affairs of the nation in general and the state in particular is amply evident from the tone and tenor of an interview in which he stated: "Running the government is getting more and more expensive. We have reached such a pathetic stage that as a nation we are now forced to borrow in order to pay wage and salaries. Our overstaffed administrative machinery is too expensive. The political machinery is even more expensive. Hard decisions are a must. If I were to run the country and if I were thirty years younger, I would certainly impose draconian laws and punitive measures to ensure that corruption does not pay."[9] In this instance also whatever Biju Patnaik had to say came straight from his heart. However, judged against the backdrop of Orissa's current harsh ground realities, it can be undoubtedly asseverated that his commitment for a vibrant Orissa was unshakable.

References

1. Orissa Legislative Assembly Proceedings, dated 01.03.1963.
2. Orissa Legislative Assembly Proceedings, dated 01.03.1963.
3. Orissa's contribution to national mineral resources can be measured from the fact that 90 per cent of its chromite, 33 per cent of its bauxite and dolomite, 17 per cent of its iron ore and 10 per cent of its limestone come from Orissa.
4. Srish Chandra Patnaik, *Industrial Development in a Backward Region: Dynamics of Policy*, Ashish Publishing House, New Delhi, 1988, p.103.
5. The Committee set up by the Reserve Bank of India under the Chairmanship of S.R. Sen submitted its report on Agricultural Productivity in Eastern India in two volumes in 1984. The Report of the Study Group on 'Agricultural Strategies for Eastern Region of India' by the Planning Commission was published in July 1985. Both these studies provide a good account of the constraints of improvement of agricultural productivity. They also suggest a strategy for accelerating agricultural growth in the eastern region, including Orissa.

The R.B.I. Committee's core strategy for accelerating agricultural growth is similar to that of the Study Group of the Planning Commission. Adequate and controlled water supply and allied infrastructure development are the spearheads of accelerating agricultural growth.

6. Dr. D.D. Panigrahi, *Centre-State Financial Relations in India*, Vikas Publishing House Pvt. Ltd., 1985, pp. 191-192.
7. Source: Rajkrishna's G.L. Mehta Memorial Lectures, *The Economic Times*, 15 May, 1980.
8. See White Papers published by Finance Department, Govt. of Orissa, March 29, 2001 and July 1999.
9. Sabina Sehgal's interview, published in *Times of India* dt.13.6.93.

Biju Patnaik : An Epitome of National Glory

16

Dr. Saroj Kumar Patnaik

"Politicians seldom had an exciting life, save their biographers - Biju Patnaik is an exception. His life and adventure made him a startling exception in the annals of Indian politics. He is one of those few octogenarian Indian politicians who would make an interesting biography, such has been his adventurous career before and after he joined politics". His long political innings has seen many highs and lows.

Julian Huxley, in his memoirs described Biju Patnaik as a "remarkable Indian whose adventures will surely fill a book".

Biju Patnaik, son of a judicial officer, Laxminaryan Patnaik, knew no poverty in his childhood, who had received inspiration from his father to be fearless in his life. He always desired that the younger generation should be fearless and straightforward in the face of all possible obstructions.

While he was a student in Ravenshaw College, Cuttack he became a pilot and joined Birla's National Airways and carved out for himself a place of honour and courage. Some of the hazardous flying missions that he undertook, first with the Royal Indian Air Force and later with the Indian National Airways earned him the sobriquet a 'daredevil pilot'.

During World War II, it was Biju who pioneered risky operations across the Himalayas to help the Chinese revolutionaries in Chiang Kaishek's China. He once flew all the way to Stalingrad on yet another mission.

The British government particularly appreciated Biju's effort to evacuate British families from Rangoon (Yangon) when the Japanese invaded Burma (Myanmar) during the Second World War. A daring pilot, who made headlines by leading the first aircraft carrying Indian troops to Srinagar in 1948 when Kashmir was threatened from across the newly created border, Biju's exploits in the sky are a legend. Biju Patnaik as a pilot was engaged in Air Transport command covering the Middle East, China and Far East during the Second World War. In 1942, along with Jaya Prakash Narayan and others and senior officers of the armed forces serving with Netaji's INA, devoted themselves in leading the underground movement after Gandhiji's Quit India Movement was suppressed by the British government. He was imprisoned for these subversive activities in January, 1943 to the end of 1945. He came to the limelight and was in direct contact with Panditji.

A close confidant of Pandit Nehru, Biju enjoyed free access to "Teen Murti Bhavan", the then Prime Ministerial residence. Nehru had entrusted him with the additional responsibility of advising him on defence matters during the Chinese aggression. He was reportedly offered to organize Guerrilla resistance in Assam if such a need arose during aggression. Once Biju Patnaik was considered to be one of the five Prime Ministerial candidates to succeed Pandit Nehru (The others being Gulzarilal Nanda, Morarji Desai, Lal Bahadur Shastri and Indira Gandhi). It's an irony of fact that all others except Biju Patnaik had adorned the office of the Prime Minister.

While his love for the country had his opposition to British rule made him plunge into India's freedom struggle in a daring and different manner as a young man, Biju Patnaik played a role in the Indonesian freedom movement also during 1946-47.

He became internationally known, when, under Nehru's instruction, he conducted sorties to Indonesia against Dutch threats to fly out several leaders spearheading their country's independence struggle at that time.

In what can be aptly described as a drama in real life, Biju Patnaik took-off an old fashioned dakota with wife Smt. Gyan Patnaik and some others on board for Jakarta where the rebels headquarters was located. As he landed in Singapore, came a Dutch message threatening that his aircraft would be shot down if it entered the Indonesian airspace.

Biju roared from his hotel room: "Resurgent India does not recognize Dutch colonial sovereignty over the Indonesian people. If my aircraft is shot down, every Dutch plane flying across Indian skies will be shot down in retaliation".

He also dashed off a message to Prime Minister Nehru: "Take necessary steps should my aircraft be shot down".

As the world watched him with admiration, the 32 year old ace pilot eluded the Dutch, landed in Jakarta and flew back to Delhi with the Indonesian leaders including Mohammad Hatta for holding confabulation with Pandit Nehru and Sardar Patel. Biju, thereafter, became the focal point of all activities relating to Indian support to the Indonesian freedom struggle.

A grateful Indonesia twice decorated Biju Patnaik with its highest civilian honour "Bhumi Putra" in return for the bravery the Indian leader had displayed at its hour of crisis. He was also called upon by President Suekarno to carry out certain top secret and important assignments for the Indonesian government with senior British Cabinet Ministers like Sir

Stafford Cripps, Mr. Bevin, the foreign Minister of the UK, having the full authority of the President and his Government. Thus, his background is one of challenge, adventure, fearlessness and seeking perfection in every sphere of his activity. He was a dare-devil freedom fighter, with patriotic adventure par excellence. His mind was as broad as the sky and as high as the Himalayas. The call of the unlimited sky made his mind romantic. He was endowed with exceptional talent and courage.

Jawaharlal Nehru was moved by his "energy and certainability" and drew him to politics. But after about more than four decades in politics, through good and bad times, he retained his spirit of adventure. The Orissa Patriarch's political career was remarkably astute, almost prophetic. For the image of the archetypal adventurer stuck to the man whom many considered a potential successor to Nehru as Prime Minister of the country. And that at a time when the country was not as desperate in its hunt for a Prime Minister as it is now. Like his role model Napoleon he deleted the word "impossible" from his dictionary, who inspired in him a deep interest in military strategy. Even Nehru used to consult him on military issues.

He missed out not only his possible hour of glory in national politics, but also lost his very own kingdom of Kalinga. The simple reason was he could never get out of the king of Kalinga syndrome and he had a vision for his kingdom. During the short span of his chief ministership of Orissa, he had made remarkable and spectacular achievements in the field of agriculture and industry. The first chief ministerial term was cut short by the Kamraj Plan which forced him to resign. It was almost providential intervention because he never again got back the same initiative.

But strangely enough, he never captured the political high ground after the early sixties when he had to relinquish the post of Orissa Chief Minister under the Kamraj Plan. His career resembled a meteor, burning brightly in the initial stage and then fading out. He remained a major figure, of course an uncrowned king of Kalinga even when out of office. He was elected to the State Assembly eight times and to the Lok Sabha four times.

During 1967, he had a bad period, and he was nearly in political hibernation both at national and state politics. His inevitable break came in 1969, when he clashed with Indira Gandhi over the Presidential election, though he stood by her during the Congress split earlier. This ideological difference has resulted in the eclipse of this great leader from the national scene. He left the Congress party and formed a regional party, Utkal Congress, after he was denied a party ticket to seek election to the Rajya Sabha. He parted ways in 1971. In the 1971 assembly polls his party did reasonably well but he himself was defeated. Indira Gandhi clinched power and was installed as Prime Minister of India. Much the same thing happened with the Janata Party and later Janata Dal incarnations. Unlike his Janata colleagues in Orissa like Samarendra Kundu, Rabi Ray and Banka Bihari Das he was not a Lohiaite or any other kind of socialist even when he made common cause with V.P. Singh. He held views on Mandal and liberalization that were opposite to his party's ideology. He has also undermined Laloo P. Yadav and H.D. Deve Gowda.

He was certainly one of the most enthusiastic mergerists, and he has been one for a long time, and is practically a politician's politician. Ever since 1974 there has perhaps been no opposition conclave with the possible merger of the parties which he has not attended. Indeed some even call him a "merger-specialist". While Choudhury Charan Singh was seriously trying to bring the opposition together, most of the leaders discouraged him but he joined his campaign very gladly. When Charan Singh formed his Bharatiya Lok Dal in 1974, Biju merged his Utkal Congress with it. Undaunted, Biju Patnaik re-established contact with his old friend Jaya Prakash

Narayan and plunged into the JP movement as it picked up momentum in 1974. When emergency was declared in 1975, he was one of the first to be arrested along with other opposition leaders. In 1976, once again there was a move to unite the opposition and he was again an active participant.

Most people think that the Haryana boss, Devilal, was the most active man behind the three opposition parties and the Jan Morcha to merge into a new party. But it was the political adventurer from Orissa, Biju Patnaik, who did most of the ground work for the merger. Incidentally, his residence was not only a rendezvous for opposition politicians but also the place where the final merger decision was announced.

During the days of the emergency, all the top leaders like Asok Mehta, Chandra Sekhar, Raj Narayan, Piloo Mody, Sikander Bakt, Shyama Nandan Mishra, Balraj Madhok, Surendra Mohan, Bairon Singh Shekhawat were put together in Rohtak jail in Haryana. Visibly, Rohtak jail turned out to be a leader's jail and Biju Patnaik, its unrivalled mentor, for all his distinguished friends. He was telling them about the episodes of his 'political adventure but not on record. He was taking care of all of them whenever they required any particular attention. The unification of political parties to form an alternative to the Congress was hatched out in the jail of which he was the chief architect. This led to the formation of Janata Party during the period of the emergency, which clinched power after the 1977 elections. For this opposition unity he will be ever remembered in the annals of political history as a pole star. Further, when there was a crisis in the coalition he was the king-pin to solve the problem as a crisis manager.

He was released from jail in 1977, and got elected to the Lok Sabha for the first time and became the Minister of Steel and Mines in both the Morarji Desai and Charan Singh governments. The collapse of the Janata Party government at the Centre and the resurrection of Indira Gandhi pushed him into a political wilderness. He went back to Orissa and retained his Kendrapara Parliamentary constituency in 1980 and 1985, despite the sympathy wave in favour of Congress following Indira Gandhi's death.

He always wanted to be at the centre stage of politics. Beginning with the famous 1977 experiment, when for the first time in India's political history a non-congress government was catapulted to power, he was the architect of this new power game. Whenever Janata and its various outfits were given the mandate - however fragmented, he was the chief architect. But he could not make any headway for his own place in the national politics during the decade, 1980-90.

With the defeat of the Congress (I) headed by Rajiv Gandhi in 1989, he bounced back into the political limelight, but after playing a key - behind-the-scene role in maneuvering V.P. Singh to the Prime Minister's post, he again chose to go back to Orissa and to prepare for the Assembly election. He came back to power in 1990, as Chief Minister of Orissa when the Janata Dal won a spectacular victory bagging 123 seats out of 147 in the Orissa Assembly polls. After Janata Dal lost power in 1995 assembly polls, he again chose to be elected to Parliament from two seats Cuttack and Aska. He retained Aska seat till his death.

Biju Patnaik, a colourful personality, a politician of a different mould and a secular to the hilt, would go down in history as a fighter for causes without regard for the consequences. He demonstrated it during the independence movement, his difference with Indira Gandhi and when he was imprisoned during the emergency. At the height of the Mandal politics he defied the Dal's national leadership to candidly state that 'there are only two castes - the poor and the rich. I do not believe in any other caste which the Mandalites profess". He stood by it until he was pressurized to change his stance. But everybody knew that he never believed in casteism, regionalism or religious bigotry.

Whether in politics or out of it, he never took care to calculate the risks his decisions would bring in. Indeed, this foresightedness, or rather the lack of it, put him more often than not in political *faux pas*. Then, that was the dynamics of his political philosophy. He gave no forethought to his decisions, for he had no time to think before he leapt. A typical man in a 'hurry'.

Although part of it himself, he did not think the United Front had much of a chance. He laughed it away as a "cluster of lobsters fighting among themselves". One month before his death he gave his colleagues the jitters by suggesting that both the Congress and the left join the United Front government. If he thought it could work, he did not give a damn about ideological and other hangups.

Whenever he left Orissa to take part in Delhi's occasional political parade, he was virtually left in the cold. Where others had put their feet firmly in the saddles of power, he had to content himself as a passive onlooker - having not much to do in the new regime.

True, Biju Patnaik like anyone else nursed the dream of becoming India's Prime Minister in the wee hours of his political clock, but as he himself said many times he did not have enough MPs with him to stake claim for the post of premier, however short-lived it would be. If he were born in any other state like UP, West Bengal, Bihar or Tamil Nadu, he could have become the Prime Minister or the President of India. He followed a kind of politics which was clearly out of the system with the changing times. In 1996 Lok Sabha election, a coalition government of 13 political parties was formed at the Centre. H.D. Deve Gowda of Karnataka became the Prime Minister. But on reasons best known to them tactfully and surreptitiously he was kept out of the ministry what to speak about the post of Prime Minister. He was kept in a shameful and uncomfortable political situation. Had he been freed from all the corruption charges levelled against him, he could have been the Prime Minister of India. It is unfortunate that the pioneer of the concept of coalition politics, which was the order of the day is no more remembered by the reigning leaders of our country and Biju Babu has been relegated to the background. He remained an enigma for the future generation. It is an irony of time when the 13 party coalition at the Centre was facing a serious support crunch, Biju Babu instead of being present in the saddle to provide the wherewithal was struggling for his own survival. It was for the first time, perhaps the last, that he was not taking up the role of 'trouble-shooter' a job which he was managing with tact and intelligence.

Even his return as Janata Dal Chief Minister in 1990 was like the flickering of an unsteady flame, for it was clear that national events were bypassing Patnaik. At the same time, he was not restrained enough to acquire the position of an elder statesmen. He had been in politics for too long and inquiries into his administrative functioning had not been too complimentary. Few were surprised, therefore, when he lost in 1995 and his party men became restive about remaining in Janata Dal. In his last years, he was like an ageing Zamindar living in an ancient palace something to which the people of Orissa, especially the poor, are accustomed. He did talk of industrialization and built the Paradeep Port, but the State has remained backward and feudal, known for the killer droughts of Kalahandi, which even an energetic politician like him could do little to change.

His exemplary courage and personality had made him extremely popular in the country. With his death the country lost a great pillar of its democracy. As a Central Minister and Parliamentarian he never hesitated to place boldly before the Centre the manner in which Orissa had been neglected. He was denied his rightful place in the national scene only because he took pride in being an Oriya.

With all the glorious qualities he was never adorned with any prestigious national awards of India during his lifetime (one who has instituted the Kalinga Award and received the 'Bhumi Putra' award from Indonesia). With so much of his contribution to the national glory during early hours of our independence and after, he definitely deserved the highest civilian award of our country if not during lifetime at least posthumously.

Biju Patnaik strode the scene like a giant. But he stopped caring about the ground his feet touched, with his head touching the sky. His youthful passion for flying and adventure made his political life much of a myth. He had no time for the pettifogging world of today's politics. In turn, this made him an anachronism well before his end.

The people of Orissa today know Biju Patnaik as their most eminent political leader but they, particularly the younger ones—have something more to know about him. The challenge to India's unity and integrity and sovereignty has to be met by the young men and women born after India's independence. Mindless terrorism prevalent in the country today is born of cowardice and lust for self-aggrandizement. The masses should be mobilized to defeat the conspiracies that destabilize India. Imperialism is not dead; it has only changed its tactics. He belongs to that dare-devil genre of old patriots who in their younger days shirked no challenge to respond to any patriotic calls of adventure for the cause of their country. For those young men of Orissa, and of the other parts of the country as well, who aspire to experience the thrill of the adventure of life, not merely for any empty excitement but in fulfilment of a higher cause—Biju Patnaik's life is a beckoning example before them.

It is very difficult to draw the real valuation of Biju Patnaik in a limited sphere. He was a multi-faceted personality. His personality has so many stiff edges; what he was telling or doing was quite spectacular and different from others. He was no doubt an epitome of national glory but he was not appropriately rewarded to get his deserved place in spite of all his life-time achievements. He strode the political scene in Orissa, and for sometime at the centre, as a colossus. 'His loss can never be replaced and there can never be another person like him'. Biju Patnaik may have died, but his memory can never be erased from the history of Orissa.

Biju Patnaik, the custodian of the pride of Orissa, will be remembered as such for thousands of tomorrows to come. He had dreamt many dreams. But his fond dream of proliferation of dashing Oriya youth to conquer every sphere as the true descendents of Mahameghabahan Aira Kharvel remains unfulfilled. We can propitiate his soul, if we fulfil that dream.

Biju Patnaik : The Chief Minister of Orissa

17

Dr. Shridhar Charan Sahoo

Bijayananda Patnaik popularly known as Biju Patnaik was the Chief Minister of Orissa from 23.06.1961 to 02.10.1963 for a period of twenty seven months. After a long gap of twenty seven years, he again occupied this key position for five years from 05.03.1990 to 15.03.1995. This personality who ruled over Orissa as Chief Minister for about seven years and three months in total was a unique and multi-faceted personality. He was a pilot, a freedom fighter, an industrialist, a crisis manager in national politics, a facilitator of opposition unity and 'a crowning statesman of national and international repute'[1] all rolled into one. Over and above, he was 'a champion of Orissa's pride, glory and greatness' reminding us of Utkal Gaurav Madhusudan Das and also a veritable symbol of 'courage and adventure' like Netaji Subhash Chandra Bose like whom he was also educated in Ravenshaw Collegiate School at Cuttack[2].

In his personality and style of functioning, in respect of his initiative and drive, his firmness and dare-devil approach in administration, Biju Patnaik as Orissa's Chief Minister is somewhat unique and different from all the Chief Ministers of Orissa.

To evaluate the achievements of a unique and multi-faceted personality like Biju Patnaik appears to be a herculean task or, as has been said, to evaluate this 'profound personality' means to delve deeper into a mysterious and multi-dimensional entity[3].

In our opinion, Biju Patnaik as Chief Minister whether in terms of his achievements or his style of functioning can be rightly judged with a glimpse at the evolution of his personality and distinctive traits of his character. The parameters of our evaluation are not merely to judge him in terms of a few controversial things he said here and there but to understand him and his mind-set in a holistic and total perspective.

Evolution of Biju Patnaik's Personality

(a) Impact of Parents

Biju Patnaik was born to Mr. Laxminarayan Patnaik and Smt. Ashalata Devi at Cuttack on March 05, 1916.

His father, even though a Munsif under the British Raj, was one of the leaders of the Orissa Renaissance and a pioneer of a separate Orissa movement of the early thirties.[4] Like many other leaders of the Orissa Renaissance and of the separate Orissa movement, he had a sense of pride as a self-conscious Oriya and was also a lover of Oriya literature sincerely committed to its growth and development[5]. In the light of what has been said above, one would feel that the impact of his father shaped his personality to subsequently emerge into an articulate champion of Orissa's pride, glory and greatness. Apart from this he also inspired Biju to be fearless and courageous. One story goes that Laxminarayan never allowed his children to come home being bashed up. "Moreover, he inspired Biju to face hardships and challenges in life and is stated to have said to Biju "unless you go through hardship, you cannot be a man."[6]

Biju's mother Ashalata Devi hailed from a patriotic family whose sons had sacrificed their lives in the struggle for independence. Biju's maternal uncles-Bijoysri, Debo Prasad and Anando-prasad were the revolutionary youths who along with Surya Sen were responsible for the Chittagong Armoury Raid of 1930.[7]

This heritage of suffering and sacrifice in the service of the motherland must have inspired Biju to be ever-prepared for suffering and sacrifice in the nation's cause almost with reckless courage and unconcerned abandon. His role during the Quit India Movement or his fearless courage in landing the first plane in Srinagar in the service of the motherland bear ample proof of the possible impact of his maternal uncles both as regards their love of the motherland and their courage and fearlessness.

Even his birth place Cuttack contributed to the evolution of his personality, a personality that was 'fearless and unyielding in spirit'. It may be submitted that the historic city of Cuttack where Biju was born and spent his childhood was 'a place of many battles' and a place which saw 'the rise and fall of many dynasties'. As has been rightly said "his mental and physical prowess was shaped collectively in the environs of Cuttack".[8]

(b) Biju: A Brave Boy from Childhood

Biju who was blessed with an eye-catching and out standing height with a very good physique was a brave boy right from his childhood. He is said to have shown remarkable strength to bravely bear the pain of a surgical operation for appendicitis in 1923 when he was hardly eight years old. This bravery and courage became subsequently a distinctive facet of his personality and career. As has been said "His life was full of acts of heroism". As a child, he once broke a police cordon to touch an aeroplane. As a football player, he always dominated the play ground. As a student in Ravenshaw College, he undertook an adventurous journey by bicycle from Cuttack to Peshawar. As a pilot, he displayed exemplary skill and courage by bringing revolutionary leaders from Indonesia in the face of stiff opposition from the Dutch. He undertook dangerous missions such as flying to the Russian territory in aid of Russia's campaign against the German forces. Patnaik and other Pilots used to fly to Teheran to load their Dakotas with arms and ammunition supplied by the U.S.A. From there they left for Stalingrad re-fuelling their planes at one or two places.[9]

Biju was a devoted student of history and the history of Orissa ever impelled him to be brave and adventurous. As he often said in his addresses: Orissa has become a small little place; one day it was the greatest empire of India. Its army defeated Alexander's army and threw them across the border of India. Kalinga was the largest maritime power ever known in the world. What better dream can I have than dream of those magnificent days. When Orissa was vital, when Kalinga was the greatest empire of India, when the sailors of Kalinga did not know fear, when the soldiers of Kalinga did not know fear, when the mothers of Kalinga were known as "Biranganas."[10]

(c) Evolution of Biju's personality during School Days

In 1926 when Biju was a student of Ravenshaw Collegiate School, he got the bitter taste of colonial brutality when the British S.P. Mr. Hargrieve cruelly assaulted him for his audacity to rush towards Gandhi to have a closer look of the acclaimed leader of India's struggle for freedom. It is said that this cruel assault which caused profuse bleeding from him head made him somewhat a nationalist. In the words of his brother George Patnaik who was an eye-witness of the assault on Biju "this event created in his mind a spirit of revenge against British colonialism". From that day a new consciousness emerged in his mind and in his heart of hearts he now decided to free his country from the British Raj.

Apart from a nationalist consciousness, another dimension added to his evolving personality was his distinction in foot ball and hockey winning laurels for his school in inter-school foot-ball championship.

(d) Evolution during College Days

Biju's days in the Ravenshaw College, Cuttack in 1930 where he took a science course showed his qualities of organisation and leadership in the sports arena apart from bringing out his traits of character as an adventurer unmindful of any hardship, suffering or risk.

He was the athletic champion for three years in the Ravenshaw College, Cuttack but what is more remarkable and memorable is that he proved to be a champion in the realm of adventure when in the company of two of his friends he 'undertook an adventurous journey by bicycle from Cuttack to Peshawar covering a distance of more than four thousand kms'.

In those days young boys who were lovers of adventure took up 'flying as a sport and adventure'.[12] Biju who was a follower of Haldane's words 'Life without adventure has no charm'[13] developed a fascination for flying and joined as a pilot in 1934 the Royal Air Force before completing his B.Sc. final. He became a distinguished pilot and served as the head of the Air Transport Command during the war years of 1940-42.[14]

(e) Role in India's Freedom Struggle

As has been indicated, Biju had developed a nationalist consciousness in course of the evolution of his personality and hence even though a pilot under British employment he was a nationalist at heart.

It is said that in 1940 he came in contact with the firebrand freedom fighters of the day and was inspired by the mass movements led by Gandhi, Jawaharlal Nehru, Sardar Vallabhai Patel and was mesmerised by the manoeuvres of Subhash Chandra Bose.[15]

Biju now joined the Quit India movement of 1942 when 'Do or Die' became the revolutionary slogan with Gandhiji's exhortation "we shall free India or die in the attempt". He worked underground with leaders like Jaya Prakash Narayan and Aruna Asaf Ali[16] and gave them hidden air-lifts from one place of India to others in his transport plane.

Biju Patnaik helped the freedom fighters in more than one way during the Quit India Movement even though he 'could not take active part in the national movement as a Pilot in the British employ'. He undertook 'sacred and secret errands to distribute movement posters and pamphlets' or 'the so-called seditious literature' in his plane. "He unreservedly helped the revolutionaries with shelter and cover who were in hiding to avoid arrest and imprisonment. In the words of his renowned daughter Gita Mehta "he was so much engrossed 'in protecting the revolutionaries from the cruel paws of the imperial police by providing them shelter and ease that his house was nicknamed absconder's paradise.[17]"

Recalling Biju Patnaik's role during the Quit India Movement, Aruna Asaf Ali says, "Among the thousands of young men and women who came to the fore-front of the freedom struggle inspired by the call of 'Do or Die' of Gandhi, Biju Patnaik, the Chief Pilot of Dalmia Jain Airways, was a burning example of fearlessness. It was he who provided the leadership and inspiration to his fellow Pilots to extend all their help to the under ground directorate which consisted of Jaya Prakash Narayan, Achyuta Patwardhan, Ram Manohar Lohia and people like me and others. Without their courage and fearlessness, we could never have established contacts with our comrades working from Bombay, Madras and New Delhi"[18].

Thus Biju Patnaik even though a Pilot under British employ now developed into a fearless patriot and committed nationalist assisting the cause of India's freedom struggle. Due to his help to the freedom fighters at the time he underwent imprisonment from January 1943 to the end of 1945.

(f) Biju and Indonesian Freedom Struggle

Due to his association with the Quit India Movement and his imprisonment, Biju Patnaik came in direct contact with Nehru[19] and became 'one of his' trusted friends.[20]

Jawaharlal Nehru who had now developed immense faith in Biju's courage and adventure as a nationalist pilot wanted to use his services in Indonesia's fight for independence in 1946-47 for which he had his full sympathy. Hence, at the instance of Nehru, Biju at the risk of his life "flew clandestine missions into Indonesia and brought Shharir and later Mohammad Hatta for personal conference with the Indian Prime Minister Nehru".[21] For this noble and heroic act of Biju during the crucial days of Indonesia's freedom struggle, he was awarded "Bhumi Putra" the highest Indonesian award and a rare distinction ever-granted to a foreigner. Biju's death-defying and dare-devil act of adventure in rescuing the entrapped top-rung patriots of Indonesia transcended the traditional connotation of a patriot. As has been aptly said that 'His Indonesian expedition shows that he was a patriot of a different kind, an International Patriot. His patriotism was not confined to the borders of a country, it was confined to the border of humanity'.[22]

(g) Role in Kashmir Operation (1947)

Another memorable addition to Biju Patnaik's nationalist and patriotic personality and his fearless courage came out in bolder vein in 1947 when Pakistan invaded India.

When in the face of this invasion of Kashmir, by Pakistan the top echelons of the Air Force in India could not have the guts to land troops in Kashmir, and it was Biju who took up the challenge and 'was able to land the first platoon of troops at Srinagar Air Port on 27th October 1947 at 10 hours'.[23] Thus Kashmir was saved for India and it was Biju who made it possible.[24]

(h) From Freedom Struggle to Industry

One of the powerful facets of Biju Patnaik's personality is his sincere love for industry.[25] Hence coming out of jail in 1945, he set himself to build industries in Orissa as he was 'terribly interested in making Orissa a rapidly industrialised State'.[26]

Regarding his achievements it has been said "Mr. Patnaik through the agency of Dr. Mahtab and Mr. Nehru established some major industries in Orissa. The notable among them were Orissa Textile Mills, the Kalinga Refrigerator Works, the Orissa Textile Industry, Kalinga Airlines and Kalinga Tubes'.[27]

In respect of those industries established by him, he is considered a pioneer industrialist. As has been said he promoted - the first textile mill in Orissa, the first tube mill in India, the first refrigerator factory in India and the first low shaft furnace in India.[28]

In those days, he was among the few industrialists in the country. It need not be said that those industries 'helped the industrialisation of Orissa, opened up job opportunities for Oriyas and added to State revenue apart from enriching him personally'. Thus Biju Patnaik apart from being a pilot and freedom fighter now evolved into an industrialist creating a place of his own in the minds and hearts of our people.

(i) From Industry to Politics

Dr. H.K. Mahtab, the Chief Minister of Orissa in 1946 wanted to utilise the youth and dynamism of Biju Patnaik in Orissa politics who by now had built up reputation as a fearless patriot and avowed industrialist with his vision of an industrialised Orissa. He had also the blessings of Nehru behind him. He was also convinced in his mind that his dream of an industrialised Orissa could be actualized 'through the instrument of political power'[29] over and above his inner urge or what has been called 'the punching of his urge' led him to decide to join Orissa politics. He started his innings in politics by being elected to the Provincial Orissa Assembly from the Cuttack seat in 1946.[30] There was no looking back. He now got himself fully involved in politics leaving behind his own industrial empire. Several times, he got himself elected to Orissa Assembly until he became the Chief Minister of Orissa in 1961.

He became the Union Cabinet Minister for Steel and Mines from 1977 to 1979 and Union Minister for Steel, Mines and Coal from July 1979 to January 1980. He was a Member of the Lok Sabha from 1980-85. He became the Leader of the opposition in the Orissa Legislative Assembly from 1985 to 1989 and was sworn in as Chief Minister of Orissa for the second time on 5th March 1990.[31]

Emergence of Biju Patnaik as Chief Minister

The Political Background (1956-1961)

H.K. Mahtab, the Governor of Bombay (1955-56) was appointed Chief Minister on the 19th October 1956[32] after he managed to force Naba Krishna Choudhury to resign from the post of Chief Minister and leave politics virtually permanently.[33] In his coming back from Bombay as Orissa's Chief Minister, Mahtab was assisted by his 'political lieutenants Biju Patnaik, Biren Mitra and Nilamani Routray'.

In the General Elections of 1957, the Congress could not secure absolute majority but as the leader of the single largest party he formed a minority government on 6th April 1957 'with the backing of CPI, Jharkhand and a few independent members'.[34]

This minority government of Dr. Mahatab 'proved shaky' and in consultation with Biju Patnaik he now formed a coalition ministry on 22nd May, 1959. In the words of Morarji Desai, Mahtab and Biju had been very insistent about making this coalition.[35]

The afore-said coalition ministry was made with the hope — 'the possibility' that some of the members of the Ganatantra Party would join the Congress in course of time. But when this possibility disappeared a few months after the coalition, it created serious differences of opinion between Sri Mahtab and Sri Patnaik. Analysing the cause of the differences which estranged the relations between Sri Mahtab and Sri Patnaik, Morarji Desai observes: "Sri Mahtab was of the view that when fresh elections were held, the Congress would not get a majority in Orissa and a coalition government have to be formed. Biju Patnaik was an ardent supporter of the coalition but he wanted the coalition to end before the election if the members of the Ganatantra Party did not meanwhile join the Congress in good numbers'.[36]

Late Dr. Sreeram Chandra Das, an eminent political scientist of national repute, records the raging power struggle between Dr. Mahtab and Biju Patnaik before the latter's emergence as Orissa's Chief Minister. As he writes: 'The invisible forces of the Congress who had brought Dr. Mahtab back from Bombay and managed the party after the Second General Election — felt restive and showed symptoms of an anxiety for actual capture of power'.[37] As he further observes: "The younger group led by Sri Patnaik and Sri Mitra first ousted the President in February 1961 in a bid to capture power from Dr. Mahtab and elected Biju Patnaik as President of the P.C.C. Soon after his election, the P.C.C. passed a resolution demanding resignation of the Coalition Cabinet and Dr. Mahtab had to resign on the 20th February 1961 when the Governor dissolved the Assembly and recommended to the President to take over the Government of Orissa under Article 356 of the constitution".[38]

After a short spell of President's rule, midterm elections to the Orissa Legislative Assembly was held in June, 1961 under Biju's leadership with a massive mandate of 82 seats for

Congress in a house of 140 members, it was for the first time in independent Orissa that Congress party secured an absolute majority.

Biju Patnaik as the leader of the Congress party was sworn in as Chief Minister on June 23, 1961. From the steering wheel of an aeroplane, Patnaik now came to occupy the steering wheel of Government. With the massive electoral victory Patnaik emerged as the undisputed leader of the State and his group thereafter became dominant in the Legislature as well as in the party.[39]

Biju Patnaik: The Chief Minister (1961-63)

The achievements of a Chief Minister depend upon a variety of factors. A Chief Minister who does not have an absolute majority of his party behind him and heads a coalition will have obvious constraints. He has to take the coalition partners along with him either in Cabinet formation or on matters of policy and development. On the other hand, a Chief Minister who has an absolute majority of his party behind him will certainly have greater freedom in decision-making so as to go ahead and fulfil his plans and programmes. That apart, the personality of the Chief Minister who is at the helm of affairs in the State administration counts a lot in either getting adequate Central funds for his State or giving a shape to a State's progress and development. In a federal system, the Chief Minister of a State who has good equation with the Central leadership and more particularly with the Prime Minister can obviously ensure the availability of adequate funds from the Central pool for his State's development. But a Chief Minister who apart from having good equation with the Prime Minister also belongs to the party ruling at the Centre will have greater advantage to go ahead and actualise his plans and programmes.

When Biju Patnaik became the Chief Minister of Orissa on June 23, 1961, he had already built up a national reputation as a firebrand and dare-devil nationalist displaying remarkable courage during the Quit India Movement, or in his Indonesian expedition or in saving Kashmir. Over and above this, he had established his credentials as an imaginative industrialist with a splendid vision of an industrialised Orissa.

The afore-said factors endeared him to Nehru but what further added to his stature as a leader is that for the first time since independence the Congress party under his dynamic leadership secured a massive mandate in Orissa.

It has been said that Prime Minister Nehru now took him as 'an expert in electoral campaigning' and that was why he put him 'in-charge of elections in Punjab'. Even the Parliamentary elections of 1962 reinforced his talent as an election strategist since the Congress party in Orissa won 18 out of 20 Lok Sabha seats.

Those electoral achievements proved to Nehru his credentials as an efficient leader and a mass mobiliser. He became, as has been said 'a smart boy in Nehru's estimation'.

This good and favourable equation of Biju Patnaik with Prime Minister Nehru proved to be a great blessing for Orissa's progress and development. What deserves mention is that 'the Third Plan allocation for Orissa was increased from Rs.160 crores to Rs.230 crores for different projects'.

Biju Patnaik not only showed his talent in the arena of electoral politics winning laurels for the Congress party in Orissa but more importantly he displayed his talent as an architect and builder. People still remember with nostalgia the 'feverish pitch of industrial activity pronouncedly seen during the brief tenure of Biju's government in the early sixties.[41]

In the second half of the forties, as has been discussed, Biju had established some major industries in Orissa like the Orissa Textile Mills, the Kalinga Refrigerator Works, the Orissa Textile Industry, Kalinga Air Lines and Kalinga Tubes. In an era of colonial bondage when few could dream of establishing any industry in the private sector, it was Biju who had the courage to go ahead in almost this untroden field and as has been rightly said 'it was an extraordinary saga of industrial adventure in Orissa.[42]

In 1945, when he came out of jail and set himself to build industries in Orissa he could possibly have entered the realm of power and politics but he was a different man. To him what primarily mattered was his vision - the vision of an industrialised Orissa. Behind his vision of an industrialised Orissa lay his love for Orissa and its people. 'He had clearly one thing in mind and that was altering the fate of Oriyas'.[43] That Orissa in spite of its rich natural resources would remain backward and poor was unbearable to his inner urge which dreamt of a prosperous and powerful Orissa. His exposure and impression of the developed world made him convinced that it is industrialisation and modernisation alone that could lift Orissa out of its grinding poverty and backwardness.

It may be mentioned that the industrialisation of Orissa or an industrialised Orissa was the central theme of his election manifesto in the midterm election of 1961. People had seen his youth and dynamism in the 1940s when he had established a number of industries in Orissa. The catchword of industrialisation now the caught people's imagination and was transformed into votes, giving the Congress a massive mandate.

His election manifesto proclaimed schemes for rapid industrialisation, drinking water in rural areas, employment for the unemployed and a development-oriented machinery for the people. In place of primitive methods of agriculture like wooden plough, he proposed steel burrows. Rice hullers were to replace the traditional dhenki, oil mills, pumping sets and tile roofs were many other things he held out before the electorate.

Though all those promises could not be fulfilled or were not possible to be fulfilled in his brief tenure of Chief Ministership from 23.06.1961 to 02.10.1963, his record of achievements in the area of industrialisation of the State is certainly outstanding. Even his worst enemies in politics will be constrained to recognise his achievement. In our opinion, this brief spell of his Chief Ministership may be considered as the golden age in Orissa's progress and development particularly in the field of Industrialisation.

(a) High Priest of Industrialisation and Development

It was the good fortune of Orissa to have a Chief Minister who at the same time was an imaginative industrialist[44]. With political power at his command, he now set himself to actualise his vision of an industrialised Orissa. For that he encouraged and motivated small and large industrial houses to put up industries in Orissa and he also saw to it that existing and ongoing projects were completed on time. As has been said, "At the helm of affairs in 1961, he encouraged small and medium entrepreneurs to set up their units and contribute to the industrialisation era of the State. He invited large industrial houses and magnates to put up some of their units in the State. He accelerated completion of major projects like the Rourkela Steel Plant and Hirakud Dam Project which lagged behind completion schedule or slowed down in respect of isolated minor works.[45]

It may be said here that Biju Patnaik as an administrator belonged to the school of development administrators who emphasised on a time frame work a definite time schedule of completing projects. He hardly possessed the patience to bear bureaucratic delay or red-tapism. As it were he was a leader in a hurry for the sake of Orissa's rapid progress and development either in the sphere of industrialisation or in relation to any other sphere of development.

Apart from accelerating the completion of major projects like the Rourkela Steel Plant and Hirakud Dam Project, another memorable achievement of Biju Patnaik in the field of Orissa's industrialisation was the establishment of the Mig Engine Factory at Sunabeda in the tribal district of Koraput. The establishment of this factory at Sunabeda was virtually the outcome of a battle royal which Biju fought with Nehru even going to the extent of sounding a note of warning to Nehru that if the Mig Factory was not established in Orissa he was going to resign his Chief Ministership. It was no small thing to stand up and fight Nehru to extract a Central project. But Biju could do it with his strong and convincing personality. 'Koraput got a Mig Factory along with two others in Nasik and Lucknow.'[46] It shows the impact of personality on the politics of development.

The Mig factory at Sunabeda provided job opportunities to many Oriyas and also urbanised an underdeveloped area in Koraput district apart from helping the nation in defence preparedness.[47]

As an imaginative industrialist, Biju started on his own initiative and with the State's resources two power projects since it was of absolute necessity for the industrialisation of the State. Thus Balimela multi-purpose project in Koraput district and Talcher Thermal Power Project in the present Angul district were launched during his first spell of Chief Ministership.

However, the most outstanding supplement to his achievements was the construction of the Paradeep Port 'on a massive scale'. The way he took up the construction work of Paradeep Port quickly smacked of his dashing and go-ahead disposition as an administrator. As has been rightly said he had no patience for 'hundred and one clearances' from the Central government nor could he wait for the sanction of funds by the Central government. He was not the man to bend or succumb to the 'stiff opposition from the Orissa bureaucracy' or to be thwarted by the 'do delay for delay's sake' attitude.[48]

As is known he lost no time to earmark funds in the State's budget for the construction of the port and 'spent 19 crores from the State's contingency fund to complete the first phase of the port's construction'.[49] Justice H.R. Khanna who headed the Khanna Commission instituted against him in 1967 rightly said "My own view of the matter is that Paradeep Port was to some extent a creation of Sri Patnaik.[50] This Paradeep Port which was the brain child of Biju Patnaik became 'the pride of Orissa and the gateway to its prosperity'.

The way he almost snatched the Paradeep Port from Nehru speaks of not only his guts and conviction but his persuasive, convincing and diplomatic finesse as well.

The Daitari Paradeep Expressway 'which is the indispensable ancillary project of the port project was also constructed simultaneously and in the same swift manner as the port work was undertaken'. Apart from making transport to Paradeep cheaper it made it possible to go into the interior areas hitherto inaccessible. It was because of this highway that Orissa government was able to tackle the devastating cyclone in Rajnagar area.[51]

Over and above, Biju Patnaik implemented his scheme of Panchayat industries for the socio-economic development of rural areas. 'Several industries-medium and small-came up throughout the State. This was an innovative scheme of rural development and Jaya Prakash Narayan came to study this scheme.[52] It also got due attention at the Central level and it was rightly said "If Balwant Rai Mehta is the father of Panchayat Raj, then Biju Patnaik is the father of Panchayat Industry in India".[53]

Biju Patnaik also established Rural Engineering works organisation to offer engineering expertise and service in the execution of small but numerous rural road and building projects. Minor irrigation projects constructed by this organisation added to the irrigation potential in a small but momentous way.[54]

(b) Rapid Expansion of Technical & General Education

During his Congress Chief Ministership, Biju opened the eyes of Orissa[55] in various other ways like rapid expansion of engineering, medical and agricultural education. He persuaded and prevailed upon the Union Government to set up a Regional Engineering College at Rourkela and with munificent grant from the Central Government, he founded the University of Agriculture and Technology at Bhubaneswar.[56] Burla Engineering College and the Regional College of Education at Bhubaneswar were also established during his first spell of Chief Ministership in the State.

(c) Mushroom Growth of Colleges

Patnaik's regime also witnessed mushroom growth of general colleges which helped democratisation of higher education. Through his encouragement, thirty four private colleges were established[57] making it possible for the poor and middle class students to have the benefit of higher education at their door step. The establishment of those colleges by the positive encouragement of his government led to greater politicisation.[58]

(d) Popularisation of Science

Popularisation of science through general education was also accorded top priority and in this respect Biju played the role of a promoter of science. Like Nehru, he had immense faith in and commitment to science. Biju believed in the modernisation of society on a scientific foundation and he was for 'inculcating a scientific temper' in people.[59] What deserves special mention in regard to his role as a promoter of science is that Biju in the 1960s instituted the prestigious Kalinga Award for the dissemination and popularisation of science. This award, it may be noted, has accorded respectability and status to the State of Orissa in the international community.[60]

(e) Creator of Planning Board at State Level

Biju Patnaik was a 'hard-boiled economist and practical-planner'.[61] He is said to have done an original work in setting up a Planning Board at State level on 15 June, 1962. Its utility was subsequently realised by other states and now it has almost been accepted by most others.[62]

(f) A Student Friendly Chief Minister

Scholarships and stipends to meritorious and poverty stricken students also multiplied during Biju's Chief Ministership. More particularly his government was quite liberal in extending scholarship to students prosecuting technical education. It was a matter of policy of his government and in fact, the Governor's address to the first session of the Orissa Legislative Assembly on 21.08.61 said: 'My Government proposes to tackle the problem by seeing to it that no promising student ... who aspires to receive technical education in the future is deprived of the necessary educational facilities because of his poverty. Scholarship for such deserving students will be freely provided'.[63]

Biju's regime also displayed its special concern for the academic improvement of Adivasi students. The construction of Adivasi hostels multiplied with the liberal provision of funds. As Biju Patnaik in reply to a question of Sakila Soren, dated 6th October 1961 said 'The Government have estimated an amount of Rs.1 lakh and 4 thousand for construction of hostels'.[64]

Scholarships to Adivasi students for the study of science and engineering was also specially encouraged with Rs.27 per month and Rs.75 per month for the science and engineering students respectively.[65]

Apart from government scholarships, Biju's Kalinga Foundation Trust helped brilliant students of his beloved Orissa to progress and prosper through financial support.

(g) Saviour of Cuttack: Role as an Able Crisis Manager

Biju Patnaik as an administrator is noted for his quick and swift decision-making ability. In 1962, when there was a sudden and unprecedented flood in Mahanadi creating a crisis situation, the possibility of Cuttack city being submerged and swept away by the rushing flood waters was very much there. Biju Babu, without any ifs and buts, ordered the Chief Engineer to detain the flood waters in Hirakud Dam and Cuttack city was saved.

Thus Biju Patnaik the Chief Minister proved to be an able crisis manager in the face of the flood crisis and saved Cuttack from being submerged by the flood.

(h) Role as a Defence and External Security Consultant and Diplomat

During the Chinese aggression of 1962, Nehru invited Biju to render advice at the time of this national tragedy. Independent India's military history will record his name 'as the only civilian whom Nehru consulted on every conceivable matter of warfare and matters concerning the external security of India'.[66] It may be noted that as the civilian adviser to Prime Minister Nehru, he was given a separate chamber in the external affairs ministry.

Over and above, Biju was given a diplomatic assignment as a special envoy of Prime Minister Nehru to impress upon President John F Kennedy to come to the aid of India. The precious role that Biju played in securing the support of the Kennedy administration was recognised by B.M. Kaul, the Chief of the General staff, in his book 'Untold Story'. He unhesitatingly recognised his unfailing and successful role as a diplomat when he said that Biju's American Mission was very much in keeping with the personality of an unfailing leader.[67]

At the height of the Indo-Chinese war when Tezpur, headquarters of the 62nd Infantry Brigade, was abandoned, he accompanied Home Minister Lal Bahadur Shastri and Assam Chief Minister B.P. Chaliha to discuss the modalities of Indian operation there. It is said that braving the danger, he made a marauding effort there in the interest of his motherland. It led B.M. Kaul to rightly remark that Biju Patnaik loved his country more than his personal security.[68]

Biju's Kalinga Airways was also one of the few private airlines which air-dropped essential materials required by the Indian Army as the Indian Air Force did not have a sufficient number of aircraft to undertake this job.

After V.K. Krishna Menon resigned as Defence Minister following the Chinese aggression, two names were considered for this important assignment: one of Biju Patnaik and the other of Yashwant Chauhan. It was an unfortunate irony that Jawaharlal Nehru himself dropped his name[69] though he had all the requisite qualifications to become the Defence Minister after the Indo-Chinese war.

Biju Patnaik's first spell of Congress Chief Ministership came to an end when he laid down his office on October 2, 1963 as per the famous Kamaraj Plan of which he was the Co-author though 'this was not known to the public'.[70] The Kamaraj Plan advocated that Congress leaders with proven ability should step down from official positions to build up the sagging morale of the Congress Party.

Biju Patnaik's resignation as Chief Minister was really unfortunate for Orissa as his ministry successfully moved with a new orientation for rapid economic development.[71]

Evaluation as Chief Minister (1961-63)

Biju Patnaik as Congress Chief Minister in the 1960s will ever be remembered as one of the makers of modern Orissa for what he could achieve during a short spell of only twenty-seven months. Even the harshest of his critics would admit that he was a dynamic Chief Minister whose regime witnessed rapid strides in the arena of industrialisation and the overall development of the State. He was primarily a development-centric Chief Minister in a hurry to bring about rapid industrialisation and the all-round development of his beloved State. In his over-zeal to achieve results within a definite time-frame, he bypassed some bureaucratic rules and regulations to cut through delay and red-tape. This admittedly led to some administrative improprieties and commission of some 'mistakes and blunders'. But who else as a political leader or Chief Minister is totally free from mistakes and blunders? But his critics and political opponents did not spare him. When R.N. Singh Deo took over as the Chief Minister of the Swatantra-Jana Congress government in 1967, the Khanna Commission of Enquiry was instituted against him to probe into charges of corruption and financial irregularities. 'It was urged on behalf of the State government that a number of projects like Balimela Dam, Paradeep Port and Express Highway and a number of corporations like I.D.C., O.M.C. and Orissa State Commercial Corporation were started by Biju Patnaik to make illicit money'. It was also urged that most of the projects and corporations were formed 'at the cost of education and other social welfare activities'. Both these contentions of the government were rejected by the Commission. Justice H.R. Khanna while exonerating Biju was only appreciative of the speed and alacrity with which the Port was completed. Had it not been for his equivocation and firmness, things would have procrastinated, the Judge observed.[72]

In the concluding remarks Justice H.R. Khanna said 'The need of Orissa is of a leader of great calibre, inspired by the cause, dedicated, devoted and determined, who may arouse the enthusiasm, which is so far dormant of the masses, harness it to fruitful activity and thus pave the way for economic betterment and future prosperity. Biju Patnaik gave the hope of that calibre, he had the halo of an adventurous past. He had daring, dash, doggedness and the advantage of youth, a good physique and a tall imposing personality. To all these may be added a touch of flamboyance. The electorate gave Biju Patnaik a clear-cut majority in the legislature. He did a commendable job in certain spheres by introducing an element of dynamism in the administration and the work he did by translating the idea of a Port at Paradeep into a living reality is bound to make an impact on the history of Orissa and its future development.[73]

Biju Patnaik had unbounded love for his people. My Kalinga, My Utkal, My boys, My mothers, My children: this is the refrain in Biju's patriotic vision. For the sake of his people, for the sake of his State he was prepared to face calumny, 'virulent political enmity' and vicious criticism'. He did his best for his people, for their welfare and for the all-round development of his beloved State. It is rightly said 'Bhim Bhoi's philosophy of suffering and his willingness to consign his soul to hell if it could save humanity is Biju's philosophy of politics'.[74] He was ever-willing to do anything and even willing to sacrifice his life if it could save his people. In our opinion, this is the yardstick by which to judge Biju and his Chief Ministership and is the key to understand his achievements or what is called his lapses and failures.

Biju Patnaik's Second Term as Chief Minister (05.03.90 to 15.03.95)

The General Election for the Tenth Assembly of Orissa was held on the 27th February 1990 along with eight other States and one Union Territory.[75] Under the able and dynamic leadership of Biju Patnaik, the Janata Dal achieved a steam rolling majority surprassing all previous records with 123 out of 147 assembly seats to its credit.[76] It was after a lapse of twenty seven years. Biju made 'an unprecedented come-back' and became the Chief Minister of Orissa for the second time on 5th March 1990. His tenure as Chief Minister came to an end on 15th March 1995. Biju's government became 'the first non-Congress government to have stayed in power for almost the full term'.

When Biju Patnaik became the Chief Minister of Orissa for the second time he broadly fixed up three priorities for his government. They were (a) ensuring a clean and non-corrupt government in the State,[77] (b) the tasks for his administration as earmarked were: the establishment of the second Steel Plant, the deepening of the Paradeep Port, the extension of railway network, etc.[78] and, (c) the functioning of the new government in such a manner 'as to be identified with the poor.[79] In spite of all his sincerity and devoted efforts he was not able to materialise the Steel Plant even though he laid the infrastructure for the Steel Plant in Duburi.[80]

Though Biju was not able to materialise the Steel Plant, he nonetheless has some memorable achievements to his credit particularly in the field of women development, reorganisation of the districts and in the arena of streamlining and rejuvenating the Panchayati Raj and local self government institutions.

Apart from the memorable achievements in the afore-said fields, Biju's second spell as Chief Minister is noted for his controversial statements which at times created a sharp reaction from his critics.

The critics of Biju were legion and they did not spare any effort to bring out his lapses and failures.

The hefty hike in the daily wages of unskilled workers from Rs.11 to Rs.25 was denounced as revolutionary in view of the fact that the daily wage of an unskilled worker/labourer in rich Punjab, Haryana and Gujarat was much less than what was announced by Biju.[81]

Biju's call to the public to beat up anti-people and corrupt officials and Ministers made him a controversial person. His proclaimed stand on Naxalities that what they were doing was right on the very floor of the Assembly was vehemently criticised.[82]

His remark that Orissa might consider seceding from the Indian Union if the Centre continued to show its step-motherly and apathetic attitude raised many eyebrows across the country with some of them doubting his nationalist credentials.

The afore-said view points need to be addressed to in the right spirit and proper perspective while assessing Biju Patnaik's achievements and lapses. Or else, the possibility of falling into the pit of misunderstanding would be very much there.

In fact it is easier to judge like a Judge but difficult to understand a multi-faceted personality like Biju Patnaik unless the context and a holistic perspective is taken into account.

Biju Patnaik in spite of what he said here and there creating controversies had the following achievements which even the harshest of his critics cannot ignore.

Biju and Empowerment of Women

Biju Patnaik's second spell as Chief Minister will be remembered by posterity for the different steps he took for the development and empowerment of women. This is considered to be a remarkable achievement.

In a way, Biju could be regarded as an ardent feminist who not only fought against women oppression with a strong administrative will but at the same was an ardent advocate of equal rights for men and women.

In his dream of the Orissa of tomorrow he was not prepared 'to hear a whisper about oppression of women'. He dreamt of a day 'when women will play equal role with men' and 'exercise with men equal power and enjoy the same privilege'. This was his dream of tomorrow, the 21st century.[83]

Biju Patnaik was dead-against the people who oppressed women and committed atrocities on them.

Readers will remember the much publicised dowry death when the in-laws of the victim were handcuffed and paraded to the Court premises. It was on his order that the Police had meted out this humiliating punishment. This action, it may be said, did create a fear in the minds of would-be dowry seekers and would-be bride killers.[84]

He also issued instructions that a government servant against whom a prima-facie case of dowry offence is made out shall be put under suspension and, if his responsibility for the offence is established, he shall be dismissed from service.[85]

It need not be said that Biju Patnaik displayed a strong administrative will to fight against atrocities on women like a social revolutionary.

Apart from displaying a strong administrative will to fight against the atrocities on women for dowry, Biju's government constituted a State Commission for women 'with a view to ensuring rapid improvement in the status of women'.[86]

It may be noted that the Commission was empowered to 'receive complaints on the atrocities on women, deprivation of women of their rights and take immediate measures in co-ordination with the State Cell and District Cell.[87]

Today, the State Commission can take pride in the hundreds of success stories bringing relief to the women in distress.[88]

The setting up of the Mahila Vikash Samabaya Nigam was another important step of the Biju regime for the development of women. The objective of this Nigam was to 'promote entrepreneurship among the women', 'organise women in viable groups' and support group activities and co-ordinate development programmes for women.[89]

Biju had immense faith in the bravery and courage of Oriya women who were known as 'Biranganas' in the past. It may be recalled that it is he who was the prime-mover to send Nivedita Acharya 'across to Bali, some 9000 kms. fighting the high seas' during the Kalinga Bali Jatra in 1993.[90]

Biju Patnaik had immense faith in the administrative ability of women. He said that they should come up to accept the responsibilities of administration. If along with managing their family they are able to serve why can't they administer was what he said in an intimate conversation with Dr. Tanmayee Mohanty.[91]

It is significant to note that during his regime posts of Secretary, Redcross, President of the Sahitya Academy or Vice-Chairmen of Zilla Parishad were held by women.[92] An Advisory Council of Tribal Women was also constituted in his regime to advise him on the problems of tribals and tribal women.

His unstinted support to anti-liquor brigade, establishing a women bank, installing a lady Chairperson in Bhubaneswar Municipality were also commendable steps showing his faith in the ability of women.

Over and above, Biju took bold and outstanding steps for the empowerment of women. 'Before any other State had come up with a policy on women, it is Biju who showed the path towards the empowerment of women by reserving one third seats for them in Panchayat Raj institutions. It was certainly a bold, stimulating and decisive step which Biju took. It requires no further evidence that thirty thousand women in local bodies have come to assert their powers.

The other two meaningful steps Biju took were that the Office of the Vice-Chairperson of a Panchayat Samiti will be held by a woman. Even the policy of keeping apart one third of the staff strength for women was extended to government jobs. In all the classes barring Class-I and Class-II, women were to be given a one third representation.[93]

Biju Patnaik's steps in the field of women development and their empowerment were undoubtedly commendable in the specific context of Orissa which, by and large, has a patriarchal culture and ethos. Once a journalist made a comment in a lighter vein that he was a 'Ladies man'. His immediate reply was categoric "yes I am a ladies man, even Nehru was a ladies man."[94]

Priorities for Poor and Wage-hike Decision

Biju wanted to guide his government with a distinct orientation for the poor. After being unanimously elected as the leader of the Janata Dal, he said that his government 'would function in such a manner as to be identified with the poor'. That the poor and the deprived constituted histop most priority would be further evident from his statement that his government is a revaluation (if you call it) for the poor masses.[95] He seemed to be very sincere in his concern for the poor and the deprived. In his view, he had set priorities for the poor because those people 'had not made demands earlier or their voice recorded in the corridors of powers'. 'I would refuse to recognise the constitution of a country' he further said, 'if I am poor'; 'my idea of a constitution is that it should be the constitution of the poor masses'.[96]

This concern for the poor and down-trodden led him to take the wage-hike decision in March 1990 which was almost a personal decision of Biju Patnaik. By a stroke of his pen, he immediately increased the wages for unskilled workers from the existing Rs. 11 to Rs.25 per day with immediate effect. He took this decision, he said, by the suggestion of a poor old lady in a remote village in Bolangir district during the last Assembly election.[97]

Critics and courts, landowners and Zamindars, economists and administration theorists put this wage hike decision to multi-pronged scrutiny. Their views in some respects may be true; it is of course true that it was a personalised decision, an abrupt decision which was made 'by a whiff of a desire'. But whatever it is, that is Biju and his style of administration who, when convinced of some thing, goes ahead being hardly concerned with its consequences. But then he put his heart at the right place, in the poor, in the destitute and in the wage-earners who in spite of all their hard labour cannot make both ends meet and who by the sweat of their brow make us comfortable in umpteen ways.

Evaluating this decision it has been rightly said: His second term as Chief Minister of Orissa is noteworthy for the fact that the high-falutin Biju descended among the poor of the State — More than any socialist or revolutionary ideal what Biju attempted to instil in the increment in daily wages is his humanitarian approach. A man - especially the poor, wage earner-has to live a life of ease and prestige - he seems to have believed in this wage-hike decision.[98]

Reorganisation of Districts: An Administrative Achievement

The reorganisation of districts raising their numbers from 13 to 30 is considered to be an administrative achievement of Biju Patnaik's government. 'Nearer the administration greater is the feeling among people that it is their administration. Hence, it was done with a view to take administration nearer to the people's door steps'. It is rightly said that this historic step of Biju Patnaik in the face of many odds will remain a momentous event in the history of Orissa.[99]

Streamlining and Rejuvenating the Panchayati Raj System

Apart from the reorganisation of districts under Biju's leadership, Orissa became 'the first State to streamline the Panchayati Raj and Local-self government institutions to make democracy participatory and not the aristocracy of a few nit-picking intellectuals.[100]

In this connection, it may be said that 'since 1990, Biju's government took steps to revive the 3-tier Panchayat Raj system in order to strengthen grass-root democratic institutions. Under Biju's leadership, the Orissa Gram Panchayat Act 1964 and the Orissa Panchayat Samities Act 1959 were amended in 1991, 1992 and 1993. The Orissa Zilla Parishad Act 1991 was also enacted in 1991 to constitute Zilla-Parishads at the district level. This act has been extensively amended - to bring it in conformity with the provision of the Constitution Amendment Act 1992.[101] It also adds to the credit of Biju's government that 'after a lapse of eight years', it conducted elections to Gram Panchayats in the year 1992[102] for 5264 Gram Panchayats in the State.

Some salient features of Gram Panchayat, Panchayat Samities and Zilla Parishad deserve mention as these were the outcome of the amendments made during Biju's Chief Ministership to which we have referred.

In case of Gram Panchayat three mentionable points are:

(a) 'The post of Naib Sarpanch is reserved for the women members, if the Sarpanch is a male'.

(b) 'One third of the total wards are reserved for women candidates including S.C. and S.T. women candidates'.

(c) Gram Panchayats have been vested with the power of supervision of women and child welfare programme, social forestry, rural housing, small scale industries and public distribution system in addition to other normal functions.[103]

As regards Panchayat Samities the following features deserve mention:

(a) One third of the total seats are reserved for women members including women members of S.C. and S.T. category.

(b) Provision has been made to reserve the office of the Vice-Chairman for a woman in case the Chairman is a male.

The Zilla Parishad ceased to exist in the State with effect from 1968. The State Government enacted the Orissa Zilla Parishad Act, 1991, in order to transfer the power of planning, control and supervision of developmental activities to Zilla Parishads at the district level'. Obviously, credit is due to Biju Patnaik for reviving Zilla Parishads and endowing them with power in district level. After the enforcement of the Constitution Amendment Act, 1992, it became necessary to amend the Orissa Zilla Parishad Act, 1991.

The following features after necessary changes need mention:

(a) Reservation of seats for S.C. and S.T. members has to be done on the basis of their ratio to the total population of the districts.

(b) One third of the seats are to be reserved for women members including S.T. and S.C. women.

(c) The post of Vice-President should be reserved for women if the President is not a woman.[104]

The State law has provided that no person having more than two children will be eligible to contest in the election to Zilla Parishad. Similarly persons having more than one spouse have been disqualified from contesting the election.[105]

It is also said that the government of Biju Patnaik set up quite a few commissions of finance for the Panchayat Raj Institutions in order to offer methods and mechanisms for resource funding thus unleashing some purpose to the decentralisation of power.[106]

Thus Orissa under Biju Patnaik became the first State to streamline the Panchayat Raj and Local-self government institutions. That his government held election after a lapse of eight years in Gram Panchayats showed Biju's commitment to restore status and dignity to this valuable unit of self-government at the grass-root level. In a way, the amendments to Gram Panchayat, Panchayat Samiti and Zilla Parishad Acts in Orissa in his second spell as Chief Minister bear the mark of his far-sighted personality - as a path indicator in respect of empowerment of women in the Panchayati Raj system. The area of participation was not only expanded and made meaningful through association and empowerment of women under Biju's inspiration, he also rejuvenated the Panchayat Raj and local self-government institutions to function as meaningful units of self-government by endowing them with power and authority in the process of development. It may be recalled that he had also rejuvenated the Panchayat Raj Institutions in the 1960s and described each Sarpanch as Chief Minister of his Panchayat.[107]

Kalinga Kutir Yojana: Rural Orientation of Biju's Government

Orissa under Biju became a unique State to launch a rural housing scheme called Kalinga Kutir Yojana for fulfilling the low-cost housing needs of the people living in the country side.[108]

In the words of Nalini Kant Mohanty, a Minister during Biju's second stint as Chief Minister, 'No other government had launched a rural housing scheme like the Kalinga Kutir Yojana. Whatever was done was done, in the Urban Area — This rural housing scheme is a remarkable achievement of our government'.[109]

The launching of backward class development programmes, and increase in the allowance for widows and the old were other areas where Biju's government left its mark.

Apart from all this Biju Patnaik, it is said, could ensure from the Centre an in-flow of larger amounts of planned grants compared to 925 crores in 1989-90. The planned grant in respect of the years 1990-91, 1991-92, 1992-93, 1993-94,

1994-95 were 1250 crores, 1443.62 crores, 1405 crores, 1450 crores and 1951 crores respectively.[110]

The Government of India's neglect of Orissa in the matter of Railways has been a stark reality since independence. He tried his best to bring justice to Orissa in this field. The strong pressure of the All-Party Committee of Vidhan Sabha formed under his inspiration which exerted pressure on the Central government worked to some extent. It is said that through his efforts Daitari-Banaspani, Lanjigad Road - Junagarh and Khurda Road - Bolangir Railway Projects were approved, though the efforts of the former Minister of State for Railways, Kanhu Charan Lenka and Bhakta Charan Das were also noteworthy. The Kalinga Hospital at Bhubaneswar established by the NRIs was also the fruit of his effort.[111] That sought to provide the best of medical facilities for serious diseases.

Biju's Anti-Corruption Drive as Chief Minister

To ensure a clean and non-corrupt government, Biju took a very tough stand that he would be the harshest administrator in Orissa as far as curbing corruption is concerned.[112] As a part of his anti-corruption drive, Biju removed some corrupt officers at the top, organised searches of houses of many engineers, I.A.S. and I.P.S. officers including the premises of the previous Chief Minister and many of his heavy weights. In his zeal to undertake anti-corruption drive, Biju government's decision to raid the Eastern Media Premises of Sambad 'appeared to be vindictive and certainly tempered with the freedom of the press'.[113]

On November 29, 1990 Biju came down heavily on the State's bureaucracy dubbing it as corrupt and frankly expressed his feeling of helplessness to run the government. He urged the people to assault the corrupt officials to make them realise their mistakes and rectify themselves[114] and also asked them to give the same treatment to corrupt Ministers and M.L.As including him if found corrupt.[115]

This obviously extraordinary and startling statement was vehemently criticised and even the division bench of the High Court observed that the Chief Minister Biju had transgressed his limits.[116] However, it appears to be the helpless outburst of a man who even as Chief Minister could not think it possible to root out corruption which like an octopus had spread its tentacles into the whole system of administration and politics. Moreover, Biju who was no hypocrite in politics to shed crocodile tears for the poor and the downtrodden and who wanted to really do something for them found a corrupt, unconcerned and anti-people bureaucracy virtually a stumbling bloc not co-operating with him as much as it should. It is significant that a man of his doggedness frankly admitted that the administration under him was less responsive than what it was 30 years ago when he was Chief Minister first.[117]

He found to his unhappiness and anger that it had now been divorced from the people.[118]

This concern for the people, the poor and the downtrodden was at the back of his call to beat up corrupt officials and also lurked behind his admiration for the Naxalites. The cause of giving justice to the poor and the downtrodden for which the Naxalites fought drew his attention and he did not hesitate to praise it with disarming candour and frankness. He was no advocate of violence, anarchy and disorder. Through his admiration of the Naxalites he was merely underlining the need of giving a better deal to the poor and downtrodden who have not been able to get their due in the system.

His sincerity for the uplift of the poor and downtrodden in his second spell as Chief Minister was simply amazing. It really touches and straightaway enters the heart when one reads between his lines "He asks why the Naxalites have taken to violence"? And he answers "only because we are not able to give them social justice. In the areas where they are active either God or Naxalites will come to uplift the people".

On 4th January, 1991 he said, "I want to handle them (Naxalites) by being a revolutionary myself. Why the hell not? What is so wrong in a Chief Minister being a revolutionary? What is so right as a Chief Minister being corrupt and a hypocrite shedding crocodile tears for the downtrodden? Have we not seen enough of the type in this country of ours, whether of Left, Right or Centre?[119]

This was Biju Patnaik, the Chief Minister of Orissa, the development-centric Chief Minister of the sixties who possibly now was conceptualising the idea of development with a human touch - a development that has got to be addressed in right earnest to the poor and down trodden 'Who had not made demands earlier or their voice recorded in the corridors of power'.

When Biju Patnaik asked the people to beat up anti-people and corrupt officials and politicians and even admired the Naxalites, he was only faithfully voicing the just feeling of the people who have been denied the benefits of the independence and democracy they obtain in this motherland of theirs.[120]

Biju Patnaik's Mind and Out-look vis-a-vis Some Issues of Concern

A few months after his second year as Chief Minister in 1991, Biju was deeply concerned with the Centre's neglect of the State's plea in certain areas. That included permission for an integrated Steel Plant, development of Railway Projects and Paradeep Port. This enraged Biju to throw a missile - a warning that Orissa should 'secede from India if it was not granted financial autonomy'. It created a spate of misunderstanding in certain circles raising their finger at Biju's nationalist credentials. However, it was more a pronouncement of anger against the step-motherly attitude of the Centre towards the State and more the articulate outpourings of a State autonomy activist than any real intention to secede from India. What he was trying to apprise the Centre was that in the Indian federal system the States should be given appropriate authority to develop their State rather than being made a victim of the excessive power and authority of the Centre which in his opinion has given rise to strong fissiparous tendencies.

At the height of Mandal politics when Orissa was writhing under a spell of violent protest, Biju Patnaik showed his qualities as a secular politician when he candidly said "there are only two castes - the poor and the rich. I do not believe any other caste which the Mandalites professs". It was his statesmanship and talent as a crisis manager that violence in Orissa did not further escalate.

Every inch a Statesman, our Chief Minister expressed his concern over the developing crisis on account of the Mandal Commission Report and Ram Janmabhoomi issue. He rightly maintained that 'nobody should be allowed to divide the nation either on a religious or caste basis'.

Conclusion

During his 27 months of Chief Ministership in the 1960s, Biju was primarily concerned with the industrialisation and over-all development of the State. The construction of the Paradeep Port and the Express Highway, the setting up of the Sunabeda Mig Factory, the Talcher Thermal Power Station and the Balimela Multi-purpose Project, etc., bear the unmistakable imprint of his personality as a development-centric Chief Minister. It was a most fruitful 'period of engineering and construction' and even his harshest of critics would admit that he proved to be a dynamic Chief Minister whose short spell of only 27 months heralded a new era of industrialisation and over-all development of the State. It may not be far from truth to state that no other Chief Minister of Orissa after him nor he even himself in his second spell as Chief Minister in the 1990s could repeat such dynamism in the arena of industrialisation and over-all development of the State. The feverish pitch of industrial activity and the launching of giant industrial projects which marked his first spell as Chief Minister may be regarded as the golden period in the history of Orissa's industrialisation and Biju Patnaik may rightly be regarded as the pioneer of industrial renaissance in Orissa.

Biju's second spell as Chief Minister in the 1990s cannot hold a candle before the dazzling light of the achievements made during his first spell of the 1960s in respect of industrialisation and development; nevertheless he will be fondly remembered for his steps in the field of women development, of reorganisation of districts, for his sincere efforts to streamline and rejuvenate the Panchayati Raj and Local-self Government institutions and more particularly for the pro-poor orientation which he sought to give to his second spell as Chief Minister.

In his second stint as Chief Minister, Biju Patnaik of course 'was not able to materialise the Steel Plant in Orissa'; but it is also a fact that he laid the infrastructure for the Steel Plant at Duburi'.

Biju had the vision of an industrialised Orissa - a prosperous and powerful Orissa. What he had always in mind was to lift his beloved Orissa from backwardness and poverty. He made untiring efforts for this whether in power as Orissa's Chief Minister or outside when out of power. He did a lot for Orissa during his two spells as Chief Minister. He was always prepared to fight with the Central authorities where the interest of the State was concerned. It is doubtful whether a personality of Biju's stature will ever emerge in Orissa politics to steer the ship of the State. Let his vision of Orissa inspire all of us to put in our best to build up a prosperous and powerful Orissa.

References

1. D.C. Das, *Biju Patnaik: The Vision of a Patriot*, Orissa Review, April 1994, p.7.

2. Duryodhan Majhi, *Biju Patnaik: A Hero of Our Times,* Orissa Review, March 2001, Information and Public Relation Department, Government of Orissa, p.11.
3. Mitrabhanu Mohapatra, *Biju Patnaik: Formidable Phenomenon,* 71st Jayanti Smaranika, 1987, Biju Patnaik Jayanti Committee, Cuttack, p.100.
4. Bhaskar Parichha, *Biju Patnaik: A Political Biography,* Har-Anand Publications, New Delhi, 1995, p.19.
5. Kunja Bihari Tripathy, *Utkal Matar Barenya Putra Biju Patnaik,* 71st Jayanti Abhinandan Granth, p.29.
6. Kumari Binita Rout, *Swadhinata Sangramare Biju Patnaikanka Abadan*, p.77.
7. Bhaskar Parichha, *op.cit.*, p.19.
8. *Ibid,* p.20.
9. Duryodhan Majhi, *Orissa Review*, March 2001, p.11.
10. *Biju Patnaik: Orissa of My Dreams,* First Binode Kanungo Memorial Lecture Delivered Extempore on January 27, 1992 at Suchana Bhawan, Bhubaneswar, Orissa Review, April 1992.
11. George Patnaik, *Biju Tankapari Piladinu,* 71st Jayanti Smaranika, p.41.
12. D.C. Das, *Biju Patnaik: The Vision of a Patriot*, Orissa Review, April 1994, p.7.
13. Dilip Kumar Swain, *Swadhinata Sangramare Biju Patnaikanka Bhumika,* 71st Jayanti Avinandan Granth, p.83.
14. D.C. Das, *Biju Patnaik: The Vision of a Patriot, op.cit.*, p.7.
15. Hullasa Behera, *The Legendary Pilot and Live-Wire Politician* published by Gitanjali Padihani, faridabad, Haryana, 1998, p.120.
16. *Khanna Commission Report*, Orissa State Archives, Bhubaneswar, p.800.
17. Hallasa Behera, *op.cit.*, p.121.
18. Aruna Asaf Ali, *Nirvika Sangrami, He Mahajivan*, Biswamukhi Prakashan, Bhubaneswar, 1918, p.11.
19. Sukdev Nanda, *Coalitional Politics in Orissa,* Sterling Publishers Pvt. Ltd., New Delhi, 1979, p.33.
20. D.C. Das, *op.cit.*, p.8.
21. Article in *Far Eastern Economic Review*, Jan 09, 1964, Quoted Khanna Report, *op.cit.*, p.800-01.

22. Hullasa Behera, *op.cit.*, p.122.
23. D.C. Das, *op.cit.*, p.10.
24. Girija Bhusan Patnaik, *The Colossus, Kalinga Keshari, Biju Patnaik Foundation Sailashree Vihar*, 1999, p.7.
25. *Sun Times*, March 4, 1990.
26. *Bhaskar Parichha*, *op.cit.*, p.47.
27. Sukdev Nand,*op.cit.*, p.34.
28. Khanna Commission Report, p.800.
29. Bhaskar Parichha *op.cit.*, p.47.
30. Hullasa Behera, *op.cit.*, p.125.
31. D.C. Das, *op.cit.*, p.10.
32. *A Brief History of Orissa Legislative Assembly* 1937-1995, p.5.
33. B.B. Jena & J.K. Baral, *Coalition Politics in Orissa Govt. & Politics in Orissa,* Print House (India), Lucknow, 1988, p.300.
34. *Ibid.*, p.300.
35. Morarji Desai, *The Story of My Life*, vol. I, Mac-Millan, India, 1974, p.123.
36. *Ibid.*
37. S.C. Dash, *Govt. & Politics in Orissa*, Indian Journal of Political Science, 1965, p.93.
38. *Ibid.*, p.93-94.
39. Kishalay Banerjee, *Regional Political Parties in India,* B.R. Publishing Corporation, Delhi, 1984, p.101.
40. Sukdev Nanda, *op.cit.*, p.36.
41. Bhaskar Parichha, *op.cit.*, p.66.
42. *Ibid.*, p.61.
43. *Ibid.*, p.62.
44. R.P. Shastry, *Biju Patnaik: A Great Son of Orissa*, *op.cit.*, p.95.
45. Hullasa Behera, *op.cit.*, p.129.
46. Bhaskar Parichha, *op.cit.*, p.67.
47. Sukdev Nanda, *Coalitional Politics in Orissa, op.cit.*, p.36.
48. Hullasa Behera, *op.cit.*, p.133.
49. Sanatan Pany, *Jivanta Kimbadanti,* He Mahajivan, Biswamukti Prakashan, Bhubaneswar, 1998, p.64.

50. R.P. Shastry, *Biju Patnaik: A Great Son of Orissa*, Jayanti Avinandan Granth, 1987, p.97.
51. Sukdev Nanda, *op.cit.*, p.36.
52. R.P. Shastry, *op.cit.*, p.95.
53. Dr. G.K. Srichandan, *Biju Patnaik Aka Birala Byakitya,* He Mahajivan, *op.cit.*, p.143.
54. Hullasa Behera, *op.cit.*, p.139.
55. Sun Times, March 4, 1990, Article Captioned *Biju Patnaik is 75.*
56. Hullasa Behera, *op.cit.*, p.129.
57. *Dusahasi O Sangrami Biju Patnaik*, Rajya Jana Sikhya Sadhan Kendra, Orissa, Bhubaneswar, 1998, p.25.
58. Sukdev Nanda, *op.cit.*, p.36.
59. Bhaskar Parichha, *op.cit.*, p.145-46.
60. Sun Times, May 4, 1990.
61. B.K. Tripathy, *Three Months of Janata Rule in Orissa*, Sun Times, June 3, 1990.
62. Sukdev Nanda, *Coalitional Politics, op.cit.*, p.36.
63. Orissa Legislative Assembly Debates, Vol.I, No.I, Sl.No.6087 dt. 23.09.76, pp.10-11.
64. *Ibid.*, Vol.I, No.27, p.16.
65. *Ibid.*, Vol.I, No.16, 20th September 1961, *Reply to the Question of Govinda Munda* by Pabitra Mohan Pradhan dated 20th September 1961.
66. Bhaskar Parichha, *Biju Patnaik: A Political Biography*, *op.cit.*, p.33.
67. *Ibid.*, p.34.
68. *Ibid.*
69. Morarji Desai, *The Story of My Life,* Vol.I, MacMillan, India, 1974, p.189.
70. *Ibid.*, p.199.
71. Surya Naryan Mishra, *Election and Political Development in Orissa,* p.43, edited A.P. Padhy, *Indian State Politics: A Case Study of Orissa,* 1995, B.R. Publishing Corporation, New Delhi.
72. Bhaskar Parichha, *Biju Patnaik: A Political Biography, op.cit.*, p.140.
73. Khanna Commission Report *op.cit.*, p.810-11.

74. Bhaskar Parichha, *op.cit.*, p.144.
75. A Brief History of Orissa Legislative Assembly, 1937-1995, Secretariat of Orissa Legislative Assembly, Bhubaneswar, 1995, p.17.
76. Sun Times, March 2, 1990.
77. *Ibid.*
78. Sun Times, March 8, 1990.
79. *Ibid.*, March 5, 1990.
80. Gopal Mishra, *Tribute to a Legend*, Sun Times, April 18, 1997.
81. Hullasa Behere, *Biju Patnaik: The Legendary Pilot and Live-wire Politician, op.cit.*, p.17.
82. *Kalinga Keshari Biju Patnaik*, ed. by Chinmayee Mohanty, Biju Patnaik Foundation Sradha Nivedan, Sailashri Bihar, Bhubaneswar, 1999, p.14.
83. *Biju Patnaik: Orissa of My Dreams,* Orissa Review, April 21, 1997.
84. Sarojini Nayaik, *Biju and Woman Power,* Sun Times, April 21, 1997.
85. Biju Patnaik's Address at the Conference on *Human Rights*, September 14, 1992 at Delhi, Orissa Review, October 1992, p.4.
86. P.C. Mohanty, *Atrocities on Women: A Burning Social Problem,* Orissa Review, June 1993, p.62.
87. *Ibid.*
88. Sarojini Naik, *Biju & Woman Power, op.cit.*
89. Mahila Vikas Samabaya Nigam, *Orissa Action Plan 1991-92*, Orissa Review, October 1991, p.3.
90. Biju Patnaik: *While ushering into the 21st Century,* Orissa Review, September 1993, p.1.
91. Tanmayee Mohanty, *Antaranga Alapa*, Kalinga Keshari Biju Patnaik, *op.cit.*, p.12.
92. Manorama Mohapatra, *Jathartha Jananeta, Biju Babu: Sradhanjali*, Kalinga Keshari Biju Patnaik *op.cit.*, p.3.
93. Bhaskar Parichha, *Biju Patnaik: A Political Biography, op.cit.*, p.103-04.
94. Gopal Krishna Srichandan, *Biju Patnaik Aka Birala Byaktitya,* He Mahajivan, *op.cit.*, p.146.

95. Sun Times, April 23, 1990.
96. *Ibid.*
97. Sun Times, March 22, 1990.
98. Hullasa Behera, *op.cit.*, p.17.
99. Chandi Prasad Mohanty, Utkal Prasanga, August 1993, p.8.
100. Bhaskar Parichha, *op.cit.*, p.108.
101. Anuradha Acharya, *Salient Features of Panchyat Raj in Orissa*, Orissa Review, May 94, p.9.
102. *Ibid.*
103. *Ibid.*
104. *Ibid.*
105. P.C. Mohanty, *Democratic Decentralisation and Panchayati Raj System in Orissa: An Overview,* Orissa Review, June 1994, p.3.
106. Bhaskar Parichha, *op.cit.*, p.108.
107. Gopal Mishra, *Tribute to a Legend,* Sun Times, April 18, 1997.
108. Bhaskar Parichha, *op.cit.*, p.108.
109. Nalini Kanta Mohanty, *Kimbadanti*, Kalinga Keshari Biju Patnaik, *op.cit.*, p.18.
110. *Bijubabunkara Sesha Satabarsha*, Kalinga Keshari Biju Patnaik, *op.cit.*, p.14.
111. *Ibid.*, p.15.
112. Sun Times, March 22, 1990.
113. B.K. Tripathy, *Three Months of Janata Rule in Orissa,* Sun Times, June 3, 1990.
114. *Sun Times* December 1, 1990.
115. *Ibid.*, December 4, 1990.
116. *Ibid.*, April 29, 1991.
117. *Ibid.*, February 22, 1991.
118. *Ibid.*, March 15, 1991.
119. *Ibid.*, February 3, 1991.
120. Biswakesh Tripathy, *Biju a Bull in a China Shop*, Sun Times, February 3, 1991.

Biju Patnaik : The Leader of Opposition

18

Dhirendra Nath Srichandan

Bijayananda Patnaik, popularly known as Biju Patnaik, the ex-Chief Minister, Central Cabinet Minister, and the leader of the opposition party in the Orissa Legislative Assembly at different times, was a legend of Orissa. Very few leaders in India have such a dynamic and colourful personality, a saga of bravery and dedication. Biju Babu was certainly one of the most enthusiastic mergerists and he had been one for a long time. He had been a front-ranking opposition leader for a long time, perhaps the only one from the backwaters of Orissa and was almost a politician's politician. Ever since 1974 there has perhaps been no opposition conclave connected with the possible merger of parties which Biju Patnaik had not attended; indeed, some even called him a merger-specialist.

Biju Patnaik was the only legislator in the Orissa Legislative Assembly who used to speak in English except on a few occasions when utterance in Oriya was seen. He in general used to attack the government in forceful language on different subjects, though his speech at times lacked coherence.

R.N. Singh Deo, the leader of the opposition bench at different times used to speak in Oriya and also attacked government in his usual style of mild and gentle tone with facts and figures. But Biju Patnaik a towering figure with vast experience as a legislator used to attack the government on various subjects of which he had the knowledge. His speeches on industry, commerce, poverty eradication, social upliftment, education and so on were milestones in the history of Assembly proceedings.

Biju Patnaik was the only leader of the country who never believed in the security system he was given. He argued that the people were the protectors of the leaders, not the police personnel. He was speaking at a press conference during his Chief Ministership in 1994 about the attack on him by the Secretariat employees. The question was, "since you knew there was danger on your life by the striking employees, why did you not take the help of the police for your protection ?" He replied, "Today I am Chief Minister of the State. I can requisition hundred of policemen to protect me. But when I would be in the opposition bench who is to help me in case an attack is made on my life?" He categorically pointed out that the best way of protection is the people themselves. He narrated an incident which occurred while he was Chief Minister of Orissa. One day on the third floor of the Chief Minister's office an unemployed young man came and demanded a job for him. There was a heated argument by Biju Patnaik with the young man. Biju Babu who was known as a short-tempered man gave a slap to the young man out of disgust. All of a sudden an unprecedented thing happened that the young man suddenly gave a slap across Biju Patnaik's face. Some pressmen, security staff of Secretariat, Inspector and Police constables who were present on the spot were stunned at the incident. Immediately the police overpowered the young man and wanted to take him in to police custody. But to everybody's surprise, Biju Patnaik patted the young man's shoulder and took him to his office room. He paid him a thousand rupees and opined that if the young men of our country would have courage like this young man, then Orissa would not have been known as a cowardly State in India. He instructed the Private Secretary to find out a job as per his qualification. He travelled inside and outside the State without any security. During his stay at Kolkata in Utkal Bhawan he had a meeting with Jyoti Basu (the then Chief Minister, West Bengal) in Writers' Building. Jyoti Basu sent a police protection car to take Biju Babu from Utkal Bhawan to Writers' Building. But Biju Babu sent back the police security and went to Writers' Building in Utkal Bhawan car with the driver alone. Several instances of his courageous activities proved him to be a dare-devil.

As opposition leader in Orissa Assembly Biju Patnaik took things in a typical manner and his Oxford spoken style English (as narrated by many national dailies) was not understood by a section of the members in the Orissa Legislative Assembly, on account of their poor knowledge of English. Once when there was a discussion to change the name of the State, Biju Patnaik gave an appropriate speech in English in support of his argument. According to him, "If we wish to revise our defeated mind what weapons do we have, with us ? We have to capitalize on our ancient history which was glorious in its own accord. That glorious chapter would give us strength. Only a change of name whether it is Kalinga, Utkal or Orissa would not serve the purpose. The whole thing is poverty of mind. If you destroy the poverty of mind and collectively if this House can give a new direction, then that will be something worth doing".

As an opposition leader he had such wonderful speeches in Orissa Legislative Assembly on variety of subjects. His speech on Education on 23 December, 1974 should have been an eye-opener for Orissa educationists as well as the government. The extracts of his statement in the Assembly is given as follows:

"Mr. Deputy Speaker, Sir, I will now draw your attention to the failures in the Department of Education. Sir, you may recollect when you were with me in the Treasury benches, we had expanded the education of the State as has never been done in the history of Orissa. We expanded the number of colleges to 92; we set up thousands of schools for boys and girls and the number of primary schools was doubled and so on. That was an era of educational expansion of our state; you may recollect, we expanded the education budget to more than two times. Besides the Utkal University, two other universities were set up. Since then education in this State has not only been stagnant qualitatively and quantitatively, it is also deteriorating proportionately to the population increase of the State. This is a dangerous situation and at all stages I find this government is indecisive, halting and always given an impression that only force and pressure can change the lethargy of government. Take this instance of the teachers' agitation. Only today the Minister of Education placed certain amendments to the rules which could have been done long before and an unpleasant situation caused by the teachers' agitation on one hand and the government or the police action on the other hand which includes tear gassing, molestation of the lady teachers and so on. All these could have been avoided if the government took the steps that they have taken today, in proper time. Therefore, as I said, in the beginning of this debate that people have got an impression in the State that this government is not only lethargic, it is not even sensitive to the people's requirements and tries to impose its will at all times on the people in a most undemocratic fashion, resulting in a resistance which is being built up against government, especially against party which is heading the government; it has built a resistance, it is somewhat unfortunate that they give a feeling or appear to have given a feeling not based on historical background.

Therefore, I say lack of education breeds undemocratic methods. The percentage of education, of literacy is the lowest in our State, is absolutely lowest in our State. It is only a supplementary budget. In the last budget also not enough money was provided in this regard. You remember, Mr. Deputy Speaker, Sir, what new ideas we had to give to little children in the primary schools-mechanised sporting equipments and other things. Government should have a factory to produce those things to give to the children. New syllabus be prepared for the men and women of our country who will bring up the child's mind, increase its mind to new dimensions comparable to the rapid growth in the developing countries of the world. Our whole system, our whole thinking is still primitive. It has no bearing on the modern world. You think you have no power to take up these. That all emanates from the lack of upbringing at the level of the people where the right type of training is not given. This Government has not, to my mind, applied its mind to it, literally doing nothing. This is a sad commentary on the governments' educational thinking, in the field of education and its development. You take colleges even the greatest of colleges, the Ravenshaw College is deficient in so many things and the other colleges having no apparatus, nor laboratories nor adequate number of teachers nor other things which come towards making up a complete modern campus. I know all these cannot be done in a day or in a month or in few months. But there is no effort by this Government towards that. This Government has come under a sense of a crippling paralysis. It is not prepared to fight for the development of the State".

Biju Patnaik had a thorough knowledge of finance vis-a-vis planning and development. He had got so vast knowledge on the State planning combined with practical knowledge of things and foresightedness for the development of Orissa. During his Chief Ministership from 1961-63 and as Chairman, Orissa Planning Board till 1967 he could be easily called the builder of modern Orissa. When he was the leader of the opposition in 1974, he had made a wonderful speech during budget discussion in which he had given a clear picture of independent Orissa's past, and future planning. During that time Surendra Nath Dwivedy was the Chairperson of Orissa Planning Board. Criticizing the Government on the size of Orissa's plan, Biju Patnaik had compared the plan figure of 1961 with the plan figure of 1974. Since Biju Patnaik had got the thorough knowledge about the plan as the Chairman of the Planning Board, he had proved the plan figure of 1974 as unhelpful to the development of Orissa. The extracts of Biju Patnaiks' speech on planning figure of 1974 are as follows: "Then why do you present figures which are not facts. I will tell you, you have said in your report the tentative size of the State's Fifth Plan is fixed at Rs. 567.01 crores which is more than twice the outlay made during this fourth plan. If that is your contention and that is double of the fourth plan why are you crying ? Have you compared the figures at 1961, that is, Third Five Year Plan ? According to Reserve Bank of India up to March of this year the value of a rupee is 23 NP. By June it has still come down. So it is one fifth of 1961 value. You yourself have stated that the Third Five-Year Plan investment is 225 crores. According to the present value of money that 225 crores is equivalent to 1125 crores of todays' money value. Similarly we started the 4th Plan in the year 1967. Our value comes to 40 per cent. Similarly the 4th Plan target was half of the 3rd Plan target. That is the actual position. Your friend who is sitting by your side the then Finance Minister tried to make minimum need investment. He started with 4,000 crores which came down to 16,000 crores. Your Chairman Planning Board Mr. Dwivedy tried for 800 crores. But now it has come down to 567 crores. Mr. Finance Minister here lies the Secretary, Orissa has no mobility of finance. It has no mobility for resources". Biju Patnaik had a vivid knowledge about Orissa, its economy, its social structure, its people and moreover its wealth.

Biju Patnaik's knowledge of industry was well known. He himself was one of the top industrialists of the country. As the opposition leader, he was the first person who ordinarily initiated discussion on industry. He not only criticised the government's failure to industrialize the state but also offered suggestions for the development of industries and the creation of industrial climate in the State. But unfortunately in the present Indian democracy the people in power hesitate to take expert advice from the opposition party leader although they are equipped with highest knowledge on industry. This was what happened with Biju Patnaik who was the master of industrial development in Orissa. Biju Patnaik was simply ignored as he belonged to the opposition party.

Biju Patnaik had the distinct knowledge of the management of public undertakings — its pros and cons. During the debate on Public Undertakings Biju Patnaik had given a vivid description as to how corporations ought to function. He pointed out that our corporation would be entrusted with the work of construction and not to the outsiders who were making huge profits. The extracts of his statements are as follows:

"The moment Birla came to know about this he came to me and requested to give the work and indicated that he would do the work at the previous rate. But I did not give him the job. I said, you have lost the job. This should be done by the Corporation here. Do you know, how many bridges the corporation did in Paradeep and Express Highway ? 67 bridges have been done by the Corporation".

Biju Patnaik was the only opposition leader who dared to humiliate the Chief Minister on the floor of the Assembly. In 1974 during the budget discussion he made a derogatory comment on Nandini Satpathy, the then Chief Minister of Orissa as his 'lady worker' from 1967-69. Nandani Satpathy in reply told that she was always a worker. Even at that time she was a worker of the people. Likewise in 1986 during a discussion on the Governors address Biju Patnaik pointed his finger towards Janaki Ballav Patnaik and said, "You, Mr. Janaki Patnaik, I have seen you. You were not a prominent person in those days. You have started your life as a correspondent of a newspaper, you have started your career as a very little man. But you see, I have received letters from the Prime Minister which I would like to bring to the notice of the House in this context. Your Prime Minister, when he writes about me, let us know, what he has said, 'Eminent citizens and patriots like yourself.' This is his letter, dated 23rd June, 1986. This is his comment on me. Another comment, that is for the consumption of my friend the chief whip. The Governor of Orissa has said "Biju Patnaik is an outstanding leader, gifted with dynamic qualities and his contributions during freedom struggle as well as during the post independence era for the progress and development of our state and country are well known. As an industrialist, administrator, social and political leader he has displayed indomitable courage, determination and confidence in diverse fields of activity". Apart from his quality of straight-forwardness in launching attack upon the Chief Minister and other ministers on the floor of the Assembly, Biju Babu served as the leader of the opposition to the best of his ability. His presence in the Orissa Legislative Assembly could create a fear psychosis in the minds of the members of the treasury bench specifically in the Chief Minister and other ministers. In a democratic pattern of administration the role of the opposition party is very crucial and important in bringing to light the errors of omission and commission of the government. Biju Patnaik as the leader of the opposition had been discharging his functions effectively well. In Orissa, Biju Patnaik was the only leader who had served successfully both as a Chief Minister and an opposition leader.

During his life-time Biju Patnaik had a love-hate relationship with Dr. Harekrushna Mahatab. But after his demise Biju Patnaik as the leader of the opposition gave him the highest tribute. Biju Babu was a large-hearted man who used to love even the enemy. Biju Patnaik's praise and appreciation for Dr. H. K. Mahatab's contribution to the freedom struggle and construction of modern Orissa, after his demise, is quoted as follows :

"Mr. Speaker, Sir, Dr. H. K. Mahatab, a great son of India has passed away and many things have been told about him. He is practically the maker of modern Orissa with assimilation of all the States and various other developmental activities which have been written about and spoken about. I was very intimately known to him as early as 1945 when he came out of jail after three years. Sir, at that time when he came out of jail, I was doing the underground movement along with Jayaprakash Narayan and Ram Manohar Lohia. Dr. H.K. Mahatab and Mr. N. K. Choudhury, in April, 1945, came secretly to have a meeting with me in the upstairs of my Cuttack house. You know why, Sir, the thinking still was that the British would not leave us, we may have to go through a battle with the British, so we may have to gather guns and ammunitions, to fight the British force. After discussion we came to the conclusion as suggested by Dr. Mahatab that we must create an underground godown where all these guns and ammunitions could be stored. So we thought of how to give coverage to it and that is how the idea of a Textile Mill came into being and a company in the name of Orissa Textile Mills Ltd. was formed where Dr. Mahatab, Mr. N. K. Choudhury and myself were associated. That was the beginning of Orissa Textile Mills. But the wheels of fate turned differently. By September, I took Dr. Mahatab with me in my private aeroplane from Bhubaneswar to Delhi and he stayed with me in my house at Delhi. There we talked to the Secretary to the Chancellor of the Exchequer Mr. Biake, who was in the airforce and we had become very friendly during the Second World War. Dr. Mahatab and I then stayed at Delhi to have our own secret deal. Subsequently, we invited all of them to Roshamans' club. It is still written in the club book about the visit of these personalities in 1945. You may recollect that Mr. Wavell who was then the Governor-General announced Mr. Mahatab's name as a member of the interim Cabinet. These are the things which are unknown to many people. When I was mentioned to Panditjee, he called me and I met him in the house of Asaf Ali and he asked me how I knew Mr. Cripps. I told him how I knew him through his Secretary, a friend of mine. That is quite interesting. Panditjee told me, you tell Mahatab that he should go back to Orissa and become the Chief Minister. So I flew to Orissa with Dr. Mahatab and he became the Chief Minister. This is how he became the first Chief Minister of Orissa after independence. He is my political "Guru". Till his death he fought for the right of men".

Those who know Biju Patnaik as a leader of post-independent period must admit of such a rare colourful personality like him. Biju Patnaik was described by Julian Huxley in memoirs "as a remarkable Indian whose adventures will surely fill a book". He was known to Nehru "as a man of energy and certain ability". Before entering state politics Biju Patnaik had acquired a glamour by his various adventures and daring feats. He was a great statesman in his own right, a great democrat by temperament and the only natural leader of Oriyas. As the Chief Minister of Orissa, as the leader of the opposition, as Union Minister or as an MLA, his political career was totally different from that of other leaders in Orissa. The man loved Orissa and Oriyas would be imprinted in every Oriya's heart and mind for all times to come. His dream to see Orissa a most prosperous state in the map of India could not be materialized because there was no second Biju Patnaik in Orissa politics.

References

1. *Ananya*—A book on Biju Patnaik.
2. Proceedings of Orissa Legislative Assembly.
3. Suniti Ghosh, *Orissa in Turmoil.*
4. *Orissa Review*, Government of Orissa Publication.

Biju Patnaik : The Man and Mission

19

B.C. Rout

Seventeenth April 1997, the day Biju Patnaik passed away, was not only a sad day for Orissa but a sad day for the whole country. He was 82 years old. He served the country more than six decades. He was a legend in Orissa and Indian politics. He was a great freedom fighter. He played a significant role in the freedom struggle of India. He was known as "the Hero of Kalinga" and "the Kharavela of Kalinga". Just as modern India cannot be thought of without Jawaharlal Nehru, modern Orissa cannot be thought of without Biju Patnaik.

Man is born mortal, but his deeds and activities make him immortal. A mortal becomes immortal by his virtues and actions. Biju Patnaik was such an immortal man. Worshipped as the demi-god, respected as a messiah and admired as the epitome of chivalry and courage, Biju Patnaik stood like a colossus and respected by the masses for his own charisma. The man who created history, changed history and shaped history would remain as a history. And the history he created or changed was the making of modern Orissa. His mission was the emancipation of Orissa from poverty and neglect.

In 1962 Biju Patnaik as the Chief Minister of Orissa, approved the project of Paradeep Port and got it inaugurated by Pandit Nehru. The Centre sanctioned more aid for Orissa. Nehru was criticised for his decision in the Parliament for providing more aid to Orissa. To this Nehru replied, "Biju Patnaik has the courage, dynamism and zeal to work. So there is no blunder in giving more aid to Orissa". This was the appreciation for the extraordinary talent and personality of Biju Patnaik.

Biju Patnaik, the custodian of the pride of Orissa, had dreamt many dreams. But his fond dream was the rise of the dashing Oriya youths to conquer every sphere as the true descendants of Kharavel. Although practicing politics, Biju Patnaik was more than a politician, he was a leader of people, a charismatic leader, a natural one. Had he been born in any other state other than Orissa, he would certainly have become the Prime Minister of the country. In 1960s his name was speculated on the top, when the question was being asked after Nehru who ? Again he missed the chance when V.P. Singh, Chandrashekhar and H.D. Deve Gowda were made the Prime Ministers.

He faced many ups and downs in politics. Though close to Jawaharlal Nehru, he had to leave the Congress Party after his death mainly due to his uncompromising nature with the Congress Party leaders including Indira Gandhi. Such was the force of his personality that it always drew the extreme emotions from the people, blind adulation or hatred, depending on the situations. There are some who try to measure the contribution of Biju Patnaik to Orissa in terms of roads and bridges and plants and ports he built. Being a man of industry in the past, he had tried to industrialise Orissa, though not with much success. A second steel plant in the state remained one of his unfulfilled dreams.

Biju Patnaik tried his best to bring industrial revolution in the state. The Chowdwar and Barbil industrial belts, the Cuttack-Jagatpur Mahanadi high-way bridge, the Bhubaneswar Airport, the Orissa Aviation Centre, the Paradeep Port, the Express Highway, the MIG factory at Sunabeda, the Talcher Thermal Power Plant, the Balimela Hydel Project, the Orissa University of Agriculture and Technology, the Panchayat level industrial projects, the IITS and the Engineering Colleges, some of the major Public Sector Undertakings of the State, the Orissa State Planning Board, some of the major urban development authorities of the State, the reorganisation of the Districts, etc. were some of the outstanding works which made Biju immortal.

Biju as a promoter of science is known to the world. Like Nehru he had immense faith and commitment to science. He believed in the modernisation of society on a scientific basis. He established the Kalinga Foundation for the dissemination of knowledge in science. He also announced the Kalinga Prize for the promotion of scientific knowledge. His basic premise behind the setting up of Kalinga Prize was that every man should have at least a basic understanding of science in order to function well in society. The Prize, now every year given by the UNESCO, is considered by the international scientific community as some kind of a nobel prize in science communication. When Biju Patnaik contemplated this prize, he gave it the name KALINGA, an empire which existed two thousand years ago and where Ashoka, the Great was transformed from Chandashoka to Dharmashoka. Like Nehru, Biju passionately advocated inculcating scientific temper in the minds of the people. More than two thousand years ago, to be exact 261 BC, the people of Kalinga fought a battle still refresh in the annals of history. It is impossible to forget the Kalinga war, fought on the banks of the river Daya, near Bhubaneswar, the death, the devastation and the killing whereby the water of the river turning red with blood. Biju Patnaik tried to revive it in the minds of people of the state and tried to fight another battle - the battle of removal of poverty from the state. As a great statesman and a visionary man, he always struggled hard for uplift of economic condition of the people of Orissa. A man with many facets and abilities, his love for Orissa and its people was intense. Restoring Orissa to its ancients glory and to its rightful place in the country was his lifetime mission for which he worked and tried ceaselessly.

Out of about six decades in politics, he was in prison for about two years in 1943 for his participation in the Quit India Movement, worked for about three years as the Union Minister and about seven and half years as the Chief Minister of the State in two terms. The political career graph of Biju Patnaik had witnessed upward and downward trends. More than half a century in Indian politics in and out of power, in the State and at the Centre, heading ruling party and building opposition structures, enjoying the highest seat of power in the state and a prestigious position at the centre was a good show and was a good score for him. His mission and message, his ambitions and dreams made him a magnificent leader and a great man. His love for his own native state had never stood in the way of his love for the country at large. And his regionalism was not opposed to nationalism. He had some qualities of Utkal Gaurava Madhusudan Das, the grand old man of Orissa who had awakened the Oriya people from their deep slumber in the first two decades of the 20th century. Some of his critics said that he talked much and did things impulsively, disregarding the means, but history showed that whatever works done by him on the impulse of the moment were not trival but monuments for the posterity.

In success and failure, glory and ignomity, felicitation and humiliation, his outstanding presence was remarkable and never to-be-missed. He stood like a pyramid in Egyptian desert sands. The true son of the soil, he demonstrated pride and self-respect of the Oriyas. He did not bend ever before Nehru, Indira or Morarji to be in power for further personal interest. The only interest, he had, was the dignity and honour of the Oriyas. He had said many quotable in his life time. These were there in his speeches in the State Legislature and in the Parliament, in his recorded discussions and interviews to the Press, and in his letters and correspondences. Some of his sayings often quoted were:

(i) To be born poor is not a crime but to remain so is indeed a crime,

(ii) If a thing can be done now, do it at once and do not defer it to the next day,

(iii) Be loyal not to me but to the destiny of the State,

(iv) Orissa is a rich state where poor people live,

(v) Be a pride to your State and not a shame, etc.

He wanted the Oriyas to achieve excellence in every field and be recognised by the rest of their country men- both nationally and internationally. His main contribution was the world of the spirit, where an Oriya boy born seven decades after him felt proud that he belonged to the same race as Biju Patnaik. No other Oriya has even bridged such a generation gap and no one in foreseeable future to do the same. Many of the Biju's dream remained unfulfilled. His dream to industrialise Orissa could not be fulfilled. Orissa, situated in the eastern sea board of India, has a rich cultural heritage just as it has been endowed with vast natural resources. But it has also been a state neglected over the years resulting in its backwardness and under development. Biju's mission of making the state rich and prosperous remained a dream. He had a multifaceted personality—an air pilot, a freedom fighter, an industrialist, Chief Minister of a State and Union Minister, all combined into one. His life is an extraordinary saga of adventure and sacrifice, valour and dedication.

His death was an irreparable loss to the nation. Lakhs of people from all over the state bade a tearful farewell to him. People realised his importance after his death. It was clear from the number of dignitaries and VVIPs who attended his funeral at Swargadwar in Puri. Three helicopter loads of VIPs including Prime Minister Deve Gowda, Chandrasekhar, A.B. Vajpayee, Krishnakant, Devilal, Madhu Dandavate, Laloo Prasad Yadav, S.R. Bommai, Ram Vilas Paswan, L.K. Advani, etc. reached Puri to bid tearful farewel to the beloved "BIJU". He was man who never let down Orissa. He tried to follow the saying of Bhima Bhoi, a nineteenth century poet of Western Orissa, who wrote (in Oriya):

"Boundless is the anguish and
misery of the living
who can see it tolerate ?
Let my soul be sent to hell
but let the universe be
redeemed."

These are the lines which Biju often quoted and followed.

References

1. Bhaskar Parichha, *Biju Patnaik : A Political Biography*.
2. G.B. Patnaik, '*Biju, Part of a Great Heritage*'.
3. Kulamani Bark, '*Biju, the revolutionary*'.
4. '*Orissa Legislative Assembly Debates*'.
5. '*Oriya Newspapers*'.

Appendices

(I) A Milestone in the outer space for the Biju charisma Asteroid named Kalinga

The asteroid no.26214, technically a minor planet, has been named 'Kalinga'. It has been decided by the International Astronomical Union (IAU) to mark the 50th Anniversary of the establishment of the Kalinga Prize by the UNESCO. The decision comes after the crucial meeting of the IAU's Commission for Minor Planet Nomenclature (CMPN).

Bearing the old name of the present Indian state of Orissa, UNESCO's Kalinga Prize has been awarded annually since 1952 to persons who contributed to the interpretation of the role of science in service to human society. The Prize is sponsored by the Kalinga Foundation, established in 1951 by the Indian Philanthropist Biju Patnaik, a UNESCO media release said.

The Kalinga asteroid is situated at a distance of 2946 astronomical units from the Earth (an astronomical unit is equivalent to 149,597,871 kilometres). It was discovered by Perr Pravec, a Czech astronomer, in 1977.

— Courtesy : UNESCO and PTI, New Delhi,
September 28, 2001

(II) Speech of the Chief Minister of Orissa, Biju Patnaik, at the 18th meeting of the Eastern Zonal Council held on the 21st September, 1991 at Bhubaneswar

Shri Chavanji, Shri Laloo Prasadji, Shri Bhandarji and Hon'ble Ministers of Governments of Member States.

I am happy to be able to welcome you to this meeting of the Eastern Zonal Council. While we have endeavoured to make your sojourn in the State pleasant, there must have been lapses and some members of your delegations might have been inconvenienced. I would be grateful if you condoned these lapses.

I would also like to express my dismay over the fact that the Council's last meeting was held six years ago. This Council was established so that the common problems discussed by Member States are found solutions through consensus. These problems may be inter-State problems or problems between a State or a group of States and the Union Government. The institution of the Council would be devoid of all meaning and its deliberations would have little utility if we cannot find time to meet each other except after long intervals. We should meet often. For each meeting, we may have smaller agenda and our delegations too may be smaller. What is important is that life should be infused into this institution and there should be clear evidence of our concern at resolving problems. You may kindly appreciate that some of the agenda items for the present meeting have lost the relevance they had when they were originally prepared and that there are other issues which are not on the agenda but which have acquired very great immediacy.

Let me dwell briefly on some of the issues. The first is the disastrous consequence on the resources of Orissa, Bihar and West Bengal of the Supreme Court's decision that States had no right to levy cess on major minerals. Implementation of its further decision that the cess already collected shoud be refunded would result in serious erosion of our resources which are by no means abundant. We have been pleading with the Government of India to take legislative measures to absolve the State Government from the obligation to refund the amount collected. This should be expedited. It is true that rates of royalty on coal has been revised by the Union Government from 1-8-1991, but the enhanced rates do not compensate us fully. These States are relatively underdeveloped and there is an imperative need to make substantial investment on the production infrastructure. The effort of State Governments will receive a setback and their under-development would be perpetuated unless royalty rates are suitably enhanced.

Secondly, I would like you to consider whether it is a correct policy that coal should be transported over long distances for generation of thermal power. The railway and the ports facilities have been put under severe stress because of this policy. I have no doubt that a more expedient alternative would be generation of power at pitheads and its transmission through high voltage transmission lines to consumer States.

Thirdly, we should critically examine the present policy of freight equalisation in respect of iron, steel and coal. The States that have these resources have been handicapped in developing industries because the cost of these inputs is the same everywhere. Naturally, therefore, development is faster in States that have already reached a higher level of industrialisation.

Fourthly, our plea for levy of tax on Inter-State consignment of goods has so far been of no avail. We are foregoing considerable amounts of revenue which is potentially collected from production of coal, iron and steel, fertilisers, etc. We would like this proposal to be retrieved from cold storage and processed immediately.

Fifthly, I would like to draw the Council's attention to the policy of the Ministry of Environment & Forests that non-forest land equal to twice the extent of forest land proposed for dereservation should be made available for compensatory afforestation. I would like to make it clear that we are as concerned as the Ministry of Environment and Forests that the country's forest cover should be enlarged and that deforestation should be firmly curbed. Where some forest land has inevitably to be taken away, an equal extent of land should be made available for afforestation. We have vast areas of degraded forests which are forests only on the records of the Forest Department. These are actually wastelands. I do not see any reason why compensatory afforestation cannot take place on such land and why, when such land is available, we must take away land that can provide sustenance to a community and to the livestock. I would like the Council to consider the matter and recommend to the Government of India that degraded land of equal extent should suffice for compensatory afforestation.

The last point concerns a matter that must be attended to at once if we must, as we should, avoid the situation obtaining in States where terrorist activity is pronounced. Extremist activity has assumed significant proportions in some part of the State. Bihar too is experiencing this problem. I had earlier suggested that the Government of India should assist us in implementing a special programme of economic development. It must be understood that the headway extremism made in this part of the country is because of deprivation. It is not extremism produced by fundamentalism or ethnic chauvinism. This extremism is seen as a response to inequality, exploitation and poverty. These factors have to be alleviated if extremism has to be contained. We have also to give serious thought to developing an administrative system that is more responsive and more effective in resolving major local problems. Immediately, we would need support in upgrading Police manpower and weaponry. If this is seen as a normal law and order problem and we are asked to find resources, our effort at countering extremism will inevitably fail. I would urge Shri Chavan, who has to handle the problem every day, to consider this proposal earnestly and with the utmost expedition.

I have perhaps consumed more than my quota of time, but I am sure you would appreciate that I have been very brief on each point I had to make. If the list of points is somewhat large, it is because of the reason I have referred to earlier, namely, the long interval between the last meeting of the Council and the present meeting.

— *Courtesy : Orissa Review, October, 1991*

(III) Address by Biju Patnaik, Chief Minister, Orissa, at the Meeting of the National Development Council, December 23, 1991

The main item in today's agenda is the Planning Commission' Directional Paper for the Eighth Plan. The policy outlines and the priorities suggested in these papers are unexceptionable, but the National Development Council must also address itself to certain issues that are generally lost sight of while discussing the national economy and the manner in which it should be restructured. The end of the cold war and political as well as economic changes in Europe and the Soviet Union have now become the inevitable starting point of every discussion of Indian economy. The end of the cold war was neither sudden nor unplanned. In a brilliant essay he published in 1989, Francis Fukuyama had said that Marxism-Leninism was a dead ideology for all practical purposes and that future international relations will be characterised by increasing marketisation. He further said that the vacuum created by the exit of Marxism-Leninism was likely to be filled by forces of religious fundamentalism or ethnic assertiveness. This is happening all over the world. It is, therefore, not as if the world has suddenly become a better place with Communism ceasing to be a political system. Other forces which represent a more serious challenge to liberalism and humanism will become stronger and will demand greater attention. The recent developments alluded to in the Directional Paper should not be viewed as purely economic matters. We have to take note of the fact that we have to contend with new political forces. In other words, the new technique of management of the economy must be accompanied by a new technique of political mangement. If we fail in the latter, the challenge to the Indian State cannot be warded off easily. The Soviet Union is now paying the price not only of doctrinaire economics but also of failure to manage a federal polity. I hope we will have the good sense of avoiding a simplistic interpretation of recent developments and of trying to shape a new technique which inspires in every Indian the faith that his Indian identity will remain unaffected by the area he lives in, the language he speaks and the religion he professes.

It is all very well that we should implement altogether new economic policies, but let us also decide that we shall not allow the new economic order to perpetuate regional disparities that have done much to weaken our integral nationhood.

I would, therefore, submit that equitable regional development should be assigned as high a priority as macro-level planning policies. If we fail to do so, growth would be highly disparate among the States of the Indian Union at the end of the Eighth Plan. It will be difficult to convince people of States where growth was slow relative to some other States that no injustice has been done to them. I am by no means suggesting that growth rate can be totally independent of natural endowments, but if investment on exploitation of natural endowments is insufficient or if benefits of development do not accrue to some people because communication to their areas is underdeveloped or because the production infrastructure is not comparable to what is available in developed States, can we, in the long run, hold the country together ?

I agree with the Planning Commission that public sector investment should primarily be on infrastructure. The question really is whether funds should be provided to the States in consideration of their potential for development or whether allocation will be according to conventional norms. In major areas of infrastructure development irrigation, power and communcation our old principles of determining the level of Central assistance to States will no longer do. We need a much larger level of food output and many more megawatts of power and many more kilometres of roads and railways. The question we should ask ourselves is: where will this increment be possible at the shortest time, at the lowest cost and at the greatest benefit to the nation ? If we identify some areas with the largest and most cost-effective potential, we should instal a mechanism of finding investigable funds without being limited by the size of the State Plan. Let me illustrate. I regret I cannot share the Planning Commission's optimism regarding the state of our agriculture. I do not deny that there has been a significant improvement in the output of rice and wheat. The rate of increase cannot be maintained in future unless the yield rate in States where productivity is low, improves significantly. It has become fashionable to find fault with the Eastern States for their alleged failure to make agriculture in their States as productive as in Punjab or Haryana. What is forgotten is that almost the entire cultivated areas in these two States is irrigated, Irrigation development had received high priority in undivided Punjab and, after partition, the same thrust was maintained. In contrast, the irrigated area is less than 30 per cent of the total cultivated land in the Eastern States. The yield of an unirrigated hectare can certainly not be compared with that of an irrigated hectare, Remove, or at least reduce, this disparity, and you will find that Eastern States will account for the larger part of the incremental production during the next two decades. If, however, intervention is refused on the ground that irrigation development must come through the State Plan, we would perpetuate poverty and inequality. What is more, we would be unable to meet the demand for food which will be larger because our population will be larger. If you exclude unusual years when reported production was exceptionally high either because of an exceptionally good season or because of ingenuity of our statisticians, wheat production grew almost at the same rate as our population between 1980-81 and 1987-88 while the rate of increase in rice production could not keep pace with the population growth. Pulse output has remained unchanged for several years whild production of coarse grains has been failing. We must not allow recent output figures for rice and wheat to lead us to the unfounded premise that long term agricultural growth has been ensured.

What is true of agricullture is also true of all other infrastructural facilities and of the overall level of economic development in 1988-89, the per capita net State Domestic Product in Orissa at Rs. 2,438.00 was less than the All-India per capita product by about Rs. 1,400.00. The length of surfaced road per 1000 sq.km. of area is 122 kms. against 269 for India, 817 kms. for Punjab and 527 Kms. for Haryana. The Railway route length per 1000 sq. km. area is 12.7 kms. In Orissa against 19.9 for India and 43 kms. in Punjab and about 30 Kms. in Uttar Pradesh, Tamil Nadu and Bihar. The result is that Orissa today is the poorest State, judged by the percentage of its population below the poverty line. The poor are actually more numerous than the estimate of statisticians. To tolerate inequality and deprivation of this magnitude amounts to, in Gunnar Myrdal's language, neo-colonialism.

We who fought colonialism must exterminate neo-colonialism.

I would urge the Planning Commission and the Government of India to give some thought to this aspect. If our moral sense of justice is aroused, it shoud not be difficult to find methods and funds for correcting patent disparities.

I fully appreciate that the Government of India may not be able to fully meet the needs of underdeveloped States. The quantum of special assistance which should be over and above the normal Central assistance will naturally be small, but what is important is that this principle is accepted and some critical projects identified for special funding. It is also necessary that State Governments are allowed to mobilise within the parameters of national policy, external resources. I am trying to do so in areas of mineral development and energy production. I must thank the Prime Minister and his colleagues for the considerable support and understanding I have received. I would especially thank the Prime Minister who has evinced a refreshingly modern and long overdue perception and Centre-State relations and who, I have no doubt, will rejuvenate the Indian federal system.

It is good that, at long last, some Centrally sponsored schemes will be transferred to the States. It is true that the larger number of schemes will be retained by the Union Government and that the Eighth Plan outlay on these schemes will be far higher than for schemes which will be transferred to the States, but let us not argue over our shares and let us make a beginning with this overdue transfer. I would also support the recommendation that Central assistance for these schemes may be governed by the formula applicable for Central assistance to State Plans with the small modification that, for the next five years, this assistance should be wholly grant and should not carry any loan component.

We have also been asked to comment on a new formula of distribution of Central assistance and market borrowings. It was only about a year ago that a consensus formula was decided upon by the National Development Council. I think there is something in our character that prevents us from reaching a decision.

Since we seldom decide on anything, we seldom make any progress.

I would urge endorsement of the formula of October, 1990 and would most emphatically record my dissent with the proposal that the deviation method should carry less percentage points. I also do not agree that the allocation for special problems should be reduced from 15 to 10 per cent; if anything, and in view of the argument in the earlier part of my address, the allocation should have been higher. It is totally unnecessary to dilute intervention in this important area by increasing allocation for Performance which would now consist of, besides sound fiscal management, such matters as population control maternal and child health, universalisation of primary education and adult literacy, etc. Does anyone seriously believe that any State is not interested in promoting primary education or the health of its children and women ? If the performance of some States in these areas is not as good as that of some others, we have to consider whether history and other factors have not imposed a constraint. States which had a large part of their present areas under semi-literate and eccentric princes or which have a very large population of Scheduled Tribes will take quite some time to be level with the States which have had the benefit of coming earlier under relatively more modern administration or whose population largely consists of people who joined the mainstream of Indian civilisation fairly early. It should also be obvious that a State with larger resources of its own is better equipped to invest on health care and education. I fully subscribe to national priorities like population control and universalisaition of primary education, but I would strongly resent being punished for a legacy I am not responsible for and I am trying to overcome. This will be a totally unjust system of resource allocation besides reducing resources that should properly be allocated to programmes and projects in underdeveloped States.

Some of the suggestions I and other Chief Ministers have given or would give may require more time for consideration than is available to us to-day. It will be useful if the important suggestions are identified and the Planning Commission comes up with a response which can be considered by this Council in a future meeting which can be convened quickly. Once this is done, the Eighth Plan would reflect national consensus and would receive wider political support. May be this would involve some reconsideration of suggested policies, but we have, I believe, entered a phase in which shibboleths are yielding place to pragmatic action and new contours of a modern federal State are emerging.

— Courtesy : Orissa Review, January, 1992

(IV) Biju Patnaik : Orissa of My Dreams; First Binod Kanungo Memorial Lecture delivered ex tempore on January 27, 1992 at Soochana Bhawan, Bhubaneswar

I have been commissioned here in the memory of my dearest friend Binod Kanungo - not to speak but to dream. I have been told that I should project the Orissa of my dreams. What would I dream/Once Gurudev Rabindranath Tagore said, "When you dream, dream big. It is only by dreaming big things that big tasks are accomplished." We are born to die. While dreaming think of big things - Dream the biggest dream of all. In his poetry, what did he say ? "Sapan dekhi tulab ami badi, prabal dwipe manimuktar ....". This was the dream which urged the young people of those days to dream big. I have not forgotten these lines of Rabi Thakur.

When I want to dream of Orissa—what should I dream ? Orissa has become a small little place. One day it was the greatest empire of India. Its army defeated Alexander's army and threw them across the border of India. Kalinga was the largest maritime power ever known in the world. That Kalinga spread her civilisation throughout the South East Asia; relics are found in all these countries even today. What better dream can I have than dream of those magnificent days, when Orissa was vital, when Kalinga was vital, when Kalinga was the greatest empire of India, when the sailors of Kalinga did not know fear, when the soldiers of Kalinga did not know fear, when the mothers of kalinga were known as "Biranganas". That was Kalinga. Therefore that is a dream worthy of Kalinga.

In my dream of the 21st century for the State, I would have young men and women who put the interest of the State before them. They will have pride in themselves, confidence in themselves. They will not be at anybody' mercy, except their own selves. By their brain, intelligence and capacity, they will recapture the history of Kalinga. I would like my Orissa of 21st century to have excellent artisans, superb craftsmen and sculptors, greatest musicians and poets. After all it is we who built Konark. It was in Orissa or Kalinga where the great Geeta Govinda was composed. It is the same place where great mathematicians like Pathani Samanta looked at the sky and created astronomical wonders. A place where we have mathematical geniuses, great sculptors and artists, great musicians and dancers, and men and women of great culture; this should be the dream of my Orissa, should be the dream of my life.

There is no English word for "Karuna". When a young woman goes to pray before her God she asks for one blessing. "O' Lord, fill my soul with 'Karuna'. I ask for nothing else." That is the epitome of culture, which the Orissa of my dream would have.

We, the men and women of today, have shrunk. Because we do not dream big, we have become little men and women with little problems, little conspiracy, little likes and dislikes, little gain or loss. Orissa can be lifted by collective will. We are the descendants of great ancestors, look at my beautiful hills, beautiful rivers, beautiful sea, rich forests which are gifts of God, given to our people. I would like my men and women, young people of my State, in the coming years to take all these gifts that God has given and produce the greatest machines that produce wealth for all and provide employment and productive work to all. In my dream of Orissa no cultivator would go dry with his field. Every drop of water that percolates through our soil is recovered. In my dream of the Orissa of tomorrow, I will not like to hear a whisper about the oppression of women. I dream of a day when women will play an equal role with men. They will exercise with men equal power and enjoy the same privileges. This should be my dream of tomorrow the 21st century. In that time no child of my State will go hungry without food or suffer from malnutrition. And all over my land, there will be no illiteracy or ignorance.

For my farmers, I would like to dream that never, and never, his crop shall perish for want of water. Each drop of water will be conserved and used. Natural calamity, the scourge of Orissa, would be a thing of the past. All the rivers would be tamed, all the water storages reconstructed so that parched lands get that water when needed.

Yesterday I inaugurated an exhibition of the Adivasis. Those of you who have not gone, I would recommend that you spend a couple of hours there, see their style of living. You realise that 30% of our people live in this condition. I would like to see that every citizen of my State has a decent roof over his head, every family potable drinking water and all-weather protection, They must have all-weather roads and bridges, schools properly manned with able teachers and hospitals with adequate number of excellent doctors. It has to be ensured that every nook and corner of my state has proper health care, proper schooling, a proper road system and communication systems like telephones, like electronics - all that modern science has given, the average villagers must have.

The wealth of minerals that nature has endowed us with will sustain many major industries for long years to come whether it is steel, whether power from coal, whether aluminium or oil refineries and petrochemicals. All these will come to us. We should make our State a place of attraction to all people from all over the world. In India, we have today no social harmony, no religious tolerance, no caste tolerance. Certainly we cannot grow with all these divisions. In my dream of Orissa, there should be harmony, broad-mindedness, greater tolerance all around and fellow feeling from neighbour to neighbour.

In conclusion I would like to say what Maxmüller said a long time back, "If I have to look over the whole world to find out the country that nature has bestowed its best, I would point to India". We all together can make our State such that the whole world would say that Orissa is our dreamland.

— *Courtesy : Orissa Review, April 1992*

(V) Address of the Chief Minister, Biju Patnaik, at the Conference on Human Rights on September 14, 1992 at Delhi.

Mr. Home Minister and Friends,

I must congratulate the Union Home Minister for the comprehensive agenda papers he has sent us. I would like to make a small suggestion before I respond to the proposals contained in the agenda papers. The issues referred to are extremely imporatant and we must devise strategies based on mature deliberation. Some of the suggestions in the agenda notes have a bearing on Centre-State relations. Some others have serious financial implications. Some others, it seems to me, do note take sufficient note of ground realities. Before any specific decision is taken, it will be appropriate that our response, based on years of experience and first-hand acquaintances with the problems under discussion, are carefully considered. We should avoid the temptation of coming out with solutions at the end of the meeting and producing the impression that these solutions were always round the corner and all that was needed was the will to find them. I would advise that the proposals contained in the agenda notes are reviewed in the light of today's deliberations: we can meet again to discuss the result of the review and design strategies inspired by pragmatic perceptions rather than summons issued by self-appointed defenders of human rights from abroad and from within the contry.

It is odd, and certainly humiliating, that we should be treated to lessons on human rights by foreign organisations whose good will towards India is not at best doubtful. They accuse the Indian state of abridging the human rights of terrorists and of scoundrels' intent on dismembering India with the help of foreign arms and money. For these organisations, the human rights of terrorists and secessionists are sacrosant and indubitably superior to those of the innocent people they kill and of the women and children who are forced into a life of penury, anguish and insecurity. Their conscience, if any, is inexplicably dumb when thousands of families are forced to abandon their homes and properties and become refugees. These organisations and their high priests have not thought it fit to condemn terrorism or secessionism or systems of governance that openly subordinate human rights to what they think are laws of their religion. They have also desisted from condemning interference by one state in the internal affairs of another, leading to enormous human rights abuse. While the erstwhile Soviet Union was accused of human rights violation in Eastern Europe, open support for armed rebellion in Afghanistan resulting in mass killing and exile of millions of Afghans was viewed differently and kindly. Our neighbour's dirty work in Kashmir and in Punjab has also been viewed with extraordinary indulgence. Is it because Indians, Afghans and people of other Asian and African countries have no human rights unless they are murderers, robbers, or on foreign pay rolls ? Why is it that there is such clamour when one of these species is killed, and none when the basic human right — the right to live — is abrogated everyday in Somalia, Ethiopia and the erstwhile Yogoslavia?

I submit that throughout the ages as well as today India can boast of human rights record which is superior to the record of any other country. This will be evident from the fact that minority populations have grown and flourished in India whereas, in the history of the west, they have often been victims of relentless carnage. Those who raise an outcry over the reported death or torture of a terrorist in India have no word of sympthy for a Malkankit Natt who was mercilessly bashed up by the London Police or for a Rodney King who was administered 56 video-taped blows by the Los Angeles police or for the Korean immigrants who lost practically everything they had earned in the race riots that followed the acquittal of policemen who had assaulted King but who the Jurors thought were simply doing their duty.

Let us therefore say, and say it openly, that we do not mean to take these experts at doublespeak seriously at least not until they have taken up the defence of human rights in their own countries and not until they have launched an impartial campaign against outside inspiration for militancy and terrorism.

The basic objective of our freedom struggle was to restore to the Indian people the human rights they were deprived of by colonial rule. Our constitution guarantees these rights and also provides for their enforcement. I frankly do not see much merit in the proposal to set up a Human Rights Commission. I can understand a commission going into certain issues in greater detail than the Government which has its hands full with everyday problems and recommending policies, laws and procedures of implementation but actual implementation has to be the function of Government and not of an agency outside it. It is not correct that a Government elected by the people should assign its functions to an organisation outside the people's mandate. Such institutions. I am afraid, are not legitimate in terms of our Constitution. This is precisely what has been happening over the past few years. We have commissions for the Scheduled Castes and Tribes, for women and the minorities. Is the Government incapable of looking after India's Scheduled Castes and Scheduled Tribes, women and minority communities? The proposed Human Rights Commission will also, I am afraid, impinge on the powers of State Governments Public order. Police and prisons fall under the State list. Clause (3) of Article 246 vests in State Government the "exclusive power to make laws" in respect of matters enumerated in the state list. It is no doubt suggested in the agenda notes that the commission will be a fact-finding and advisory body, but it would also have the mandate to recommend prosecution of the offenders and to advice authorities about the steps they should take to uphold human rights". There is absolutely no doubt that it will function as an authority that believes that State Governments are accountable to it, especially when it is set up as has been suggested by an Act of Parliament. We may perhaps have a Commission to enquire into human rights questions and submit its report to Government, but it should cease to exist after a specified period during which it must submit its report. To go beyond this will lend strength to the thesis that the Union Government and the State Governments cannot be trusted in the matter of human rights. Let us be clear that it is the Government's duty to uphold human rights and it will do so at all costs.

Agenda item No. 2 is far more important; custodial crime is utterly reprehensible and must be curbed, regardless of the status of the offender. We should however look at the problem in its perspective. In a large number of cases, policemen responsible for such offences have been punished. This is the position in my State and is, perhaps, true for other States as well. What this means is that the State in India does not take an indulgent view of custodial crime. We should also take note of the fact that in a large number of cases, allegations of custodial torture are motivated, the motive being to force the investivating officer into a position of self-defence and thereby deflect him from the single—minded pursuit of the case. The motive may also be to win the court's sympathy. This phenomenon has been observed in several countries.

A disciplined and motivated police force is seldom guilty of custodial crime. Such crimes are committed by a few deviant members of the force, but their proportion to the number of correct and responsible policemen is no higher than such proportion in other professions.

The most effective insurance against custodial crime is the morale and the attitude of the force. *Unfortunately police morale had suffered serious erosion both due to politicisation and unionisation. For the first evil, we ourselves are responsible since we would like to use the police to protect the people whose only virtue is that they are with us and persecute the people who have different loyalties. As long as we persist in this behaviour, no system can be effective against custodial crime.* The offending police officer may have done us some service in the past or may promise to do in future. This distortion is matched by a corresponding distortion caused by the unionisation of the force. If an investigation into an alleged custodial crime is taken up against a police officer, there is a tendency on the part of others to combine and protect him. We must make up our mind that we shall not suffer this impediment and must proceed against every police officer, guilty of such a crime.

While allegations of custodial death and torture are exaggerated, such allegations are widely believed to be true because there is very little openness in enquiries and because the results of enquiry are seldom published. We can consider a system that would ensure expedition and objectivity in enquiries. There is no advantage in a mandatory judicial enquiry in such cases. Section 176 of the Code of Criminal Procedure already vests in magistrates the power to hold an enquiry into cases of custodial death including death allegedly due to suicide. We can examine whether the provisions of the Code cannot be enlarged and made more effective so that cases of custodial death and rape are enquired into by authorities other than those of the police. Greater authority to the District Magistrates or to the functionaries nominated by the State Government would go a long way in investing transparency and credibility both to enquiries and follow-up actions.

The award of financial relief should be informal and left to State Governments. I do not see why a State Government that provides financial relief to victims of natural calamities and communal riots cannot be trusted with this task and must act in pursuance of a Central Law. We can agree on certain guide-lines, but their implementation is best left to State Governments. Let us consider setting up a task force to formulate the guide-lines, but let us desist from doing under law what can be done through an attitude of concern and compassion.

I have said earlier that there is a correlation between the incidence of custodial crime and erosion of police morale. In addition to the two aforesaid causes of declining police morale, there is another, the alarming fall in convictions due largely to the present system of prosecution. The earlier system of prosecution which had succeeded in securing convictions for the larger number of criminals was replaced in 1973 by the new Code of Criminal Procedure. After the new system came into force, acquittals have far outnumbered convictions. The result is that the law-breaker is no longer afraid and citizens are afraid of the law breaker. So great is the citizens' fear that they have lost the capacity to resist the most heinous crimes committed in broad daylight. So great, again, is the erosion in the State's will to govern that several such crimes go unpunished although there is no doubt either about the identity of their perpetrator or the distress of their victims. The powerful and the rich have acquired the capacity to abuse the judicial process and to be immune to retribution under the law. We are fast moving into a situation which Shakespeare described as follows:

> Through tatter'd clothes small vices do appear Robes and furr'd gowns hide all. Plate sin with gold, And the strong lance of justice hurtless breaks, Arm it in rags, a pigmy's straw doth pierce it,

(King Lear, Act 4, Scene 6).

I would submit that it would be artificial to delink human rights from punishment of crime. It will be artificial for two principal reasons. Firstly, in a situation in which the system of punishment for a crime is ineffective, the criminal has the licence to trample upon the human rights of hapless victims. Secondly, in such a situation, society which includes the police will be compelled to devise other methods of containing crimes. The police are accountable when the crime situation deteriorates. If the normal system of investigation and prosecution does not yield results, there will be a tendency to resort to other methods; so that the police can give a good account of itself. I should think that the incidence of custodial crime should be seen in the perspective of our system of administration of Criminal Law. If amendment of the Evidence

Act and the Code of Criminal Procedure is being contemplated so that those responsible for custodial crime are punished adequately and quickly, there is clearly a stronger case for contemplating amendments so that criminals and killers do not acquire the power to dominate the society.

The need for educating police officials in human rights is both great and urgent. It should be possible for us to devise a programme of training, the cost of which can be shared between the Union and State Governments designed to promote human rights literally. Financial support to State Governments is also necessary for expanding and modernising jails.

As for crimes against the disadvantaged sections of society including women, all that we need is a strong administrative will. Crimes against these groups have come down significantly when there is clear evidence of the State's will to punish the offenders. These criminals do not belong to the under-world. They have social status, being either land-owners, or Government employees, or employees of the corporate sector or persons who prosper in their own business. I have recently issued instructions to the effect that a Government servant against whom a *prima facie* case of dowry offence is made out shall be placed under suspension and, if his responsibility for the offence is established, he shall be dismissed from service. I am aware that this will not have more than marginal effect on crimes against women but this is an illustration of State will. We do not, unfortunately, have a worthwhile social movement that creates awareness against such crimes. During the days of our freedom struggle the goal that inspired us was not only political independence but a society in which the individual, whatever his religion or caste or sex or income status, could live with dignity. Gandhiji who gave direction to the freedom struggle integrated issues like the removal of untouchability, the rights of tenants to land and freedom from poverty, with the issue of political independence.

We are incapable today of understanding his integral philosophy and have assigned the task of social engineering to thousands of non-Government organisations supported with munificent Governmental grants. Societies do not change through the work of persons who are paid to bring about change. We, regardless of the parties we belong to and the political goals we cherish, must combine to create an awarness which will not condone any crime against a Harijan, a woman, a poor man or a person who calls his God by a different name.

I am sorry I have taken a lot of time but then the issues you have raised do not admit of a summary response. I would make a final submission. *Human rights are important not because foreign human rights organisations have asked us to honour human rights but because our culture and our history have embedded respect for man in our soul.* We should device methods consistent with the realities of our situation to operationalise this respect. If these methods do not conform to the prescriptions of some self-righteous organisations, there should be no cause for distress.

- Courtesy : Orissa Review, October 1992

Biju Patnaik, as Others see him...

Both as a freedom fighter and a mass leader, who worked in various fields successfully after independence, Biju Patnaik will be adored by the people.

— **K. R. Narayanan**
President of India

Biju Patnaik's role in India's national reconstruction will be remembered for long. His role as an eminent Parliamentarian, Central Minister and Chief Minister of Orissa is noteworthy.

— **Dr. Shankar Dayal Sharma**
Former President of India

Biju Patnaik was not only a politician but also a brave warrior. He was a front-ranking freedom fighter, able administrator and the maker of modern Orissa. Whenever needed, he went above parochial party considerations and gave positive suggestions and advice.

— **Atal Behari Vajpayee**
Prime Minister of India

Biju Patnaik was a very inspiring personality. He was an utterly fearless person who inspired the youth of India.

— H.D. Devegowda
Former Prime Minister of India

Biju Patnaik was not only a great freedom fighter, but also a towering politician and social leader of India.

— Dr. Farooq Abdullah
Chief Minister, J & K

Biju is my younger brother. But he had a larger-than-life personality for which he is well-known the world over. I am proud of him. The poor and the down-trodden people always occupy a special place in some intimate corner of his heart.

— Dr. George Patnaik
Eminent sportsperson and elder brother of Biju Babu

Biju Patnaik was a symbol of unity in Indian politics. He had an open mind. Even during his weak financial position, he spent for the cause of democracy.

— Surendra Mohan
Eminent political ideologue

His contribution to uphold the democratic rights in India will never be forgotten.

— Jyoti Basu
Former Chief Minister, West Bengal

He was not confident of winning. But he did not detract from his decision. I pay respect to such a unique personality. Electoral win or defeat was just immaterial. He said whatever he believed in and he did whatever he said. That was the philosophy of life of Biju Patnaik.

— Surendra Mohanty
Eminent Writer and former Parliamentarian

He was one of the foremost mass leaders of India. He has faced many storms in life and every time he has come out with renewed vigour.

— Dr. Radhanath Rath
Eminent Journalist and Editor, Writer

Biju Patnaik was the eagle of the storm and sculptor of the clay. It is hard to believe that Biju Patnaik is no more. He has influenced the political life of the state for half a century. He was the symbol of ever-inspiring working spirit.

— J. B. Patnaik
Former Chief Minister, Orissa.

Biju Babu was very fond of reading. But he was equally unwilling to write anything. Even he was very reluctant to write letters. I have failed to make him write down his adventures that could inspire the posterity.

— Prof Samar Guha
Writer and Parliamentarian

Biju Patnaik wanted to write his autobiography ; but he could not do so. During the freedom struggle, our Delhi house was known as 'absconders' paradise.'

— Geeta Mehta
Daughter of Biju Patnaik and Eminent Writer

Perhaps Biju Patnaik was having a developed inner-self which was known to very few of his fellow-beings. He seems to have achieved many things in one life which might be impossible to achieve in a number of lives.

— Manoj Das
Internationally acclaimed writer and thinker

Biju Patnaik always tried to highlight Orissa and its people before the international community. He founded the Kalinga Award which also popularises the name of Orissa throughout the world .

— Prof Sriram Ch. Dash
Eminent Academic and
former President, Indian Political Science Association

Biju Babu's large-heartedness is unparalleled. Once we went to him to ask for a donation to establish statues of Utkalmani Pandit Gopabandhu Das in Cuttack, Puri and Sambalpur. He went through the pages of our receipt-book that carried amounts ranging from rupees five to one thousand. He wrote rupees five thousand as his contribution. We became spell-bound.

— Udayanath Sarangi
Eminent Journalist and writer

Biju Patnaik's ideas and activities were great. He was a futurist and far-sighted leader who was always concerned for his mother-land. But the only problem was that immense possibilities of his life were often imprisoned by political compulsions.

— Justice Harihar Mohapatra
Former Judge, Patna High Court and eminent writer

Biju Babu was a very daring person who accepted constructive criticism very sportively. His life-long work started with his participation in the freedom struggle and it continued for fifty years after independence.

— Nityananda Mohapatra
Freedom Fighter and Writer

Biju Patnaik took direct and personal interest in the day-to-day administration. Once he became convinced about some thing, he took strong decisions without any fear or favour.

— Prof. M. N.Das
Eminent Historian, Ex- Vice Chancellor and Member, Rajya Sabha

Biju Patnaik was a wonderful figure in politics—full of various typical characteristics. He possessed an incomparable and indomitable personality. Even his die-hard critics agree that he was the undisputed leader of the mass. He knew how to speak the unpalatable truth.

— Smt. Manorama Mohapatra
Eminent writer and Editor, The SAMAJ

Biju Patnaik was a dare-devil person. He was a modern-day Emperor Kharavela. He was given the title 'Bhumiputra' (Son of the Soil) by Indonesia for his participation in that country's freedom struggle.

— Nilamani Routray
Former Chief Minister, Orissa

Biju Patnaik was an artist of dream and a symbol of determination par excellence.

— Judhistir Das
Former Speaker, Orissa Legislative Assembly

Biju Patnaik once expressed the view that true literature should inspire readers and should create ripples in their consciousness.

— Satakadi Hota
Eminent Writer, Editor, The SAMAYA

Biju Patnaik is the hero of many legends, be it his cycle-expedition from Cuttack to Peshawar or dare-devil piloting during the Indonesian war of independence.

— Dr. Bibhuti Patnaik
Eminent Oriya Writer

Biju Patnaik always aimed at daring the impossible and to achieve what is not dreamt by ordinary individuals.

— Balaram Mohanty
Freedom Fighter and Writer

Biju was a revolutionary in the true sense of the term; a fighter till the last moment.

— Kailash Lenka
Former President, Oriya Young Writers Conference

The life of Biju is the history of pride of Orissa.

— Kanhu Charan Lenka
Former Union Minister

Biju Patnaik had tremendous self-confidence and pride. He was well above the ordinary mortals who always thought beyond the present time and expediency.

— Prof K. C. Tripathy
Writer and Publisher, The SAMAJ

We rarely find another Oriya who can surpass Biju Patnaik in relation to his love for the tradition, culture and heritage of Orissa as well as his dream to build a modern Orissa.

— Basanta Kumar Panigrahi
President, Utkal Samilani

Many people are parts of history. But few can make history. Biju Patnaik was one such personality.

— Dr. Prasanna Kumar Patsani
Writer and Member of Parliament

Biju Speak ....

"When and how I shall die- may be in a road accident or in any other manner; but not in a plane crash. I wish I should just fall down and die."

* * *

I am the descendant of the Kharavela dynasty. My culture is Jagannath culture and my tradition is Jagannath tradition. My state is `Kalinga' because it has excelled in all forms of art (*Kala*).

* * *

If we look to the whole world, we will find that nature's best creation is India. And let us try to build Orissa in such a way that the whole world will say that Orissa is our dream state.

Editors and Contributors

Rabi Ray: Former Speaker of the Lok Sabha, a renowned socialist leader, parliamentarian, writer, columnist and social activist.

Sarat Kumar Kar: Presently Speaker of the Orissa Legislative Assembly, a progressive parliamentarian, writer, orator, a former Minister and cultural activist.

Jogesh Ch Rout: A prominent leader of the co-operative movement, an able parliamentarian, a former minister and writer.

Girija Bhusan Patnaik: The Founder-Secretary of the Universe, Orissa, a prominent social activist, cultural organiser, writer and columnist.

Bhagabat Prasad Mohanty: A former Minister of Orissa, a prominent socialist thinker, writer and lawyer.

Late Banka Bihari Das: A prominent freedom fighter, socialist thinker, writer, environmentalist of national repute and social activist.

Gour Mohan Sarangi: Had a distinguished career in Orissa Civil Service, a noted writer and columnist, and served as the Private Secretary to late Biju Patnaik.

B.C. Rout: A renowned political scientist, writer and researcher, former Professor and Principal of lead Colleges of Orissa and the Director of Text Book Bureau and a member of the editorial board.

Debadutta Mohanty: A senior Reader in Political Science, a researcher, writer and cultural activist.

Sridhar Ch Sahoo: A Reader in Political Science, with specialisation in modern Indian political thought, and a distinguished writer.

Major K.P. Mohanty: A renowned political scientist, researcher, academic and writer, the first Vice-Chancellor of North Orissa University, a very senior and active Rotarian of the State, commended for distinguished services in the National Cadet Corps, has had a long and meaningful career in educational administration in the leading Colleges of Orissa, a columnist of repute who contributes regularly to the Dailies on topics of national and international affairs including those of education, society and development and Editor-in-Chief of the editorial board.

Jagdish Kr. Patnaik: A senior member of the faculty of Political Science, a writer and researcher, and a member of the editorial board.

Saroj Kr. Patnaik: A senior Reader in Political Science, Principal of an affiliated College of Utkal University, a researcher, writer and social activist, and a member of the editorial board.

Swadesh Ghosh: A senior Reader in Political Science, a writer, researcher, organiser and former Principal of a Degree College in Orissa and a member of the editorial board.

Pabak Kanungo: A senior member of the faculty of Political Science, a writer and researcher, the Secretary of the Gyanamandal Foundation (Oriya Encyclopedia).

Nishamani Kar: A senior member of the faculty of English language and literature, a writer, a researcher, critic, a visiting associate of the I.I.A.S., Shimla and a member of the editorial board.

Srinibas Pathi: A senior member of the faculty of Political Science, a writer, columnist, researcher, cultural activist, a visiting scholar in Universities of Sweden and South Africa, and a member of the editorial board.

Jugal K. Mishra: A senior member of the faculty of Political Science, a researcher and writer, and a former Secretary of the Orissa Political Science Association, I.I.P.A., Orissa Regional Branch.

D.K. Srichandan: A senior member of the faculty of Political Science, a writer, researcher and a member of the editorial board.

Guru Kalyan Mohapatra: The Chief Editor of the Utkal Prasanga (Oriya monthly published by the Department of I & P.R., Govt. of Orissa) and a journalist and poet of repute.

R.N. Burma: A senior advocate, social activist and member of the editorial board.

J.N. Mitra: Presently M.L.A. of Khurda and a prominent youth leader and a member of the editorial board.

Pradosh Patnaik: Presently the news-editor of the *Samaj*, the premier Oriya Daily and a writer, a member of the editorial board.

Aurobinda Mishra: A journalist, writer and a member of the editorial board.

Ashok Das: The Chief-editor of '*Ajira Orissa*' a popular T.V. news and feature programme, journalist and a member of the editorial board.

Capt. Debasis Das: A senior member of the faculty of English, a popular writer, critic, social activist and a member of the editorial board.

Bibhuti Patnaik: A news correspondent and member of the editorial board.

P.K. Patasani: Presently a member of the Lok Sabha, a poet and writer of repute, a former Minister, a teacher of spiritual yogic cult and a widely-travelled person.

J.K. Parida: Principal, Khurda Women's College, researcher and scholar and a member of the editorial board.

Srikanta Mishra: Principal, Prananath College, Khurda; an academic, researcher, and a member of the editorial board.

Index

❑❑❑

चित्र सं.1. आदी पुरुष (Adi Man)

चित्र सं. 2. न्यिशी पुरुष (Nishing Man)

चित्र सं.3. आपातानी महिला (Apatani Woman)

चित्र सं.4. मोम्पा महिला (Monpa Woman)

चित्र सं.5. मेम्बा जनजाति की महिलाएं (Memba Woman)

चित्र सं.6. नोक्टे जनजाति (Nocte Tribe)

चित्र सं.7. वांचो दंपती (Wancho Couple)

चित्र सं.8. पारंपरिक वेशभूषा में गारो जनजाति की महिलाएं (Garo Women in Traditional Dress)

चित्र सं.9. पारंपरिक वेशभूषा में खासी पुरुष (**Khasi Men in Traditional Dress**)

चित्र सं.10. हाजोंग महिलाएं (Hajong Women)

चित्र सं.11. कार्बी लड़कियाँ (Karbi Girls)

चित्र सं.12. जेलियांग जनजाति (Zeliangrong Tribe)

चित्र सं.13. आओ नागा बालिका (Ao Naga Girl)